YOUTH WORK AND WORKING CLASS YOUTH CULTURE

YOUTH WORK AND WORKING CLASS YOUTH CULTURE

RULES AND RESISTANCE IN WEST BELFAST

Norman Gillespie, Tom Lovett
and Wendy Garner

Open University Press
Buckingham · Philadelphia

Open University Press
Celtic Court
22 Ballmoor
Buckingham
MK18 1XW

and

1900 Frost Road, Suite 101
Bristol, PA 19007, USA

First Published 1992

A catalogue record of this book is available
from the British Library

Library of Congress Cataloging-in-Publication Data

Gillespie, Norman, 1953–
   Youth work and working class youth culture: rules and resistance
in West Belfast/Norman Gillespie, Tom Lovett, and Wendy Garner.
     p. cm.
   Includes bibliographical references and index.
   ISBN 0-335-09481-3 (hard) ISBN 0-335-09480-5 (pbk.)
   1. Social work with youth–Northern Ireland–Belfast. 2. Working
class–Northern Ireland–Belfast–Attitudes. 3. Youth–Northern
Ireland–Belfast–Attitudes. 4. Youth–Northern   Ireland–Belfast–
Societies and clubs. 5. Belfast (Northern Ireland)–Social
conditions. I. Lovett, Tom. II. Garner, Wendy, 1959–.
III. Title.
HV1441.G8B454 1992
362.7'09416'7–dc20   92-9361
                                                      CIP

Typeset by Best-set Typesetter Ltd, Hong Kong
Printed in Great Britain by Biddles Limited, Guildford and Kings Lynn

CONTENTS

ACKNOWLEDGEMENTS

We would like to thank all those who made the study possible for their support, encouragement, advice and assistance.

These include: Ballymurphy Tenants Association; Belfast Centre for the Unemployed; Belfast Education and Library Board; Cairnmartin School; Crumlin Road Opportunities; Department of Education (NI); Farset Youth Project; Lower Shankill Community Association; Northern Ireland Association of Youth Clubs; Northern Ireland Youth Forum; Standing Conference of Youth Organisations; Springhill Community House; University of Ulster (Department of Adult and Continuing Education); Upper Springfield Resource Centre; Whiterock Community Centre; Whiterock Leisure Centre; and all the people from Shankill and Upper Springfield without whom this book would not have been relevant (or possible).

We would also like to acknowledge and compliment Ann Murphy and Denise Prue for tirelessly typing the manuscript against all odds. Last but not least we would like to thank the Economic and Social Research Council (ESRC) for financing the research and the Ulster People's College for housing the project and providing administrative assistance.

The cover illustrations are based on photographs which originally appeared in 'What Is Happening To Us?', one of a series of basic learning kits produced by The Community Action Research and Education Project (CARE) at the New University of Ulster, Londonderry. The publishers acknowledge and credit the use of these photographs as follows: Bonfire Building – Peter McGuinness, Art & Research Exchange; Celebrating With A Pint – *Community Mirror*; Skipping Games – Buzz Logan, Shankill Photographic Workshop.

INTRODUCTION

There is a growing concern within the youth service in Great Britain that present provision is not meeting the changing needs of young people in an economically depressed, culturally divided and rapidly changing society. Young people today confront a barrage of social and economic problems, most of which are outside their control. Many are faced with the bleak prospect of life on the dole in a society where money is the major means of access to status and a decent standard of living. At the same time, in their personal lives and relationships, young people are confronted by major problems associated with changing moral attitudes and values. They are also attempting to come to terms with a society in Northern Ireland that is riven by sectarian conflict and blighted by almost twenty years of 'the troubles'.

It is in working class areas of Northern Ireland that these problems are felt most acutely. Here working class youth are experiencing all the problems briefly outlined above and it is here that youth provision is often most concentrated. In fact youth clubs have probably replaced the school as the major mediating institution between working class youth and the state. They are in a long tradition of attempts by the state, religious bodies and other voluntary organizations to 'do something' about, and for, working class youth.

This concern with some form of supervision of working class youth is usually located within a policing, welfare and schooling function in society and legitimized under one kind of educational label or another. It is in many respects essentially sexist in nature, concerned with the rich tradition of training boys for manhood. There is also, in Northern Ireland, an emphasis on promoting tolerance and mutual understanding *between* the two communities and combating the influence of paramilitary organizations on young people *within* the two communities.

This book is concerned with examining the youth service (and the assumptions lying behind it) and is about the values, attitudes, culture and needs of working class youth in Northern Ireland. It concentrates on investigating the nature of present provision, and the reasons why some (about 30 per cent) avail themselves of it and the great majority do not.

In the course of this investigation some basic questions are explored. Why do some young people participate in youth clubs and some not? Are there different patterns of participation by boys and girls? Are there different patterns of participation by religion and class? How do young people use their 'leisure' time if they are not involved with youth clubs? How relevant is the youth service to the culture and lives of those not participating in youth provision? Has the youth service a role to play in meeting the needs of young people? What are those needs?

These questions are often asked by those involved in youth provision in Northern Ireland and elsewhere in Great Britain. They are all too often answered by those who feel they know best what is good for young people, and who then attempt to provide a particular kind of service and ask young people to participate in it. Consultation with young people themselves is often limited in scope and imagination. The main emphasis in the work outlined in this book is on letting the young people speak for themselves, to tap into the rich working class oral tradition; to explore working class youth culture, with all its tensions and contradictions, as experienced by youth themselves.

Working class youth in Northern Ireland experience, to a heightened degree, many of these tensions and contradictions. Their views and experiences, and the response of the youth service to their needs and aspirations, is of more than purely local interest. It has something to say to all those who are concerned with an imaginative and positive response to the problems facing working class youth throughout these islands.

We start with the assumption that relevant, useful and exciting youth provision is impossible without a much fuller understanding of working class youth, their culture and their needs, and an honest appraisal of the relevance of present youth provision.

1 YOUTH AND YOUTH CULTURES IN WEST BELFAST

Since 1969 Northern Ireland has witnessed widespread social, economic and political upheaval on a scale previously unprecedented. Part of this process was a result of the transformation in the economic structure of the Province and part a result of the related political crisis (the 'troubles'). West Belfast in particular has been subject to massive changes in the physical, economic, social and political spheres. In the physical sphere it has witnessed the largest redevelopment programme in the history of Northern Ireland and the creation of an infrastructure geared towards the new market relations (urban motorways, supermarkets, enterprise zones). The local economies have been virtually destroyed (the Shankill lost 9000 jobs between 1968 and 1980) in the interests of British, European and American economies of scale. Social life has been transformed by the mass dispersal of families, a loosening in informal neighbourhood ties, increasing secularization and the influx of mass ready-made entertainments (slot machines, leisure centres, videos, pool rooms) and the decline of participatory entertainments (with the emphasis on people rather than machines). Politically, the area has witnessed the dismantling of the 'Orange System' with the fragmentation of the Unionist Party (although it has survived in a revised form). It has also witnessed a shift towards militant political stances and the growth of paramilitary organizations and activities. The area also experienced some of the worst street confrontations between catholics and protestants, sectarian murder campaigns, the Provisional Irish Republican Army's armed struggle against the 'British presence' and the sharp end of the British presence itself – British Army patrols on the streets, blanket searches, internment, plastic bullets, Diplock courts and supergrasses. West Belfast is also totally segregated now into a catholic part (the Greater Falls) and a protestant part (the Greater Shankill).

Attitudes of the people in the communities have changed corre-spondingly: attitudes to family and neighbourhood, to the opposite sex, to religion and morality, to work (or lack of it), to social life and to authority. Nowhere are the conflict and tension, the paradoxes and the contradictions, resulting from this upheaval more apparent than in the life of working class youth.

It was no coincidence that the period 1968–80 saw the mushrooming of 'community' work, in all its many manifestations, and formal youth provision. The state was heavily involved in both developments. The 1970s did, in fact, see a tremendous growth in community activity and new, dynamic and progressive forms of voluntary effort in Northern Ireland. As one prominent community worker put it:

> Pressures for social change came from a range of different sources inspired by a variety of motives, including compassion for victims of misfortune, anger at injustice, and fear of unrest. Thus, literally hundreds of local self-help community and pressure groups have emerged over the past decade – some to protest at local conditions (e.g. Save the Shankill) and some to try and meet immediate needs (e.g. lunch clubs, summer schemes, play groups). At the other end of the scale, government, motivated by a mixture of fear at social unrest and concern for the worst extremes of poverty and deprivation, backed community programmes (e.g. increased expenditure on community work, Belfast Areas of Need etc.). In the middle lots of concerned and compassionate individuals became involved in organ-isations such as those running children's holiday schemes, helping the elderly and so on.
>
> (Frazer 1980: 4)

The watershed of community development and action in the Province had arrived by the end of the decade. It was reached with the growth of Community Workshops (YOP, YTP) for the training of unemployed young people. The Department of Manpower Services and later the Department of Economic Development encouraged the growth of such projects. Resources and the responsibility for managing these workshops were given to community groups in the professed hope that training would be more relevant than that available in the government training centres.

What in effect such projects constituted was a fairly cheap means of social control (however 'well-meaning' the organizers of such schemes). It was a peripheral strategy designed to encourage young people to accept their powerlessness rather than to confront it. Management committees faced with the dilemma of pursuing 'radical alternatives' or 'conservative' means of organization, content etc., have found themselves opting for whatever will ensure their own continuance. As one commentator has stated:

This has meant the perpetuation of the belief that the development of entrepreneurial capitalist skills is an essential element in bringing about a vital economic life within the Province. Paradoxically, those who would wish to radically change society are being used to maintain the most cherished and outmoded beliefs of the status quo. Out of the most sincere motivations and because of the need to actually be doing something about the ills of this society many find themselves bound and tied.

(Eamonn Deane, quoted in Frazer 1980: 17)

A further contradiction in community development as a means of improving community relations is that neighbourhood community associations and projects tend to be parochial in nature. The function of such groups is to win as many scarce resources as possible for their community. This inevitably means that people in other neighbourhoods get less. When neighbourhoods are sectarian ghettoes to begin with this means that, willingly or not, the competition for resources (which may be based on parochial considerations) inevitably has sectarian implications.

The same is also true of local youth provision and there has been a growing concern with the state of youth in West Belfast since 1969, as young people have increasingly become involved in the street confrontations and paramilitary violence that have permeated Belfast for the past twenty years. Before 1969 specific youth initiatives were rare in the Province. In the Shankill, for instance, they were confined mainly to uniformed organizations, a few church groups and the odd Girls' Club Union or Boys' Club. The activities were mainly drill, physical activities and games, religious observance and, in the case of the uniformed groups, 'badge-work'. Formal youth work in Ballymurphy was non-existent before 1970 and its eventual development was the result of a community organization initiative, closely followed by a rival church group. Direct Board youth provision in the two areas is relatively new. The form of youth developments has often centred on 'giving young people something to do' assuming that by occupying the recipients with 'acceptable alternative forms of behaviour' the aspiration to riot or engage in other 'anti-social' behaviour, such as mugging, solvent abuse or drinking, will somehow magically disappear. There have been many other approaches, most notably attempts at integrated holidays, inter-club visits and the general development of a non-sectarian ethos in youth provision.

The aims of the Northern Ireland Youth Committee are given in Chapter 3. We should note here that most of the young people we interviewed in youth clubs did not attend, mainly, for reasons that were related to the declared aims of the Committee but for more simply identifiable activities, such as to play snooker or meet their friends. It should also be noted that the section of the youth population that gives rise to most concern does not participate in formal youth activities and would probably be excluded from so doing anyway by the ideological prejudices of many youth workers, who often view non-participants as anti-social, disruptive, negative or just plain ignorant. Such views were quite widespread in our interviews with youth workers and when one considers that as many as 60–70 per cent of young people do not participate in formal youth provision then the nature and extent of the problems and the inability of the Youth Service's attempts to remedy them are glaring.

The state and working class youth culture

Attempts at somehow controlling working class leisure by the dominant class are, of course, nothing new and have exhibited various degrees of success from the inception of the quasi-military youth brigades of the turn of the century to the purpose built leisure centres of today. Such efforts have tended to be concerned mainly with giving working class youth 'something constructive to do' (Hall and Jefferson 1976: 176). The more recent sophisticated attempts at curbing the informal activities of youth are a reflection of the changing social and economic climates. Urban redevelopment and the destruction of local economies have clearly left their mark. On the one hand there is the reality of the erosion of the traditional working class neighbourhood and community itself and all that went with it. On the other hand there was the failure to deliver the promised 'consumer society' that increased geographical and educational mobility – not to mention changes in production – was to bring. Working class youth activities became and remain the most pressing 'moral panics' (See S. Cohen 1972) of the age of mass youth unemployment in ghost towns that were originally designed as growth towns. The changes in the shape of informal youth activities are a direct reflection of the breakdown of the close interconnections between family and neighbourhood and the weakening of informal social controls (see Hall *et al.* 1978: 156–7). There has been a strong tendency to reduce this complex and uneven process to the famous, and simplistic, 'generation gap'.

Part of this process has been the re-orientation of the working class away from a general concern with their own well-being and basic needs to a more specific consumerism that can best be summed up by reference to the increased working class demand for material goods. Working class youths have similarly been subject to this process. 'We have become dependent on capitalism', as one commentator has put it (Seabrook 1983: 193). In his classic study of the working class, Hoggart drew attention to the responsibility of the minority of political activists and convinced trade unionists within the working class:

I have recalled their work for social reform and have stressed that it was inspired not primarily by a search for material goods but by a sense of the need for higher satisfactions by working people, satisfactions which could be more easily obtained once material improvements have been made . . . [Their] ideas . . . are in danger of being lost . . . material improvements can be used so as to incline the body of working people to accept a mean form of materialism as a social philosophy.

(Hoggart 1976: 322–3)

This is exactly what has happened to the working class, owing to the relative increase in prosperity since the Second World War. Material satis-factions have become the end rather than the means to achieving higher aims, such as access to a higher quality of life generally, culture, peace, a healthy environment, satisfactory relationships, higher standards of, and access to, education, real power and participation in the political system, safe and comfortable working conditions and meaningful work. The drive to achieve such standards in life has been largely lost to the vast majority of the working class because of the changes in social priorities over the past thirty years. One is reminded of the passage in *The Ragged Trousered Philanthropist* when the cynical charge-hand of the house decorators tells the trade unionist, Owen, 'Them things aren't for the likes of us' (Tressel 1985). This is an attitude that comes dangerously close to stagnating the growth of working class consciousness and undoubtedly plays a large part in the seemingly hopeless drive for escapism that has come to dominate working class culture.

Working class youth culture is often represented in terms of a distinctive sub-culture (often implying a 'delinquent' sub-culture). However, it should be stressed that the dominant elements of the youth culture are often the same elements that dominate working class culture in general (the 'parent' culture) albeit in varying degrees of manifestation. Anyone who decided, for instance, to describe a gang of mods or punks in the Shankill or Ballymurphy would be seriously misleading if he or she attempted to present this as an indication of the dominant youth culture in the areas. Such exotic sub-cultural groups tend to be peripheral, sparse and grossly unrepresentative of working class youth culture in general (the youth of the Shankill frequently referred to mods and punks as queers, dick-heads, eejits and so on). Clarke *et al.* have drawn attention to the fact that:

> We must see sub-cultures in terms of their relation to the wider class cultural networks of which they form a distinctive part. When we examine this relationship between a sub-culture and the 'culture' of which it is a part, we call the latter the 'parent' culture.
>
> (Clarke *et al.* 1976)

This should not be confused with the particular relationship between 'youth' and their 'parents'. What it means is that a sub-culture, though differing in important ways – in its focal concerns, its trends and its activities – from the culture from which it derives, will also share some things in common with that parent culture. The overwhelming desire for money, obsession with 'the other sort' and forms of escapism that are often associated with working class gangs of youth in West Belfast can also be associated with the working class in general. Youth sub-cultures must first be related to the parent cultures of which they are a sub-set. But sub-cultures must also be analysed in terms of their relation to the dominant culture – the overall disposition of cultural power in the society as a whole. We may distinguish 'respectable', 'rough', 'delinquent' and the 'criminal' sub-cultures within working class culture but, although they may differ among themselves, they all derive in the first instance from a working class parent culture. They are all, therefore, subordinate sub-cultures in relation to the dominant middle class or bourgeois culture.

It should be stressed that the great majority of working class youth never enter a tight or coherent sub-culture at all. Individuals may, in their personal life-careers, move into and out of one, or indeed several, such sub-cultures. Their relation to the existing sub-cultures may be fleeting or permanent, marginal or central. The sub-cultures are important because there the response of youth takes a peculiarly recognizable form. But in the post-war history of the class these may be less significant than what young people do most of the time. The relation between the 'everyday life' and the 'sub-cultural life' of different sections of youth is an important question in its own right.

It would be absurd to attempt an analysis of working class youth culture in West Belfast without placing it firmly within the social and economic transformations outlined at the beginning of this chapter. The impact of redevelopment on the local economy (particularly in the Shankill) has many similarities with Cohen's analysis of East London sub-cultures and his exploration of the 'intra-class dynamic between youth and parents'. (P. Cohen 1972). As in East London, redevelopment and rehousing led to a depopulation of the area, and the break-up of the traditional neighbourhood. There was a massive drift in the workforce from areas like Shankill to the new so-called 'growth centres' outside Belfast. The most immediate impact was on the kinship structure – the fragmentation of the extended family and its partial replacement by the more nucleated families of marriage.

Cohen has described how the new housing projects in East London had the effect of destroying:

> the function of the street, the local pub, the cornershop, as articulations of communal space. Instead there was only the privatised space of the family unit . . . in total isolation . . . which lacked any of the informal social control generated by the neighbourhood.
>
> (P. Cohen 1972: 16)

Alongside this was the drastic reconstruction of the local economy – the demise of small craft industries, their replacement by larger concerns often situated outside the area, the decline of the family business and the corner shop (see Wiener 1981; Gillespie 1983).

Cohen saw the formation and development of youth sub-cultures as latent attempts to express and resolve the contradictions that such forces left in the parent culture. He suggested that such sub-cultures represented an 'imaginary relation' (ideologically speaking) between the social reality of working class youth and the 'real relations' (objective structural reality). Cohen's position allows for an analysis in which *specific* economic and political forces (de-industrialization, redevelopment, powerlessness) create the conditions in which (but do not necessitate that) sub-cultures emerge. Furthermore, his position allows for an analysis whereby working class sub-cultures possess a 'relative autonomy' of their own. This means that although they may have specific conditions of existence it does not necessarily follow that their actions are given directly by those conditions. It is the sub-culture's relation to wider class formations that is the crucial determinant. This overcomes the problem of ideology, which is so often ignored in non-sociological accounts of sub-cultures and youth in general.

This approach allows us to analyse the informal structures of ideological practices, which are not directly given by the economy. In the Northern Ireland situation there is a specific combination of national, racist, labour aristocratic and ethnic ideologies (not given by the economy) which determine the particular form of ideological social relations. That is, they prevented the assimilation of protestants into the Irish nation, which sustained pro-British protestant ideology, which sustained minority antipathy, which produced republicanism. Here we have *specific* economic and political conditions; plantation, uneven development of capitalism, partition creating the conditions in which two forms of nationalism, a cross-class political alliance and a labour force divided on ethnic identification emerged (while not necessitating their emergence). It is quite common for unemployed youths from the Shankill to describe their plight in terms of 'all the Taigs coming up from the South and getting all the good jobs'. This of course has no foundation in *objective reality* but it is grounded in the *social reality* of the subject and its consequences will undoubtedly be real.

Working class sub-cultures take shape on the level of the social and cultural class-relations of subordinate classes. Hall *et al.* (1978: 440–5) have argued that they are one of a number of strategies (negotiation, resistance, struggle) adopted by the working class to counter its subordinate position.

They argue that a developed and organized revolutionary working class consciousness is only one among many such responses and that it must be seen as such. To define everything else as a token of incorporation imposes an abstract scheme on to a concrete historical reality. We must attempt to show how, and under what conditions, the class has been able to use its material and cultural 'raw materials' to construct a whole range of responses. Such responses – the repertoire of resistance specific to the history of the working class – form an immense reservoir of knowledge and power in the struggle of the class to survive and win space. Working class sub-cultures serve to win space for the young: cultural space in the neighbourhood and institutions, real time for leisure and recreation, actual room on the street or the street corner. They serve to mark out and appropriate territory in the localities. They focus around key occasions of social interaction – the weekend, the disco, the bank-holiday trip, the night out, the 'standing-about-doing-nothing' of the weekday evening, the Saturday match, the eleventh (of July) night, Internment night. They cluster around particular locations. They develop specific rhythms of interchange, structured relations between members: younger to older, experienced to novice, stylish to square. They explore focal concerns central to the inner life of the group; things 'done' or 'never done', a set of social rituals that underpin their collective identity and define them as a 'group' instead of a mere collection of individuals.

While different sub-cultures provide for a section of working class youth (mainly boys) one strategy for negotiating their collective existence, they cannot resolve the problematic of a subordinate class experience. This can be 'lived through', negotiated or resisted but it cannot be *resolved* at that level. There is no solution in the sub-cultural milieu for problems fused by the key structuring experiences of the class. There are no sub-cultural solutions to working class youth unemployment, educational disadvantage, compulsory miseducation, dead-end jobs, the routinization and specialization of labour, low pay and the loss of skills.

Working class sub-cultures are a response to a problematic that youths share with other members of the parent class culture. But class structures the adolescent's experience of that problematic in distinctive ways. First, it locates the young, at a formative stage of their development, in a particular material and cultural milieu, in distinctive relations and experiences. These provide the essential cultural frameworks through which that problematic is made sense of by the youth. This 'socialization' of youth into a class identity and position operates particularly through two informal agencies: family and neighbourhood. Family and neighbourhood are the specific structures that form, as well as frame, youths' early passage into a class. For example, the sex-typing roles and responsibilities characteristic of a class are reproduced, not only through language and talk in the family, but also through daily interaction and example. In the Northern Ireland context the home is where primary socialization into sectarianism is located:

> The catholics have big families and they won't work. Daddy says we're poor because the Government takes his money to give to the catholics and all their children and their priests to keep them in luxury because they don't work. In the South they wouldn't get any money and would have to work for it. Here they keep us all poor and don't appreciate what they get.
>
> (Fraser 1973: 96)

In the neighbourhood, patterns of community sociality are embedded partly through the structure of interactions between older and younger youths and children. It is largely through friends and relations that the distant but increasingly imminent worlds of work or of face-to-face authority (the rent man, social security, the police) are appropriated. Through these formativė networks, relations, distances, interactions and orientations to the wider world and its social types are delineated and reproduced in the young.

Working class youth inhabit, like their parents, a distinctive structural and cultural milieu defined by territory, objects and things, relations, institutional and social practices. In terms of kinship, friendship networks, the informal culture of the neighbourhood and the practices articulated around them, the young are already located in and by the parent culture. They also encounter the dominant culture, not in its distant, remote, powerful, abstract forms, but in the located forms and institutions that mediate the dominant culture to the subordinate culture and thus permeate it. Here, for youth, the schools, work and leisure are the key institutions and agencies of public social control. The school serves this function, but alongside it is a range of institutions, from the 'hard' coercive ones, like the police, to the 'softer' variants – youth and social workers.

Youth culture, as a whole, must be understood as a response to the problems posed by a framework of *bourgeois* institutions, but that response is the response from a working class experience of those institutions. The problem is to decide in what sense that response equals resistance and under what circumstances that resistance has political implications. In West Belfast there is undoubtedly a specific working class youth response that equals resistance and has political implications among certain sections of protestant youth. It is a resistance to the perceived threat posed to protestant survival by militant republicanism. In catholic West Belfast it is an 'armed revolutionary struggle' against the perceived injustices of 'British imperialism'. Thus resistance in West Belfast is not the 'resistance through ritual' of sub-cultural youth groups in Great Britain.

In conclusion it must be stated, with Corrigan and Frith (1976), that any political analysis of youth culture must focus on the culture's working-classness rather than on its youthfulness. This is not to deny that young people are in a special situation (largely because of their relative – and only relative – freedom from family and occupational ties) but emphasizing this makes political analysis impossible. For a start it means exaggerating the differences between youth culture and its class context at the expense of the continuities. The concept of 'generation gap' (derived from theories of middle class youth) is inappropriate and incorrect for working class teenagers. Even if they are involved with different institutions from their parents (schools, youth clubs etc.) all the evidence is that their response to them is based on similar values. And a focus on the youthfulness of youth culture means a focus on the psychological characteristics of young people – their adolescence, budding sexuality, individual uncertainties and so on – at the expense of their sociological characteristics, their position in the structure of the social relations of capitalism.

Working class young people are, in sociological terms, an actual and potential labour force and it is this (not their youth) that determines their social situation and structures their institutional relationships (and it is this that unifies their diverse experiences, links them to their elders and gives their culture its political potential). All relevant institutions must also be connected in any sociological analysis of youth culture, just as they are in working class experience. The reality of the teenage world is the *combination* of family, school, apprenticeship, job, police (or army), courts, youth clubs, social workers, commerce and mass media, and it is this combination to which youth culture is a response. We should stop trying to isolate youth culture with respect only to commercial leisure or to the school or to the law.

2 Two Communities in West Belfast: the Shankill and Upper Springfield

The Shankill

Growth and character

The protestant Shankill area of Belfast is one of the city's oldest quarters although its growth was a result of the development of heavy engineering, and particularly shipbuilding, after 1860.

The backbone of the shipyard's labour force and the engineering industry was concentrated in areas such as the Shankill, which mushroomed during the city's second phase of industrialization (linen accounted for the first). The relative prosperity of such areas gave birth to a wide range of auxiliary industries that were locally based. Street-end factories and workshops flourished throughout the Shankill and the Shankill Road itself became a thriving commercial centre and a busy shopping street that catered for customers from all over Belfast. Corner shops were also dotted frequently among the many side-streets and served useful social functions as well as being economically competitive because of their numbers.

The social and economic background: family, neighbourhood and community

The basic living unit on the Shankill before redevelopment was the extended family (see Wiener 1980: 71–3). It was not unusual for three or four generations of the family to live in the same street or neighbourhood and sometimes in the same house. This pattern was not unique to the Shankill but was characteristic of other working class areas of Belfast and industrial areas of Britain as a whole (see, for example, Young and Wilmott 1971). The basic reason for the continuation of the extended family system was that there were few economic advantages to be gained from moving that could have compensated for the communal benefits of life in a close-knit community.

Extended families were centred on neighbourhoods – which consisted of a few adjacent streets joined together through interlocking families (Wiener 1980: 73). The 'neighbourhood' was characterized by: one or more corner shops, which not only served as meeting places but often remained open until the early hours; often a street-end factory or mill, for instance a small clothing firm; some backyard businesses, such as a timber merchant or scrap dealer; occasionally a garage or coal merchant, located in a merchant's premises or one of the 'courts' (basically these were converted stables). All of these, together with the corner pub, served important social functions and enabled at least some of the neighbourhood population to work locally. Children would play in the streets, which were, in effect, an extension of the house. A whole set of relationships was constructed, centred on family but including most people in the neigh-bourhood. The neighbourhood, then, was a kind of Coronation Street with extended families, friendship networks and local businesses. Older people played a significant part in the neighbourhood by frequently 'minding the kids' and thereby allowing the mother to go out and work.

Communities on the Shankill consisted of a number of such neighbour-hoods. These communities, such as the 'Hammer' and the 'Nick', consisted of about 30–50 acres and contained some 2000 to 4000 people (Wiener 1980: 75). Each community had an individual character, related, originally, to differences in employment skills. The community was the main living area for people in the Shankill. It contained pubs, shops, small businesses, churches and meeting halls. To many people the community met all their needs and, except for going to the Shankill Road, they would rarely leave it.

Each community on the Shankill was joined to others by the Shankill Road, which has always been one of the main shopping areas in Belfast. On Saturdays in particular, people from all parts of the Shankill as well as from other parts of Belfast would meet on the Road to shop and talk. The Shankill Road provided the different communities with a common identity and sense of purpose that was celebrated in particular on occasions like the anniversary of the Battle of the Boyne (12 July).

The Shankill, then, had most of the attributes of an urban *Gemeinschaft*, such as a sense of belonging, capacity for common action, a high degree of face-to-face interaction, shared goals and interdependence. All of this, of course, helped to cope with the many difficulties and deprivations that existed, such as unemployment and poor housing.

As well as in small local businesses and shops, the Shankill's population was employed in the larger linen and flax mills that surrounded the area. These were traditionally the largest employers in West Belfast. In addition to this there was a long tradition of shipyard and later aircraft production workers from the area, although the work was located across the River

Lagan in East Belfast. The engineering firm of James Mackies on the Springfield Road recruited a large proportion of its workforce from the Shankill. Mackies employed 4500 workers in 1968 and was a valuable source of employment, particularly for men, while women tended to be employed mainly in the textile and clothing industries and the many local retail, service and catering concerns. Clothing was, to an extent, the 'hidden base' of Belfast employing, at its peak, more people than ship-building and engineering. The largest clothing company on the Shankill was Ladybird (NI) Ltd, which closed down in 1977 having previously been a crucial source of employment for female workers (300 in 1976). Most of the textile firms had also gone into steep decline in the course of the 1970s, mainly because of factors associated with the decline in Britain's textile industry generally, with a loss of over 5000 jobs (Shankill Community Council 1983: 23–4).

Added to this crisis were the declining fortunes of the shipyard, which lost nearly 20,000 jobs between 1960 and 1980, and Mackies, which was forced to cut back its workforce by 3000 in the late 1970s and early 1980s. A further 500 jobs were lost in North Howard Street industrial complex on the Falls/Shankill divide over the same period, making the spiralling unemployment problem the most critical onslaught on traditional life in the Shankill by the 1980s.

Connected with this problem and magnifying its worst effects was the massive redevelopment programme that decimated the Shankill community throughout the seventies. The Shankill was Belfast's biggest redevelopment area and by 1985 some 80 per cent of the wards that constitute the study area had been completely rebuilt, with a resulting population decline from 30,000 (1971) to 17,000 (1981) (Census of NI 1971, 1981).

Industrial decline and the Shankill redevelopment experience

The economic background
Much of the present poverty can be directly attributed to the redevelopment programme, which caused a greater amount of physical, social and economic disruption to the area than the worldwide recession throughout the 1970s and 1980s and the political crisis that coincided with this period. There were hardships before redevelopment but the communal living patterns of the time helped to cope with these, and the results of redevelopment that were deemed to be advantageous by the planners to compensate for the break-up of such living patterns – increased employment opportunities and general prosperity – did not materialize.

The Hammer, a part of the Lower Shankill, lost all its local employment, most of its people and nearly all its houses. To replace these there was a grossly underused recreational complex and a regional youth centre. Together with an impressive leisure centre nearby and the glaring open spaces for car parks the Shankill became what some community activists had always strove to avoid – 'a mad Disneyland of expensive leisure centres, motorways, car-parks, and uninhabitable flats and supermarkets' (Birch, in Shankill Community Council 1977).

Some 3000 jobs, or 90 per cent of local employment opportunities, were lost in Shankill redevelopment areas between 1968 and 1981 as small businesses were bulldozed out of existence and larger firms relocated despite having experienced years of success in the area (Shankill Community Council 1977). Of 760 jobs in the wholesale, warehouse, dealing, building and haulage sectors (which are a peculiarity of the older proletarian back-street economy) that existed in 1968 not one remained by 1981. Employment in the retail sector dropped from 820 to 140 (nearly all on the front of the Shankill) and manufacturing employment fell from 400 to 40. There was a decline in catering and consumer services from 225 employees to 105. According to the Shankill Employment Report (Shankill Community Council 1977: 62–3) the Shankill lost a total of 9000 jobs between 1968 and 1981. Of the 3000 lost in redevelopment areas 90 per cent were in relatively small businesses.

The young people of the Shankill, and particularly school leavers, are the most vulnerable section of the population to the effects of massive reductions in employment opportunities. The only alternative for many is a year on a Youth Training Project (YTP), which has been the major government strategy at easing unemployment among young people. The YTP and other projects, such as WEEP (Work Experience on Employer's Premises), have been woefully inadequate and serve no purpose except to tinker with the unemployment figures and attempt to prepare young people for jobs that do not exist.

Youth and youth work initiatives
Traditionally, formal youth provision on the Shankill has been in the hands of church and (mainly church-connected) uniformed groups. Although the uniformed organizations are of long standing in the area, church youth clubs are, generally speaking, relative newcomers. Many of them emanated from the early days of the 'troubles' when 'concerned' clerics and lay-Christians attempted to curb the rising problem of street confrontations and general 'lawlessness', which were both widely associated with young people under 25. A significant part of such work was inspired initially by what can best be described as the 'radical evangelicism' of the leaders. These were largely young people themselves, who were practising informal evangelical Christianity (sometimes, but not necessarily of a particular denomination) and who combined their religious beliefs with a 'radical' approach to social problems as a means of at least understanding the confusion of the period (the early 1970s). They had a commitment to 'getting kids off the street for their own good' (that is, to divert them from rioting and petty crime) and perhaps to influencing them into 'thinking more positively'. Many of them had become disillusioned with traditional church provision and approaches, realizing that such

strategies could never significantly reach the vast majority of young people who were on the streets, because of their aversion to formal religion and scepticism towards the motives of church-based clubs. As one such worker informed us:

> The troubles were starting – there was a lot of riots on the Shankill and all that sort of thing and I discovered the irrelevance of church youth work of which I was a part in terms of the church, so . . . two of us . . . left our involvement in the church . . . Shankill Baptist . . . and established a sort of open house. We rented . . . a terraced house and ran something which originally was run from some sort of Christian motivation in a house called 'The Way' . . . which moved over a period . . . to some sort of more radical Christian position . . . to one that had absolutely no connections with Christianity at all . . . I was 19 myself and the kids coming in would have been a bit younger than that . . . It was people who had nowhere to go – they were rioting every night and it was very often people who were thrown out or barred from the youth club round the corner – St Saviour's as it was then – and there was nights there would be 80 people in this wee terraced house. The amazing thing was there was absolutely nothing there for them – there was a broken down old record player, there was no room to have anything, it was just a place to go – it was theirs or everybody that went and at the start a lot of them became sort of Christians. We were involved in what was called the Jesus Movement at the time – that sort of West Coast American thing that landed here with Arthur Blessed . . . [We] discovered that the ones that did become 'Christians' . . . immediately abandoned their mates and friends and the group that they knocked about with and became a sort of separated group which was nearly as bad as like a church . . . The house became more of a community house really . . . although I didn't know any of the terminology at the time . . . The kids who became Christians eventually got sort of forced out and these other kids would come round with a lot of pluck . . . that they had stolen and leave it in the yard . . . like the railings off Eastland Street playground . . . after they had closed it . . . sawed all the lead railings down and brought them round. They'd white boots on to make it seem they were from the Corporation and it was obvious things were getting a bit out of control in that respect. Other positive natural things had happened; like I remember with all the houses getting knocked down just below where we were, they used to start bringing the doors round you know and sawing them up and making window boxes and start selling them to people up the street . . . like a wee unofficial mini-industry started; none of these kids were working.
>
> (Redpath 1986)

Such an 'impulsive' initiative did not last for a significant number of years because of the growth of alternative activities and the channelling of the organizers' energies into the more pressing problem of the time – housing. Nevertheless, the 1970s did see a development in church youth provision in the Shankill area (encouraged by the state) as a response to the growth in social problems associated with young people and also in an attempt to stem the rising secularization of the period.

The inability of formal youth work initiatives to have positive influences on aspects of 'anti-social' behaviour has been recognized by officials in the Youth Service itself. As one prominent figure remarked on cut-backs in expenditure on youth work and the growth of social problems involving young people:

> I don't think there is a correlation. We had problems in the seventies and money was plentiful then. Cuts in expenditure are not the basis for social problems. There are more important conditions. Economic problems, for example, such as employment. There has also been a significant rejection of law and order which is not due to a lack of money but political activity. There is also the growing influence of Western society – materialism. The cuts are not the basis of increasing social upheaval . . . Such problems can't be dealt with by *normal methods* [emphasis added]. We must look at the causes not the symptoms. There are quite a number of homes where the parents have lost control through apathy or because the old man is in Crumlin Road [prison] or because of their lifestyle or because they don't have sufficient resources. I don't know whether it's because young people can't, like you or I did, look forward with a relative degree of certainty of going into a job. These are the factors that need to be considered.
>
> (Hearst 1985)

It would seem then that some prominent officials were aware that the problems of youth could not be divorced from the problems of modern urban society: social deprivation, materialism, inner area decline, social disintegration, unemployment. Formal youth provision is obviously not in a position to affect such conditions and is therefore a peripheral activity that can never really be expected to 'get to grips' with problems associated with youth. Perhaps the most widespread manifestation of social disintegration has been the eradication of kinship networks and the consequent undermining of the more informal agents of social control:

> There used to be this thing in the old Shankill if you fucked about you got a crack in the ear. Somebody came out. It might be a neighbour, maybe your granny or somebody. The thing could be nipped early in the bud you know. Now there's none of that and people are essentially afraid.
>
> (Redpath 1986)

Part of the reason why people are now afraid is that the ranks of paramilitary organizations have been swollen by the recruitment of young people.

There has been widespread condemnation in the Shankill, since redevelopment, of how State provision of education and youth projects has been prioritized:

> What I think is a ludicrous provision in the Shankill . . . is something like the Hammer Youth Resource Centre. It was a crazy idea . . . *nothing a leisure centre couldn't do that place is doing* [emphasis added]. That money would have been better spent in community centres, in local youth clubs and so forth.
>
> (Redpath 1986)

The project mentioned here is available for use by youth organizations and projects throughout the North and West Belfast areas. Most of its facilities are of a leisure/recreation nature that is broadly in line with formal youth provision in Belfast, i.e. there is a concentration on games and sports. Some resentment in the area arose because it was situated on a site that was orginally intended for the provision of a local community development project and some because at the time of this construction there was no statutory youth club in the immediate area (the only one in the Shankill was, at the time, an exclusive boys' club).

The Education Board has also been criticized for its lack of flexibility in relation to supporting community centres, particularly in places where community centres are also the only source of youth provision:

> There's the disgrace in terms of the voluntary provision where people have struggled in those areas like the Lower Shankill to get a bit of a community centre together for kids and the Education Board has been so fuckin' inflexible in its attitude. Ainsworth is another example where it has just not been possible to provide anything decent in terms of resources in those places for the kids. They're absolutely starved of resources and proper support and the fuckin' youth officer for the whole area . . . like a fuckin' policeman. You know, he essentially operates on a negative basis protecting what he has . . . and you know the sort of rules, like if you are a community centre you have to attend ten sessions a week before you even qualify for funding or something. No way can a small community centre do that because they are going to become a youth club centre. So they have got an option. They can either build community centre youth clubs, which they haven't done, or work within ways that community centres work. They should be doing both in fact. The other thing is that absolute abandoning to cuts of the idea of detached youth workers. I would be very strongly in favour of people who have no commitment to books and administrating things, who can just go and work with kids. That's where I think it counts.
>
> (Galbraith 1985/6)

'The legacy'

The resulting alienation of the young has manifested itself in a growth of 'anti-social', 'self-destructive' and 'negative' behaviour, such as solvent abuse and mugging. The ranks of paramilitary organizations have been swollen. The summer of 1984 saw the most serious outbreak of rioting on the Shankill for over ten years. The participants were overwhelmingly from the under-25 age group. On the surface the riots appeared to be, and were presented as, a direct reaction to the supergrass system of justice (the use of paid informers to implicate their alleged accomplices in serious crimes in return for certain privileges, such as immunity from prosecution). Although the disorder was undoubtedly precipitated by the start of one of the biggest supergrass hearings implicating 46 local men and one woman, there were significant underlying factors that contributed to the material pre-conditions necessary for the generation of rioting as a social practice. The editorial of the local newspaper (*Shankill Bulletin* no. 45, September 1984: 3) focused its attention upon the politicians who condemned the rioting without 'looking behind them at the causes'. It noted:

> the build up of despair and frustration in the weeks and days before the riots . . . The Government should have learned that you cannot beat down a community, lock up its people without a fair trial, on top of doing nothing effective to alleviate the growing, grinding poverty without a fierce reaction . . . The Government . . . should build a massive and co-ordinated programme to eliminate poverty in Northern Ireland. A programme to release all our people from the worst depression since the 1930s concentrating on better education for our children, looking after the elderly and defeating unemployment.

Significantly, the 1984 Shankill riots were the climax of a summer that saw; an outbreak of mugging, a dysentery epidemic and the destruction of Mid-Shankill (called the 'heart of the Shankill') by redevelopment. Fewer than one in five young people were finding jobs within two years of leaving school (according to a survey in the *Shankill Bulletin*, October 1983). By 1984 the situation had deteriorated). When widespread rioting broke out again in 1986 in response to the Anglo-Irish Agreement, it was once again young people who suffered the most.

Conclusion

The Shankill, then, has experienced considerable changes over the past 20 years or so. Despite this, a significant amount of the traditional character of the area has survived, particulary in the retention of the Shankill Road as a shopping street. Despite the onslaught of redevelopment and the 'troubles' there has been a willingness to strive for better conditions and many old customs have survived, although being limited by changing social and economic patterns. Many of the disrupted communities have to an extent reconstituted themselves in the new housing developments. The area has, however, been permanently scarred – physically and socially.

The effect of the efforts of the planners who claimed to be attempting to alleviate the deprivation of the Shankill people was the creation of widespread disruption and decay. The changes in terms of redevelopment and employment opportunities, etc., which were held to be taking place to benefit the working class, were in practice an attack on their living standards. Professor Peter Townsend, author of *Poverty in the United Kingdom*, said on the eve of redevelopment in 1968, of the Shankill: 'I had never before seen anywhere in the UK where there were so many evident signs of poverty' (Townsend 1979: 6).

Despite all the plans, development programmes and redevelopment strategies that have uprooted the area since then, the only fact that has changed is that the prime indicators of poverty – particularly unemployment – have considerably worsened.

Upper Springfield

The catholic Upper Springfield area of Belfast is a complex of post-war housing projects located on the outskirts of the city, about four miles from the centre. The study area comprises the Whiterock Ward, which is composed of Ballymurphy, Westrock, Springhill, Moyard, New Barnsley and Dermott Hill. Whiterock Ward is in West Belfast and is bounded on the north by the protestant Highfield and Springmartin estates. Across the Springfield Road to the west is the countryside, dominated by the Black Mountain, and to the east is the catholic Beechmount aross Britton's Parade. To the south is the City Cemetery and to the south-west the Turf Lodge estate.

Ballymurphy is the biggest estate in the area and is fairly typical of the social, physical and economic character of the Upper Springfield. Some of the smaller estates though, in particular Dermott Hill and Springfield Park, contain newer up-market housing and are the residential neighbourhoods for the local professional classes and socially aspiring families. According to the 1981 Census Report for Northern Ireland, the population of the area was 8644.

History and development

The Ballymurphy housing project was a result of housing put back following the Second World War. The estate was effectively completed in the early 1950s. One early occupant of the estate and community activist recalled that:

> There was an enormous waiting list because there were no houses built after the war and the idea was to build as many houses as they possibly could in a small area. There was very little imagination in the lay-out or the design of the houses.
> The notion was to build the houses as quickly as possible . . . they

were an absolute failure. There was dampness, draughts and they were too small in any case for the large families.

(Cahill 1985)

A full-time Community Worker in the Whiterock Resource Centre saw the initial problems in terms of demographic and social service factors:

There was a concentration of problem families that were moved in at the same time and there was no back-up resources. There was no proper social service facilities or home help or community nursery, or any proper facilities to support families and the idea seemed to be just create a so-called 'second class' status – dump all your problem families in one area.

(de Bariod 1985)

Father Des Wilson first came to the area as a priest in 1971 and since then has been involved in 'bringing the Church to the people'. Adopting this stance has led to an ongoing dispute with the Catholic hierarchy which, at times, has had a bitter flavour to it:

It [Ballymurphy] was an artificially contrived population and the whole programme was geared towards concentrating the 'lower level' tenant in the one area. It was originally 25 per cent protestant and was a settled, stable community in terms of family life and so on.

(Wilson 1985)

It became a liability to have a Ballymurphy address and many of those who could have contributed to its improvement moved elsewhere while others avoided it altogether.

By the late 1950s the estate's reputation for bad rent payers was well established and the Estates Department of the City Council suggested it to one researcher for the purpose of a *Study of Unsatisfactory Tenants* (Field 1959). The description shows that the social condition of the estate had already deteriorated considerably:

The general appearance of the estate is most depressing. The roads and paths are always strewn with paper, metal scrap and glass (I could not see a single litter basket on the estate). Very few of the gardens are neat and there are no trees. Vacant spaces in and around the estate are rough and full of weeds. The shop frontages are very dirty and the broken ventilators under each shop window look like gaping holes in the wall. The doors to the flats are covered with scratched names and epitaphs. All the windows in the dentists' surgery appear to be broken and some are boarded up.

The amenities, apart from shops and buses, are very poor for an estate of this size. There is a large Catholic intermediate school for boys immediately below the estate but no primary school closer than the Falls Road. Nor are there any churches or buildings for Catholic or non-demoninational community activity on or near the estate. There are no proper playgrounds for young children, although the older ones play on the open ground that exists around the estate at present.

The tenants in the sample have large families (the average number of school and pre-school children per household is 4–8), and more than two-thirds of the population is under 18. Three-quarters of the wage earners are unskilled or semi-skilled. Only half of the male householders were working at the time of the survey. The average income of the household was largely dependent on state benefits . . . Two-thirds of the front gardens were cultivated . . . The large majority of living rooms were not adequately furnished. By original definition this description was given to rooms where there was some floor covering, curtains, an easy chair, a table, sideboard of some kind and a couple of straight chairs. Only a few rooms were coded either as well furnished or as barely furnished . . . only a few houses and persons on this estate were coded as dirty. The remainder were equally divided into the categories clean and indifferent.

The study was very critical of several aspects of the housing management of the Estates Department and made a number of recommendations. They were not implemented.

There was a period of 13 years from 1950 during which there were no schools to facilitate the population and the nearest schools were unable to cope with the overflow of population from Ballymurphy: 'The only way they could deal with it was to give them half days' education' (Cahill 1985). In other words, an entire generation did not receive a full education in Ballymurphy when it was something that was being taken for granted elsewhere. This in turn exacerbated the already acute social problems and more significantly hampered the employment prospects of anyone who came from an area which needed all the incentives it could get in this field.

Early self-help developments – the formation of the BTA

The Ballymurphy Tenants Association (BTA) was formed in 1963. It represented an effort by the leading residents to halt the demoralization of the estate:

> I think the formation of the Tenants Association came through frustration . . . They [the local people] decided to have a public meeting to discuss some of the problems and difficulties in the area and counteract some of the things that were said, like the people in Ballymurphy were dirty, lazy and vandals and that they could not manage the budget, and kept the coal in the bath.
>
> (Cahill 1985)

The BTA developed two lines of strategy. The first was to work with the statutory and voluntary authorities for the general improvement of the estate. But its officers found that one after another their suggestions were turned down. Even when agreement was reached for new arrangements of procedures (for example, with repairs) they were soon ignored. By the late 1960s the officers were convinced that appeals to public authorities on grounds of equity, fair play and justice were useless. Gradually they turned to threats of legal action, political demonstrations and extra-legal actions, such as rent strikes. The second line of strategy was to develop a community centre for the estate. The first stage of the centre was completed at the end of 1970, with half the cost being met by the Ministry of Community Relations.

By this stage, events in the area and in Northern Ireland generally had taken a dramatic turn with the outbreak of widespread civil disturbances in August 1969 and the entry of the British Army to the streets of West Belfast. The Ballymurphy Citizens Defence Committee (CDC) was formed at this time as a reaction to the increasing number of sectarian confrontations and the lack of confidence in the RUC as an impartial force. The CDC was initially concerned with defence and helping refugees from other areas but proceeded to develop new roles in peace keeping (between local youths and the troops), policing (organizing vigilante patrols) and youth work. It was split into two factions, one for the lower part of the estate, based at St Thomas' School, and one for the upper part, based at St Bernadette's.

From the start the Catholic Church was sceptical (and/or suspicious) about independent groups developing their own programmes and exercising control. The complex relationship between the authority of the Catholic Church and local secular organizations can be traced to this period:

> Their (the Church's) idea was to be in control of whatever was happening. The Tenants Association resisted that notion and were determined that anything that they would do they would do it on their own and the people of the area would be in control of it.
>
> (Cahill 1985)

The Church/voluntary dichotomy was to become much more complex after 1970 with the development of secular voluntary organisations and attempts by the Church to re-assert its authority in face of the ascendant republican movement. But perhaps the most significant episode in this period and the most crucial, in terms of control, was the development of youth work initiatives.

Early youth initiatives

The lower Ballymurphy CDC had by the end of 1970 become actively engaged in youth work, running sports activities under the title of Corpus Christi Youth Club and using St Thomas' School for training sessions. It also took an active part in raising funds for the school's field centre and hostel and for the church of Corpus Christi, opened in 1971.

The lower Ballymurphy CDC had in effect been 'taken over' by the catholic middle class and the Catholic Church following the split in the republican movement in early 1969. This period saw the beginning of a church-controlled youth club – Corpus Christi – and an independent youth club, organized by the BTA in the community centre.

The BTA received 1200 applications for membership for its youth club in the first week, which led to it having to scrap the idea of a structured club because of lack of accommodation. There were considerable problems at first, which were connected to the civil unrest in the area. The BTA set up a youth committee, which attempted to organize youth activities throughout Ballymurphy:

> We were using the schools in the area for discos but we had to abandon that because any rows that developed during the week between the two different gangs of young people invariably ended up inside the discos on a Saturday. At the end of the day they had to abandon this particular activity. The final straw was when a gang of young people arrived in a van one night and produced a gun and we could not take the risk any more.
>
> (de Bariod 1985)

The early 1970s was the period when the government began to allocate substantial financial support to youth programmes. Much of this strategy was an attempt to defuse as much as possible the escalating political crisis and increasing regularity of street confrontations involving groups of young people in areas such as West Belfast:

> There was a lot of interest in youth work from the government as well, because they somehow had the idea that youth work would solve the problem of, you know, it was the old notion of getting the kids off the streets. The added thing here was reconciliation, community relations and all the rest and that was basically the inducement that the government had.
>
> (de Bariod 1985)

Reconciliation has always been a key aim of youth work in Northern Ireland and the authorities have attempted to achieve this by a number of strategies, such as integrated outings, visits to clubs in other communities, children's holidays, exchange visits and, to some extent, 'social education'. Social control is the other side of the same coin and government interventions in youth programmes (to keep young people off the streets, to make them think positively, to give kids something constructive to do) were a direct response to the break-down of law and order, alienation and endemic inter-communal conflicts, all of which were rampant by 1973. Even within relatively small areas such as Ballymurphy there were regular struggles as rival factions vied for supremacy. Unlike the Church versus secular contest they were not always confined to a war of words and often exhibited violent manifestations.

There was a lot of friction in the greater Ballymurphy area between the Officials and Provisionals or supporters of the provisional and official republican movement and this tended to make its way into the youth club and we in the BTA had to abandon the discos sometime early in 1973. We had a riot on our hands that basically developed into a gunfight in the estate afterwards. The same thing happened in St Damian's here when there was a kind of Mexican stand-off between two groups of young people armed with rifles. St Thomas' had to abandon their discos when a nail bomb and a Thompson sub-machine gun were brought into their disco, and this was reflected all across the city at the time. It was very difficult to operate a youth work programme within the building . . . We attempted to develop a local project in . . . houses in Divismore Park. Unfortunately the empty houses proved an attraction for the army and they used them for observation posts. They were breaking into them and leaving the doors open. The kids were then getting in and out, people were becoming quite afraid of the houses because they knew there was an army presence there from time to time and that particular scheme collapsed as a result of that.

(de Bariod 1985)

It was such a trajectory of events that led, almost inadvertently, to the establishment of 'detached work' in Belfast:

The other house was in Ballymurphy Road . . . we set up a permanent residence there. There was no support from any direction . . . started to fund raise. Six months after the job was established the Belfast Education and Library Board had come to know about it and thought they would like to get into it. Into . . . detached youth work without any idea of what they were letting themselves in for or having any real policy on it or positive ideas on it. They created a job as a detached youth worker in the Ballymurphy area.

(de Bariod 1985)

Limitations to youth work

The only voluntary youth club in Ballymurphy (although there was another in New Barnsley) was the BTA club, which received gradually depreciating support from the government from its inception in the early 1970s. It received the salaries of the staff and £250 a year. This kind of support was seen by the local community activists as being grossly inadequate.

The BTA reiterated the need for voluntary youth provision in the area, particularly in view of the fact that the formal education system was seen to represent 'an alien culture' and statutory youth provision was perceived as an extension of this:

It is middle class culture full of ideology, full of values and traditions to which working class people do not relate . . . There is no input at all by parents . . . The whole value of the Youth Service going back to the Industrial Revolution had been from a middle class ideology base and basically from middle class fears of large groups of working class young people.

So you have got the traditional lies coming through from those times, through the youth service. You can see it if you look through the structure of management in the Belfast Education and Library Board and . . . if you look at the sort of background they come from. They come from the kind of church organization, the established type youth clubs and so on. You don't have a great many people coming from, say, radical working class backgrounds in the higher structure of the Youth Service . . . certain rules are set down . . . which again you wonder where that kind of value comes from.

Like the so-called four letter words and so on, which would be banned in a youth club. You know, there is a clash of values there immediately. I think that the Youth Service is available to younger people, does fulfil the needs of some people, but I do not think it comes anywhere near fulfilling the needs of the majority of young people and I do not think it even sits down and works out what these needs are. If you walk into any youth club you will find the same thing . . . your table tennis table, your snooker table, your darts board, your TV . . . I think that the detached youth work . . . in this area and in some other areas as well, certainly had some potential towards travelling along some of these roads because you were not restricted by a building, by large numbers, by having to provide equipment and then police equipment so that it did not get wrecked. I think that can come out by the fact that the boards very quickly clamped down on detached youth work . . . I think you had a more truthful and natural relationship between the adults involved and the young people involved because they weren't involved simply in some kind of table tennis competition or debating societies or whatever. But there was an overall involvement also in all the community activities and that is something some people were asking all the time that you cannot divorce youth work from an overall concept of community work, that the problems that affect the community affect the young people . . . I think when you have the problems of a community being defined by people from outside of their community, outside that environment, and the solutions, their so-called solutions, just don't relate to what is going on. That spills right on to the street where you have most young people in this area, standing on street corners . . . They don't come into youth clubs and that has always been the case.

(de Bariod)

Increasingly the Board came to prioritize direct formal provision as opposed to informal, basically controlled projects. This strategy tended to operate against the most deprived areas. The Ballymurphy estate itself had only the precarious provision of the voluntary club and the church-controlled Corpus Christi project. The strategy was a direct consequence of stringent cash limits being imposed from central authority and attempts by the Board to re-assert its control by giving priority to club-based projects. Detached work projects, either because of the informality of the organization involved, or because of the radical nature of the work, were first to suffer.

Certainly by the mid-1980s the diverse problems of Ballymurphy were being exacerbated by cut-backs in public expenditure and an increasing unemployment problem, which some community workers claimed had reached 87 per cent. The allocation of resources became much more selective throughout this period as a result of cut-backs and the question of control became the overriding factor as voluntary projects were axed and church groups received any support that was available. Local people saw this as a case of the authorities making value judgements in terms of 'respectability'.

The BAN report and Ballymurphy

The report of the BAN project team on *Belfast Areas of Special Social Need* (1976) identified the Whiterock Ward as an area of highest overall social need. The then Minister of State, Lord Melchett, set up a Belfast Areas of Need Sub-group, which consisted of public officials and residents' representatives as a means of enabling the community to be involved in the future planning and decision-making processes that would affect the Ballymurphy area. The sub-group produced a report in 1980, which indicated that the problems of Ballymurphy and the Whiterock Ward were at least as 'deep and difficult as any experienced, or likely to be experienced elsewhere in the British Isles' (BAN Sub-group 1980). On top of the serious social and economic problems there was the continuing political disorder, which expanded the complexity and extent of the socio-economic problems.

The BAN report rated areas of social need according to 20 indicators of social and economic deprivation. Whiterock Ward was shown to be the ward most in need according to this, which would make it one of the most deprived urban areas in Western Europe. As is usually the case, such an accumulative mass of problems tends to create a culture and ongoing cycle of deprivation that is likely to enfold within the children born into such circumstances.

There was, in fact, a high proportion of dependent children in Whiterock Ward, with over 63 per cent of households having at least one child and over 28 per cent having three or more dependent children (the Belfast Urban Area averages were 37 and 12 per cent respectively). Of the Ward's population 32.19 per cent were aged less than 15 years (BUA average 11.9 per cent) and the mean age for the ward was 19.7 years (BUA average 30.5). Household size was also relatively large, with an average of 4.5 persons per household as compared to 3.0 for Belfast as a whole (all these and subsequent figures, unless otherwise stated, are taken from the BAN Sub-group Report 1980). There was also a high incidence of one-parent families (12 per cent in Whiterock compared to 5 per cent throughout Belfast).

Social facilities

The primary sources of youth provision in the area were the youth clubs. Two of these, Ballymurphy Tenants Association Youth Club and the church-controlled Corpus Christi, were in Ballymurphy. The Board controlled Matt Talbot Club was in Moyard, the voluntary Newhill Club in New Barnsley and St Aidan's Primary School part-time club was between the Ballymurphy and Turf Lodge estates.

The Whiterock Leisure Centre, with sophisticated modern facilities for sport and leisure, was opened in the autumn of 1984. However, it does not appear to be an attractive venue for the youth of the area. As one senior worker in the centre has stated: 'the concept of leisure centres is a middle class concept' (Morgan 1986). The BAN Sub-group report (1980) indicated: 'for those caught in such a syndrome [the cycle of deprivation] the provision of better leisure facilities may be very low in the list of priorities.'

Much of the commercial provision for young people, such as cinemas and dance halls, has been curtailed, partly by the troubles. There are, for example, no cinemas operating in West Belfast. However, hotels, pubs and social clubs have stepped in to cater for the potential market. This has been fairly successful, but one by-product has been a serious under-age drinking problem. There has been a change in drinking habits in recent years, with a large increase in the numbers of licensed social clubs.

Sports facilities in the area are limited. There is one 'gaelic' (all weather) pitch at St Thomas' school and another (grass) at the adjacent Corrigan Park. An indoor swimming pool is available at Whiterock Leisure Centre. The swimming pool, however, is, with the leisure centre in general, excluded from or exluded by the local population. As the centre under-manager has said: 'More employed people use this leisure centre as opposed to unemployed', to which a prominent local youth worker has added: 'People need to know how to use recreational facilities . . . prices are too high in Leisure Centres'. In our survey of youth club participants (see Chapter 5) in the area only 14 per cent of the first choice alternatives to club activities and 10 per cent of the second choices were other clubs or recreational facilities; 32 and 40 per cent respectively spent their time in informal activities ('hanging about the streets' or 'sitting at home').

There are a number of community centres, usually controlled by local residents and catering for most age groups. The emphasis tends to be on adult social evenings and licensed social functions. Apart from Ballymurphy there are centres at New Barnsley, Newhill and one in the new Whiterock Leisure Centre.

The Upper Springfield Resource Centre is an important community facility created and controlled by local community groups and concerned with resources from the point of view of adult education. It has sponsored local public enquiries into education, unemployment and a variety of cultural activities. It also publishes a local community newspaper, *Resource*, which focuses on diverse issues, such as housing, cultural and social activities, welfare rights, youth programmes, women's issues, prisoners' rights and local political commentary. The community house at 123 Springfield Avenue is also a major adult education facility, with upwards of 100 people weekly participating in a variety of courses recognized by the Rupert Stanley College of Further Education.

The Ballymurphy Handicapped Association is the main voluntary organization working with the handicapped in the area. It should be remembered that the prevalence of mental and physical handicap in the estate has tended to be up to three times the rate found in Belfast and Northern Ireland generally (Spencer 1972).

Educational indicators and facilities

The BAN Sub-group report indicated the extent of educational disadvantage in the Whiterock Ward. Over 90 per cent of the people residing in Whiterock Ward left school without passing any examinations. Of those persons in the ward sitting examinations, only 10 per cent passed, and over 50 per cent of 11-year-old Whiterock pupils had a reading age of 9 years of less, compared to a Belfast average of 24 per cent.

The BAN survey thought that variations in educational attainment were more closely linked with family and community characteristics than with educational provision. The closest links of retarded readers were with low income and unskilled occupations and those of school exams and occupational qualifications were with social class. They concluded that educational disadvantage measured in terms of the number of pupils leaving school without reaching the level of attainment of which they are capable seemed more likely to be reduced by a broad approach than by education provision alone.

Table 1 illustrates one of the indicators of need examined by the BAN Sub-group study – those in receipt of free school meals. When we consider that the girls' comprehensive school (St Louise's), which has the highest rate (9 per cent) of those paying full or part, is located outside the study area and draws many of its pupils from 'more respectable' neighbourhoods in West Belfast then these figures become glaring.

It seems almost incredible that every single pupil at the boys' secondary

Table 1 Number of pupils receiving free school meals by school

School	Daily total	Free	Paying full or part
St Bernadette's	226	210	16 (7%)
St Aidan's (primary)	324	318	6 (2%)
St Thomas'	191	191	0
St Louise's	690	628	62 (9%)

school in Ballymurphy was receiving free school meals (we may reasonably assume that the socio-economic conditions of the girls from Ballymurphy who attend St Louise's were basically the same). Providing more schools or more teachers may not be the answer to such a problem even in terms of raising the standard of education. The BAN Sub-group report recorded one of the most specific needs in the educational restructuring of schools in the area, as perceived by the community, as 'changes to the school curricula to meet the needs of pupils. Concern was expressed about the relevance of school programmes to meet the needs of the majority of pupils' (BAN Sub-group 1980: 42).

Economic indicators

Forty-three per cent of the total population in Whiterock and 39 per cent of the heads of households were between the ages of 15 and 39, which indicates a long-term continuation of demand for employment. The corresponding figures for Belfast were 35 and 25 per cent respectively (according to the Belfast Household Survey 1978).

The level of demand for employment is one of the factors determining the economic health of the community. The figures for heads of households in the 'economically active' category (excludes those who are listed as retired, housewives, or never worked) show 48 per cent unemployment in Whiterock, compared to 14 per cent (in 1978) in Belfast. The Belfast figure at the time of the study was 18 per cent (Department of Economic Development, press release, 1986) and we may safely assume that there was a corresponding increase in Whiterock. In fact, allowing for the spiralling unemployment rate of the 1980s, and if we include married women in the figure, we are talking about an unemployment rate in Whiterock in the region of 80 per cent, or 60 per cent for head of households. The BAN Sub-group in 1980 quoted data from the Department of Economic Development showing that 7.3 per cent of the registered unemployed at the time were from Whiterock while only 1.8 per cent of all heads of households were residents of the ward (para. 11.4). The situation for the future can only be expected to deteriorate, as Whiterock has a significantly higher proportion of young people, who are not yet available for employment, than the rest of Belfast. One of the major aspects of this problem is the unavailability of local employment opportunities. Whiterock Ward has nearly 2 per cent of the total heads of household in Belfast and less than 1 per cent of the total employment opportunities. Limited occupational status and low income contribute to the pressures of high unemployment in the area. Some 80 per cent of the heads of household in Whiterock are in manual occupations with over half of these classified as unskilled (compared to 62 and 41 per cent respectively for Belfast) (NIHE 1978). Ballymurphy was not only an unattractive site for industrial developments, it was virtually impossible for local people from the estate to find employment elsewhere because of the reputation it had as well as its physical isolation: 'I really believe they should change the name of Ballymurphy. This estate has [always] had a notorious name' (Spencer 1972: 79).

There were some attempts by the local figures to encourage employers to give jobs to people from the area but these were merely peripheral measures and frequently met with failure:

> Father Wilson was speaking to industrialists asking them if they would offer jobs. There were two jobs but unfortunately it was 35 miles away from Ballymurphy and people would have to travel there for work. He made the announcement on the Sunday at Mass saying that two jobs were available and the next morning there were over 90 people queuing up to get in for the interviews for those two jobs. That was the indication of people wanting to work.
>
> (Cahill 1985)

A local employment project was established eventually on a 13 acre site adjacent to the estate which had previously been a farm. Three units were established with some government aid and a training unit was established. Over 100 young people were being trained in work skills each year:

> We knew that a training programme would be needed . . . if we were going to redress that balance [of an over-preponderence of unskilled labour] and that went on for a period of five years . . . and that . . . stimulated the confidence here. They were being placed in jobs fairly quickly and they were doing their exams in the technical college and they were getting very good results there as well.
>
> (Cahill 1985)

However, yet again the hope of any form of improvement in the local economy was thwarted. On this occasion the continuing military crisis had a direct bearing:

> Some weeks later the British Army came into the factories . . . and advised the owners . . . they [the army] were taking over the entire

site . . . to build a fort . . . That put paid to any effort to create employment in the area.

(Cahill 1985)

That was in 1979 and the result was an increase in demoralization and a feeling of hopelessness within the community. The Northern Ireland Census in 1981 estimated that well over half (56 per cent) of the economically active male population of Ballymurphy was out of work. This is probably a conservative figure as many of the Census forms were destroyed in a ritual burning as a protest in support of the hunger strike at the time, in which ten republican prisoners fasted to death in protest against the 'criminalization' policy of the British government. The hunger strike had the effect of further alienating a large section of the community and embittering attitudes against the British. Two years later Gerry Adams became the first Provisional Sinn Fein candidate to win a seat in the Westminster elections. It was no accident that he did so in West Belfast. It was a significant victory, even allowing for a split in the 'constitutional' nationalist vote. The Spencer Report in 1971 quoted one middle-aged woman as saying:

Street names which have Ballymurphy in them should be changed . . . as I am sure it prevents one from getting a job and one feels like a criminal when giving one's address.

(Spencer 1972: 139)

By 1981 the street names had been changed. They were translated into Gaelic by local inhabitants in a mood of nationalist stridency.

3 THE YOUTH SERVICE IN NORTHERN IRELAND

The Youth Service in Northern Ireland owes its origins to the development of the Youth Service in England. It would appear that youth organizations sprang up around 1833, taking on the form of Christian, uniformed movements.

> There were also a wide range of commercial leisure agencies touched on here which deliberately set out to appeal to children and adolescents, such as Penny Dreadfuls and the Penny Theatres, while in the second half of the nineteenth century adult organised youth movements, such as Boy's Clubs and cadets were becoming more common.
>
> (Springhall 1985)

During this time the Youth Service's philosophy was embedded in a theory of character building. As Dr Thomas Arnold noted, 'The Youth Service is to endow boys with the bodies of men strong and active, their minds clear, rich and versatile, spirits able to control body and mind to direct their physical and mental powers to the service of God' (Blach 1980).

It may be argued that the creation of youth organizations was based on the ethos of controlling working class young people, and males in particular. Bearing in mind that most of these organizations were created by middle class philanthropists it is no surprise that their ambition was to control the working class male. As John Springhall suggests, 'The most noisy customers for the new forms of the leisure industry were among those unmarried men who, without family responsibilities, were becoming independent of their own parents and had sufficient wages to lead an active social life' (Blach 1980).

It is obvious that youth organizations were patriarchal in their attempts to do something for working class males. As Springhall asserts, 'much female leisure has been concealed simply because it took place either in the privacy of the home or only when accompanied by the opposite sex' (Springhall 1985: 23–4). The nature of the female relationship with the leisure industry has largely been ignored in the various studies surrounding a history of the youth service. This point will be considered later.

A few organizations were created for females around the middle of the nineteenth century in England. Such organizations emanated from the Girls' Club Union (1833 in England, 1909 in Northern Ireland). Yet it is not surprising that these organizations were controlled by the middle classes and geared towards the ethos of character building.

Working class youths have for the most part been defined as 'delinquent' and the creation of youth organizations was seen as a valid way of controlling them. These organizations felt the need to 'save' adolescents from the 'evils' of their parent culture – 'gambling, moral laxity, animal excitement, theatres, cinemas and the curse of drink' (Leslie 1985: 23–4) – with the intention of directing working class leisure into respectable channels with a religious or military bias or both.

The Boys' Brigade and the Boy Scouts were two of the best known character building organizations created around the turn of the century to assist young men through the presumed storm and crisis of the newly diagnosed adolescent period. These organizations expected loyalty from their members.

> This loyalty was but one strand in a complicated web of national identity and the connection of the one to the other was achieved in various ways by different movements.
>
> (Blach 1980)

Such organizations, including the Boy Scouts, Boys' Brigade, Army Cadets, Naval Cadets, Church Scout Patrols and the Jewish Lads' Brigade, were closely connected to the army. Thus their members wore uniforms, practised drill and were often superintended by an ex-army officer. The concept of wearing uniforms and practising drill served to reinforce an ethos of discipline. Resulting from this the leadership and models were essentially patriarchal. Females were awarded a subordinate role in the fabric of the nation as reproducers. Young males were seen as the essential contributors to society. While many uniformed organizations recruited members of the working classes, they were essentially middle class in outlook and character.

There were repeated attempts by the state to maintain control over the working class adolescent. One attempt to exert this control is illustrated by the Russell Committee in 1917. This committee sought to control the working class adolescent by co-ordinating and encouraging the provision of facilities for most young males in an attempt to combat juvenile delinquency via the creation of local juvenile organization committees. More recent attempts to divert the attention of the working class adolescent were highlighted in the state's creation of community centres and the availability of grants for unemployed adolescents. This appeared to be an innovative development.

This policy was directed into the Youth Service in Northern Ireland in an essentially different way. From 1917 to 1943 many youth organizations were created, such as: Youth Hostel Association of Northern Ireland (1931), Young Men's Christian Association (1934), Federation of Boys' Clubs (1940), Army Cadet Force, Catholic Girl Guides and Catholic Boy Scouts (1943). The creation of these organizations was treated with scepticism by many working class adolescents. As Jeffs (1985) suggested, '16% of the youth population was affiliated to youth organizations'. It would seem that the character building ethos of these organizations was largely unattractive to most adolescents of that time.

In its attempts to conceal the character building ethos built into the Youth Service, the Ministry of Education made a half-hearted attempt to provide a Youth Welfare Act. This act (1944) did very little for youth but provided a youth committee. Its function consisted of recommending applications for grant aid and making deputations to or presonal contact with local authorities in several areas with regard to provision of playing fields, gyms and swimming pools. The youth committee mainly grant-aided clubs, which were recreational in outlook.

In England from 1944 to 1947 there were many debates about the future of the Youth Service. Such issues as the role of the Youth Service and its relationship with the national education system were of great concern. There was concern over whether the Youth Service should be a statutory duty on the part of every local education authority. Such debates had obvious consequences for the Youth Service in Northern Ireland. Resulting from this many organizations were created: the Northern Ireland Council for the YMCA, the Churches Youth Welfare Council, the Catholic Diocesan Youth Council, Down and Connor, the Federation of Boys' Clubs and the Federation of Girls' Clubs. Such organizations sought to attract the working class adolescent via their character building ethos.

The Youth Service in Northern Ireland made consistent attempts to attract working class adolescents. But by 1948 out of a total of 135,000 adolescents between the ages of 14 and 20 only 65,000 were being catered for in individual units of youth organizations. Training for youth workers, however, was limited and by the onset of the 1950s the social role of youth work was the inculcation of discipline and kindred 'respectable' moral values.

During the 1950s society witnessed a major restructuring. Working class people in general were *relatively* better off than before the war with the advent of the welfare state, and there were a number of social changes as a consequence. Increased production and higher levels of income made the subsequent increase in consumption a realistic goal for sections of the working class. Working hours became shorter, which led to an increase in leisure time.

Similarly, the 1960s were also a dramatic time of change for many working class adolescents. For the first time the working class was to become involved as a major participant in a consumer-orientated society. Many youths had more time on their hands and leisure was dominating a large section of their lives. This shift in emphasis from production to consumption meant more leisure. Leisure facilities were concentrated in city centres. Working class youth, in particular, were involved in a competitive, consumerized society whose competitive efforts were manifested in the increased provision of leisure and youth facilities. At the same time the abandonment of conscription only served to increase the number of young males on the streets in England. As a means of competing for the attention of this 'new consumer' the state implemented more plans in the way of youth provision. The Albemarle Report (1960) was one indication of the state's continued attempts to control working class young people. In it 'It was hoped that youth workers, properly trained and equipped, would offer the young a "Constructive Alternative".' The report directed most of its attention to working class males. Like many other reports in the past, Albemarle was viewed by many as a commendable but limited document. It was completed in less than 12 months and four recommendations out of 44 were accepted on the day of publication.

At this time, the Youth Service in Northern Ireland did little in the way of responding to the new distinctive form of adolescent lifestyle. In terms of providing an outlet for this new consumerized adolescent the youth service merely served to provide youth activities that reiterated the themes of character building. The Youth and Sports Council Act 1962 did little for working class adolescents, as did the reports that dominated the Youth Service from 1960 to 1968. However, in 1971 there did seem to be some recognition given to the role of young people: 'There was a need for services for the young; particularly those who had left school and whose environment was inadequate' (Northern Ireland Youth Committee 1973: 10–12). But there were no governmental attempts to alleviate the problems faced by young people who lived in 'inadequate environments'.

The philosophy behind the Youth Service in Northern Ireland was only clear about one thing: its need to maintain control over working class youth. Such an ethos had over-shadowed the Youth Services in England and Northern Ireland for more than a century. The state's constant attempts to disguise its intentions were illustrated in its seemingly benign interest in the role of young people. In England this was reflected in such things as: '13 million pounds expenditure on the Youth Service, 100 Detached Youth Workers, Youth Counselling expanding, Youth Wings sprouting; 700 Teacher/Leader posts, Youth Tutor posts, National Association of Youth Clubs, the establishment of Community Industry Scheme for the unemployed, alternative youth movements established such as Street Aid, Arts Labs, British Youth Council' (Milson/Fairburn Report 1975). All these initiatives were seen as an attempt to compete with the leisure industry within which working class young people seemed to assume a 'real' role, that of a consumer.

The effects of the post-war economic boom had produced a generation of young people with a different set of attitudes, ideas and lifestyles. These attitudes often manifested themselves in a variety of ways of which their right to participate in a democratic society was very significant. In 1969 many young people became involved in street riots in Northern Ireland. This chance to participate in street confrontations with the state authorities was very significant in that for many it was an alternative to existing youth provision. Young people also became involved, to an alarming extent, in paramilitary activity.

It is not surprising then that the state-funded Youth Service developed dramatically during this time. In 1973 the Recreation and Youth Services Act asserted: 'Each Board shall secure the provision for its area of adequate facilities for recreational, social, physical, cultural and youth service activities and for services ancillary to education' (Northern Ireland Youth Committee 1973: 10–12). The main assertions in this act dealt with the Boards' responsibility to maintain a Youth Service as a statutory obligation. This response was seen as a reaction by the state to street confrontations, which were increasing in intensity, frequency and scale.

The 'alarming' rise in street disorder and juvenile 'anti-social' activity was viewed with serious concern by both the state and community leaders alike, which precipitated a number of initiatives seeking to direct working class adolescents' time into 'more constructive channels', as the adults saw it. As one local community activist and former youth worker asserted:

> The whole values of the Youth Service going back to the industrial revolution have been from a middle class ideology base and basically from middle class fears of large groups of working class young people.
>
> (de Bariod 1985)

However, this view is not representative of all community activists. It would appear that most of them see youth work in conservative terms, just as many working class adults see 'youth on the rampage'.

Within Great Britain and Northern Ireland it might be said that post-war social policies leading to the redevelopment of traditional working class communities were another attempt by the state to sectionalize the community in order that social control could be made easier. One facet of this sectionalization was the creation of a separatist Youth Service that served to alienate many young people from the community and the real issues within it. Yet many local community activists viewed such extensive youth provision as plausible, as it served to take many young people off the streets. It did, however, result in a loosening of the more informal agents of social control that were inherent in traditional working class communities.

Much of the concern for young people has been channelled into youth projects that appear to concentrate heavily on giving young people something to do, assuming that by occupying the recipients with acceptable alternative forms of behaviour, the aspiration to riot or participate in anti-social behaviour would magically disappear. Such policies, however, tend to ignore the causes of 'anti-social' behaviour, such as deprivation, alienation, social disintegration and racial and religious discrimination.

From 1977 onwards the Youth Service produced a series of reports that gave little insight as to its future direction. The aims of these reports served to reiterate 'personal development and social education'. However, they were somewhat vague in regard to the meaning of such concepts and how these were to be implemented.

The most radical development in this period was the creation of a programme of 'detached youth work'. Such projects were widely welcomed by community leaders and youth workers. Initially they concentrated on work with young people who did not use formal youth provision. This placed the worker in a unique position of facilitating for the young in their 'natural environment' without the formality of a club and all the restrictions and rules that go with it. It was a radical form of youth work in that the worker was able to relate to the young on their own level and participate with them. Such youth provision did offer young working class people a chance to participate in a programme that was not only decided by them but also related to their needs. This was one of the state's more effective ways of dealing with the issues facing young people.

In an attempt to give working class young people access to the decision-making powers within the Youth Service the Northern Ireland Office established a Youth Forum and a Youth Council (Department of Information Services, press release) in 1979. It asserted:

> Young people should be involved in the operation of a youth service . . . Young people can take decisions and exercise real responsibility . . . Within the Forum they will discuss and comment on any issue that it wishes.

Alongside this 30 youth councils were created. These intended to give young people a chance to discuss the real issues affecting their lives, at a local community level. It may be argued, however, that such a forum was a tokenist gesture on the part of the state and catered for those who could articulate their views best. It is obvious that many working class young people have been deprived of the educational avenues through which such articulation was made possible.

At the start of the 1980s the monetarist cutbacks affected the major state controlled institutions of society. The youth service was also cut back, which led to a greater emphasis on the voluntary sector. In interviews, Youth Service staff were asked: 'Do you think there is a significant correlation between the cutbacks in public expenditure on Youth Work and the apparent increase in social problems involving young people?' As the Divisional Youth Officer (DYO) for West Belfast said, 'Cutbacks have had a devastating effect on the Youth Service' (Donnelly 1985), and as the DYO for the north of the city of Belfast stated, 'There is a fair correlation between the world recession and social problems' (Steven 1985). Most significantly, the reduction in detached work projects was a direct result of cutbacks in public expenditure.

Such widespread cutbacks have affected the state-sponsored youth service and the quality of its delivery within specific working class communities. The Senior Education Officer for the Belfast Education and Library Board has asserted:

> Recent cuts on the Service have started to bite, we are depending greatly on the good will of the people to keep going and that is very dangerous . . . It will lead to the stage where there is no other option but to close provisions and declare redundancies amongst paid staff . . . and this will seriously affect the youth service.
>
> (Northern Ireland Assembly 1983)

Despite the cutbacks, the 1980s witnessed a drive towards providing programmes of social education within youth clubs. The Birley Report (1977) stated: 'The Youth Service has the responsibility to provide social education for young people'. This report identified the Northern Ireland Youth Service as being much more than a recreation-based service. The Birley Report appeared to acknowledge the need for the Youth Service to centre its philosophy on social education.

One major outcome of this role was the increase in moneys available to those who worked with young working class youths. During 1984/5, £665,000 was handed into the Youth Service from the Department of Economic Development (Youth Committee for Northern Ireland 1986) for special projects for the unemployed. The Youth Committee has suggested that in an era when permanent employment cannot be guaranteed, it may be necessary for the Youth Service to compensate by providing opportunities for young people to 'grow towards maturity' (YCNI 1986: 10). Corresponding amounts for similar purposes were provided throughout Great Britain.

This 'growing towards maturity' undoubtedly refers to the process whereby unemployed school leavers with no future will come to terms with their position in life. Such thinking has permeated youth policy in Great Britain and Northern Ireland since the late 1970s. This emphasis on 'social education' and personal development and creative use of unemployed 'leisure time' in youth work policy and practice serves to normalize such things as unemployment, crime, poverty etc. The 1986 Youth Service review (Youth Committee Northern Ireland 1986) concluded that 'it is important to stress that one of the main themes of the report is the extent to which the youth service should be meeting the specific needs of young people against a background of social change.' It is clear that the most pressing need arising out of this rapid change is the need to find a job and to acquire a better lifestyle. In our survey areas fewer than one in five young people were finding a job within a year of leaving school. It is obvious that their greatest drawback is their social class and/or religious or ethnic identification. The Youth Service is absolutely powerless to meet this need because it is a class and ethnic issue.

Byrne (1979), among others, has drawn attention to the process of acculturation and the part it plays in the ideological reproduction of the reserve labour army in Northern Ireland. Acculturation programmes are designed to affirm and reinforce the discipline of labour, the continuation into the post-school experience of the hidden curriculum of the school. Basically, acculturation programmes can be divided into those for school leavers without job experience and those for adults who have become unemployed. Doing something about youth unemployment clearly is an essential task for legitimizing government in a mass democracy that is faced by extensive structural unemployment among school leavers, but it is also crucial in its own right. School leavers have to experience the practice of work and the ideological implications carried by that practice, so job creating programmes including Young Help, Enterprise Ulster and the Youth Training Programme are established to provide what the productive industrial structure itself cannot because of de-industrialization. This process ensures the reproduction, at the ideological level, of the reserve pool of labour.

Such an approach is to be found right across the range of the state's educational and training programme and is explicitly *correctional* in character. Such a stance, it has been argued (Bell n.d.), has 'articulated well with official constructions of sectarianism as a "social problem" to be tackled by clearly delimited state sponsored educational and youth work initiatives'. Sectarian divisions in Northern Ireland are usually approached from a position of high moralism and are usually attributed to a defect in Irish character and culture – the irrational preservation of ancient animosities or a 'cultural lag'. Direct rule presents the opportunity of transferring British liberal and social democractic sensibilities to the recalcitrant Irish. Social and educational policy announces as one of its aims the combating of sectarianism, which it understands as a structure of personal prejudice rather than a complex web of ideological social relations encompassing a political conflict that articulates a struggle between divergent forms of national aspiration, ethnicity and oppression against a background of widespread social and economic deprivation.

The Youth Service itself functions to facilitate the acculturation process in reproducing ideological relations in Northern Ireland. In June 1986 there were 45,830 young people under 25 registered as unemployed in Northern Ireland and a further 7550 involved in the Youth Training Programme, representing 43.7 per cent of the 16–24 age group (Department of Economic Development 1986). The emphasis on social education, personal development, recreational provision and making responsible in Youth Work policy and practice serves to institutionalize unemployment to a large extent. The 1986 Youth Work Committee report is permeated by references to the changes experienced in youth work to meet the problem. The unemployment problem is particularly marked in West Belfast (according to Youth Workers in Upper Springfield/Ballymurphy, none of the participants in any of the five youth clubs had jobs) and this exacerbates the tendency towards the ghettoization of an already segregated residential life; this, in turn, reproduces and re-affirms ideological definitions of social and political reality.

The Youth Service seeks to provide youth facilities in working class communities where social problems are high, in the hope that what is provided will channel the energies of a section of the young people in such areas away from 'negative, anti-social behaviour'. The task of making such provisions attractive to a large proportion of the youth in Great Britain and Northern Ireland is a daunting one given the nature and extent of alternative forms of behaviour and the degree of alienation. It is especially daunting in areas with particularly high incidences of social deprivation. The resistance of the young, in the streets of West Belfast, Brixton, Handsworth, Toxteth or Broadwater Farm, to authority has a distinctive political and ethnic character.

Social education should be about increasing awareness of areas that have shaped the lives of individuals. To this end, it has been argued, the individual needs to be aware of the broader social and economic forces and interrelationships that have contributed to his or her life experience (Finnegan et al. 1982). The Youth Service clearly does not concern itself with this. The consequences for the young people of West Belfast are that they are faced with an embittered empty shell of a life on the dole, with the only legal respite coming in the form of ready-made social facilities, such as video games and pool tables, that stifle self-examination through interaction and participation. Can it then be of any wonder when they turn to unofficial, more informal and at times blatantly self-destructive behaviour in order to get a kick? The price to be paid by society for maintaining this ideological strait-jacket intact is likely to be excessive and, at times, disturbing. The rest of this book will consider these issues.

4 YOUTH WORK IN WEST BELFAST

Introduction

This chapter contains analyses of a survey of youth workers in the Shankill and Upper Springfield areas which was conducted during our research project. We were concerned with discovering the divergences that existed not only between the two areas (one protestant and one catholic) but also between workers involved in different types of clubs (statutory, church, uniformed and voluntary).

We were concerned with ascertaining comprehensive information on the state of youth work in the two areas as perceived by the workers themselves. We obtained basic quantitative data on number and type of clubs, qualifications, activities, problems, functions and so forth. Added to this was an analysis of work satisfaction and the rationale of the workers involved. Last, but by no means least, we collated data on how youth workers perceived the needs of young people in the two areas, how they thought these could be met, and to what extent they believed that their particular club or organization was able to contribute towards the alleviation of the social problems in the areas and satisfy the needs of the young people themselves.

There was an unevenness in the survey that was largely inbuilt because only five clubs existed in the Springfield whereas the Shankill had 48 (three of which did not respond). Sixty-two workers subsequently participated in the Shankill sample but only 11 in the Springfield sample. This was also partly due to a failure to return questionnaires (particularly in the voluntary sector). We included in our sample the 'leader in charge' (where possible) of each group and a random sample of other workers from each group (sex and type and duration of experience were controlled, however, to ensure a representative sample).

Young work participation levels in the Shankill and Upper Springfield

There was a marked divergence in the types of youth work practised in both areas. Briefly, the Shankill tended to be permeated by church clubs and affiliated uniformed organizations (93 per cent of participants compared to 35 per cent in the Springfield). Statutory clubs accounted for 40 per cent of participants in the Springfield as opposed to only 5 per cent in the Shankill. Secular voluntary projects accounted for 25 per cent of the participants in the Springfield as opposed to only 2 per cent in the Shankill.

The difference can best be explained historically. Formal statutory youth provision is relatively new in Northern Ireland and really only took off in the 1970s. Uniformed groups had already firmly established themselves for generations before this. However, these have always tended to be more associated with protestant churches (again for historical reasons, such as the identification of such groups with Great Britain). There are no catholic uniformed organizations in the Upper Springfield, and if we were to omit membership of such groups in the Shankill area from our analysis then the difference in church group participation between the two areas, although still significant, would be much less glaring.

Another factor is that it is the stated aim of the youth division of the Belfast Education and Library Board to provide youth projects only where 'needs' are not being met by already established groups (in the Shankill there is practically one church group for each neighbourhood). Non-uniformed church groups in the Shankill were quick to organize themselves in face of the massive social problems created by the political, geographical and economic upheavals after 1969. The church group in Upper Springfield was much slower off the mark.

The youth workers

There were significant differences between the two areas in terms of personnel because of the nature of youth work practised in both communities. The Shankill is permeated by small voluntary, church and uniformed groups, where the workers are involved with youth work for one or two evenings a week on average. The Upper Springfield, however, tends to practise a more 'professional' full-time approach. It should perhaps be noted that full-time statutory work in *both* areas is essentially a male domain. There were no full-time females in our sample of statutory club workers. The only full-time female worker in the entire sample was employed by the church club in Upper Springfield. The only female worker in the statutory clubs in both areas was also the only voluntary worker. The mean age of youth workers in both areas was the same, 32, although there were differences depending on type of club.

The clubs

The clubs in the Springfield were, on average, over six times the size of the clubs in the Shankill in terms of numbers. This is a reflection of the shortage or provision in the Springfield (basically a collection of housing estates) as opposed to the Shankill (an old working class area with a preponderance of social and, now vacant, commercial property). It also represents the small size of the groups on the Shankill, which is a reflection of the diverse religious interests. The 11 church clubs in our survey were affiliated to different churches. In comparison, the Catholic Church is monolithic and this is reflected in the Upper Springfield sample. There is only one church in the Upper Springfield – the Catholic Church – and hence only one church youth club. Some of the Shankill clubs were, however, quite big, with the largest church and male uniformed groups having over 100 members.

Organized youth work in every category has existed much longer on the Shankill (although the mean age of church clubs on the Shankill is slightly lower). The most significant factor here is that youth work on the Shankill clearly preceded the present phase of the troubles (with the exception of the single voluntary club). On the other hand all youth work in the Upper Springfield is post-1969. This would appear to suggest that formal youth provision in the Springfield was (in part anyway) a reaction to the street confrontations that increased in intensity and scale in the area after 1969. Local community workers and youth workers in the statutory, church and voluntary sectors have confirmed that there was an increasing concern with young people. Although the approaches to the problems associated with the young of the area may have varied depending on the ethos of the individual club they all shared a common concern with the state of youth. It was felt that something was needed to offset the negative aspects of life for young people in their free time and that the best way to achieve this would be by providing social and recreational facilities, activities and so on, with the objective of keeping them occupied. Voluntary organizations would tend to be particularly concerned with de-escalating the spiralling local social problems associated with youth since 1969. It was evident that the Upper Springfield was one of the major centres for the 'hoods' (informal gangs of young people engaged in 'anti-social' behaviour), and this gave the area (particularly Ballymurphy) a notoriously bad reputation.

The church was undoubtedly concerned with the sharp decline in 'moral standards' and those attending mass. It has been pointed out that the rate for those actually practising Catholicism in the area is perhaps as low as 20 per cent, which is well below the Northern Ireland average, and that the rate for young people in their late teens and twenties is significantly lower than this again (interview with Fr. Des Wilson).

The statutory sector involvement, under the Belfast Education and Library Board (BELB), was the most recent youth work development in the Springfield and would suggest a direct attempt by the state to defuse the massive feeling of alienation that young people in the area have experienced. Traditionally, the state would have preferred to curb such feelings by supporting Catholic Church initiatives (as in the case of schools). However, it has become apparent in the Upper Springfield that the traditional dominance of the church in social life is being seriously challenged by secular voluntary community groups.

Experience and qualifications

Formal youth work qualifications were significantly more prevalent in the Upper Springfield than the Shankill. This partly represents the different types of youth work practised. This is explained by reference to the statutory sector, where the difference is much less significant. Nearly 60 per cent of the total Shankill sample had no relevant qualifications whatsoever. In comparison over 90 per cent of the Springfield sample had some form of relevant qualifications. This illustrates the divergent forms of youth work practised and workers involved. The statutory clubs tended to employ only professionally qualified youth workers. On the other hand, the uniformed organizations, and to a lesser extent the church clubs, tended to be dominated by part-time voluntary workers.

Motives

The most striking differences in motives for participation were those concerning spiritual reasons and professional or personal advance (to help promotion, part of job, for financial reasons, further vocational experience). Professional or personal advancement only accounted for 1 per cent of the responses in the Shankill (2 per cent of the respondents), compared to 28 per cent (36 per cent) in the Springfield. This perhaps indicates two factors. First, it may represent the greater emphasis on professional youth work in the Springfield (although more of the workers in the statutory clubs in the Shankill indicated this as a motive). Second, it may be indicative of the discrepancies in economic and career opportunities between the two areas.

Spiritual reasons accounted for 20 per cent of the responses for the Shankill (26 per cent of the respondents) compared to none for the Springfield (not even in the church club). They were particularly high for the church clubs and male uniformed organizations in the Shankill (which was not surprising) and relatively low for the female uniformed organizations (which was).

The activities

The most striking feature of activities was the overall dominance of games and sport, which was mainly due to the pre-occupation of church clubs with such activities. This is especially true of the Shankill church clubs, where this category accounted for 75 per cent of the activities. The exception was the female uniformed organizations, where it came second to creative and educational activities, which accounted for one-third of the programme.

Creative and educational activities were second overall in the Shankill (22 per cent) but came third (17 per cent) in the Springfield, behind social activities (23 per cent). Social activities in the Shankill, in comparison, came a poor fourth (7 per cent) while spiritual activities came third (11 per cent). These tendencies reflect, to some extent, the overall divergence in ethos of the dominant types of clubs in each area. However, when we consider more closely the individual types of clubs the discrepancies are not so apparent, although they still have some significance. The statutory clubs in the Shankill varied considerably from the overall (or church-orientated) activity content in the area and, to a certain degree, from the statutory clubs in the Springfield. Creative and educational activities scored highest (37 per cent) in the statutory clubs in the Shankill compared to second (31 per cent) in the Springfield. Social activities came second in the Shankill (26 per cent) compared to third (23 per cent) in the Springfield, and games and sport scored third in the Shankill (21 per cent) compared to first (39 per cent) in the Springfield.

There was a strong emphasis on discipline in the male uniformed organizations in the Shankill (19 per cent) compared to the female organizations (4 per cent), where there was a stronger emphasis (18 per cent) on spiritual activities. Spiritual activities scored surprisingly low with the church clubs in the Shankill (4 per cent), although the lack of formal spiritual activities need not necessarily detract from the overall ethos of the club. The same may also be true of the Springfield church club, which did not have any formal spiritual activities (prayer meetings, Bible study, testimonies, religious singing).

We asked the workers which activities they would ideally like to *develop* given the time and resources. Despite the fact that sport and games already dominated in the Shankill clubs this category still headed the list, scoring more than the other activities combined (41 per cent). The statutory clubs were a major exception here, with creative and educational activities dominating the responses (64 per cent). This category scored highest in the Springfield sample overall (41 per cent) followed by sport and games and outings (19 per cent each). Outings came third in the Shankill sample (12 per cent).

There was a noticeable lack of interest in 'integrated activities' (bringing catholic and protestant young people together) in both areas. The only exception was the voluntary club in the Shankill, which already participated in such activities (during the summertime). A significant number of respondents mentioned 'more participants' (getting young people to attend), which is not an activity but was nevertheless included in the analysis to demonstrate the emphasis placed on this by youth workers (the numbers game).

Support and local knowledge

Approximately one-third of the workers in each area had never lived locally although a much higher proportion (58 per cent Shankill, 64 per cent Springfield) had resided in the areas for at least five years, indicating a high degree of local awareness.

Most of the workers were satisfied to one degree or another with their relationship locally. However, it was apparent that workers were not as satisfied with the *support* they received from the local population. This was particularly true in the statutory sector but not in the voluntary sector. We did not measure the satisfaction of the local population with the service provided by youth clubs and organizations but perhaps the participation levels are an indication of this.

The functions

We asked the respondents to indicate the main *official* functions of the youth clubs in the two areas. This was an 'open' question for which each respondent could name four functions. On the whole, assistant workers were in agreement with leaders-in-charge on what these were. Altogether there were 151 responses from the Shankill and 23 from the Springfield (where three of the eleven workers did not answer the question).

There were a number of differences concerning the functions of the clubs between the two areas and also between the types of clubs. Spiritual development scored highest (22 per cent) in the Shankill but second lowest in the Springfield (4 per cent). This undoubtedly reflected the tendency for youth work on the Shankill to be church and uniformed organization based, bearing in mind that all but one of the uniformed organizations were 'attached' to a church (there is, anyway, a strong spiritual code enshrined in such bodies; for instance, the motto of the Boys' Brigade begins 'to advance Christ's Kingdom').

'Social development' (developing friendships, working together, understanding of others) scored second highest in both areas (27 per cent in Springfield, 20 per cent in Shankill) and was particularly high in the statutory and voluntary clubs in the Springfield. This would support the objective of the Youth Service to 'foster stable social relationships and social confidence among young people' (Youth Committee for Northern Ireland 1977, 1981).

In the Springfield sample, 'personal development and caring' (caring, counselling, giving service or advice, help to unemployed, giving a place to go) and 'education' (teaching skills, domestic skills, extension of school, social education), scored jointly first (17 per cent), significantly higher than in the Shankill sample (fourth, 12 per cent, and fifth, 10 per cent, respectively). Significantly, personal development and caring and education scored joint highest in the statutory clubs in the Shankill (25 per cent) and first (24 per cent) and joint second (18 per cent) in the Springfield. This undoubtedly reflects the 'professional' background of workers in the statutory clubs, bearing in mind the emphasis placed upon personal development and social education in formal youth work training and in the objectives of the formal youth service.

'Social control' scored a significant third (15 per cent) in the Shankill. This included discipline, keeping young people out of trouble and, in the case of the uniformed organizations, drill. It scored second (20 per cent), behind spiritual development, in the uniformed organizations in the Shankill, which gives an indication of the ethos of such groups. Another significant factor was that although social control scored low (8 per cent) in the Springfield overall it was the only 'positive' response given by the only voluntary sector worker who answered the question.

'Getting young people to attend' (numbers game) and 'keeping young people off the streets' scored 25 per cent for the church club in the Springfield and 12 per cent for the statutory clubs. They only scored 3 per cent overall in the Shankill but 8 per cent for the statutory clubs. This would reflect the greater concern attached to 'feasibility' by the professional workers and clubs.

Undoubtedly, the most significant difference in functions between areas was the concentration of spiritual motives in the Shankill and the greater commitment to professional-type work in the Springfield. A fairly representative reply to the question in one of the church clubs on the Shankill came from a female voluntary youth worker, aged 38, who had been involved in part-time youth work for about three years in a club with 23 members: 'The main reason is to introduce young people to the Gospel of Jesus Christ and that this is the answer to unanswerable problems and questions they face throughout life'. She then went on to quote the Bible: 'Therefore if anyone is in Christ, he is a new creation, the old has passed away, behold the new has come' (2 Corinthians 5: 17). The old Shankill may have passed away but the new is hardly a sight to behold. Perhaps the scriptural reference was coincidental but it more or less underlined the tragic irony between seeking a 'spiritual salvation', which would earn rewards in the afterworld, and the realistic material emancipation that most young people in the ghettoes of West Belfast would much rather settle for in this life.

There was little disagreement between what workers saw as the official functions and what they thought they *should be*. The only significant difference came in the statutory clubs in the Springfield sample, where social development scored almost twice as much in the 'should be' category. This should not be surprising given the degree of disillusionment experienced by many of the statutory workers in the area. One worker (age 32) who had been involved in youth work voluntarily for eight years and worked part-time for two years in a statutory club listed the official functions as:

1 Proper administration.
2 Meeting deadlines.
3 Maintenance of building.
4 Youth work.

Points 1 to 3 were uncodable as functions and were not scored, but the example should nevertheless be given as an indication of how some workers view formal statutory provision in the area. The voluntary worker stated that the functions should be: (a) youth work; (b) social education.

The only other significant factors to emerge in Springfield came in the church club, which put a greater emphasis (40 per cent) on getting young people to attend as one of 'what the functions should be', and in the response on social control (50 per cent), which did not change in the voluntary sector. In other words it was admitted not only that social control was the major function of the club but also that the youth worker agreed with that position and did not think the club should have any other functions.

The role

Respondents were asked to rate (1, 2, 3 and so on) how they interpreted their role regarding young people in order of importance, against nine given categories. They could rate as many of the categories as they wished. The responses were scored in reverse order. First choice scored 9, second 8 and so on. Those not rated did not score.

'Developing their personality' scored joint highest (mean 6.5) in the Springfield sample and second (mean 5.4) in the Shankill. It scored significantly higher in the statutory and voluntary sectors in the Springfield than in the church sector. It scored highest in the statutory sector in the Shankill (7.6) and relatively low in the uniformed sector (4.9). These results tend to reflect the emphasis placed, in youth work in general and statutory work in particular, on personal development.

'Developing their natural abilities and skills' also scored 6.5 in the Springfield sample but was only ranked fourth in the Shankill (5). It did, however, score much higher (6) in the statutory sector in the Shankill sample, which would tend to support what was said in the last paragraph.

'Caring for them' scored highest (6.1) in the Shankill sample and third (5.5) in Springfield. This tended to score particularly high with the church groups in both areas (6 in Springfield and 6.5 in the Shankill).

The most striking discrepancy in role perception between the two areas was in 'helping them to become better citizens', which scored second highest (5.9) in the Shankill and second lowest (3.6) in the Springfield sample. Significantly, it scored a clear highest in the Springfield church category, gaining the highest score all round for the area (8), and lowest in the other two categories (3 in each). It also scored lowest in the statutory sector in the Shankill sample (2.2). However, it scored highest in the uniformed organizations (6.7). These results would tend to support the view of commentators who claim that uniformed organizations in prot-estant areas and church organizations in catholic areas give a high priority to promoting conformity.

'Encouraging them to be independent' scored 5.2 in the Springfield compared to 3.8 in the Shankill. This may, perhaps, represent the growth of radicalism in the Upper Springfield area, particularly in the past 20 years, which has manifested itself most profoundly in rejections of traditional moral and religious authority and in attempts at self-help. The church versus anti-establishment debate has many faces and this may represent one of them, bearing in mind that youth and community workers of the non-church variety tend to be more anti-authoritarian (at least in rhetoric) than most people. 'Encouraging them to think positively', which is similar, scored 4.9 in the Shankill sample and 4.7 in the Springfield.

'Controlling them', although rated lowest in both the Shankill (2.3) and Springfield (2.9), scored high in the voluntary clubs in both areas (6 and 5). 'Educating them', although rated low all round, scored high in the church (6) and voluntary (6) sectors in the Springfield.

The non-participants

Youth workers were asked to indicate why young people did *not* use their clubs. The two highest rated reasons in the Springfield sample were 'undesirable alternatives' (negative thinking, anti-social alternatives, street gangs, drinking, laziness, they don't want to be taught, TV, ignorance, paramilitary influence, political influence) and 'limitations of club' (dislike of or lack of activities, would be bored, decor). Each accounted for 25 per cent of the responses. Both, however, scored significantly lower in the Shankill. 'Undesirable alternatives' was rated fourth (13 per cent) and 'limitations of club' second last (7 per cent).

'Limitations' did score significantly higher in the voluntary sectors in both areas, which would reflect the relative shortage of resources in such clubs. The score would appear to indicate that facilities and resources are more readily available in the Shankill (particularly in the church and uniformed sectors) than in the Springfield.

It was also found that the church groups in the Shankill rated 'undesirable alternatives' highest (29 per cent) despite its low position in the Shankill sample. It was also rated joint second (20 per cent) in the statutory sector and highest in the Springfield statutory sector (33 per cent). Surprisingly, though, the uniformed organizations in the Shankill rated this third lowest (7 per cent). We may explain this, partly at least, by reference to the highest rated category in the Shankill, which was 'formality/control/restraints/discipline'. This category contained dislike of formality, won't wear uniform, dislike discipline, and too rowdy as the most common responses and, not surprisingly, it scored highest (28 per cent) in the uniformed sector. This factor illustrates an important point. It appears that when looking at why young people do not use or join their organizations, uniformed leaders tend to look at *their own* structures for reasons while statutory and church groups tend to look for alternative activities *unconnected* to their own club or group. Another related factor is that church groups in the Springfield and statutory groups in the Shankill do not see formal controls and restraints as a factor in non-participation. As we shall see from the responses of non-participants, this is absurd.

'Competition or physical barriers' (leisure centres, inconvenience, bad night, location) was rated third in both samples (16 per cent Springfield, 15 per cent Shankill). Many of the clubs, mainly in the Shankill, only opened for one or two nights a week, perhaps a Friday or Saturday, and some of the workers referred to these as being bad nights on which to get young people to attend. We can only speculate that this was because of the array of alternative social activities on such nights. Both areas contained modern leisure centres (the Shankill has one of the biggest and best in the UK). However, in our informal discussions with non-participants it did not become apparent that leisure centres played a significant part in their social lives. In fact they often complained that the centres were not for them or were too expensive. It is also difficult to imagine 'location and inconvenience' as being a major barrier to participation. There is at least one club in each area within easy walking distance for everyone.

'Social influences' (growth of individualism, parental influence, ridicule of peers) scored significantly higher in the Shankill (15 per cent) than the Springfield (6 per cent). Significantly, the Shankill had recently experienced a breakdown in traditional community relationships because of the restructuring and redevelopment of the area since 1969. As we have seen, this manifested itself in, among other things, the virtual destruction of the extended family and a growth in individualism. Such trends would inevitably have a particularly detrimental effect on the uniformed organizations and, indeed, they scored in this category a high 21 per cent. Ridicule of peers would also be most felt here. It was quite often pointed out by the members of such organizations that they were singled out and made fun of. A number of boys involved told us that 'they (non-participants) think we're all fruits', or words to that effect. This was probably due to the uniform and the fact that the organizations tended to be single sex. Reference was made to the church or school connections of clubs (12 per cent Shankill, 3 per cent Springfield) and this was higher in the Shankill because of the greater concentration of church clubs. Members of church clubs were often considered to be 'holy Joes', although this was usually far from the case.

Sex, age or social background limitations scored low in both areas. We believe, however, that these factors were grossly underestimated. It was often stated, for instance, that members of uniformed groups in the Shankill were thought of as snobs, and as we shall see later there was a significant difference in social class background from the uniformed groups, down through the church and statutory groups to the voluntary clubs. Sex was an obvious barrier in groups such as the Boys' and Girls' Brigades, Girl Guides, Girls' Clubs, Church Lads' Brigade and Scouts (although the Venture Scouts, the senior section, is mixed).

Age was an obvious factor. Some clubs only catered for young people up to 14 or 16. Non-participants in the 16–18 age group frequently complained that youth clubs did not offer attractive activities for them. Those in the over-18 age group were rare. These factors were acknowledged most by the two statutory clubs on the Shankill. One of them had evolved from being a traditional boys' club. The other, which had just opened, catered only for juniors (under-15s).

Remarkably, 'promotional difficulties' scored lowest (3 per cent) in the Springfield and second lowest (7 per cent) in the Shankill. This referred to lack of publicity and lack of incentives. It is remarkable to the extent that workers, in suggesting other reasons for non-participation, often complained that it was because of misconstrued perceptions of the club image (especially the church and uniformed groups). It is also remarkable in that the workers were admitting that two-thirds of the young people in the areas did not attend their clubs and that this was not because of poor publicity. It is also one of the aspects of work on which workers would like, ideally, to spend more time, as we shall see later.

Finally, it was brought to our attention by a youth worker in the Springfield area that parts of the area have 'different political affiliations' and that 'sections of the community are split up into pockets', and that this would account for attendance or non-attendance at certain clubs. For instance, the church club and the statutory clubs may not be appealing to republicans, while one voluntary club had frequently been in conflict in the past with church authority and was organized by the 'radical' community association.

Perhaps the most honest answer came from a worker in a club attached to a school in the Springfield, who said that 'this club just doesn't suit certain types'. It was, of course, a major objective of this study to investigate why this is so and who exactly the 'certain types' are.

The needs and how they can be met

The respondents were asked to name up to five needs of young people in their area. Responses overall were significantly higher in Springfield (85 per cent) than in the Shankill sample (45 per cent).

The first category consisted of 'structural needs', such as jobs, housing, standard of living, incentives and better environment. This scored 50 per cent in the Springfield and 28 per cent in the Shankill of the total responses. This possibly reflected the marginally more deprived status of the Springfield, generally, as well as the greater inclination for profession-ally qualified youth and community workers to consider the wider social structure. (It should be noted that the church sector in the Springfield scored 86 per cent in this category and that this does not detract from what has just been stated, as the workers were professionally qualified.) Although it scored 28 per cent in the Shankill overall, the corresponding score for the statutory sector was 45 per cent.

The second category covered 'personal needs' (stable home, parental care, sympathetic ear, acceptance, love and friends). This was rated a low fifth (7 per cent) by the Springfield sample but second (18 per cent) in the Shankill. There does not appear to be any particular explanation for this as the statutory clubs in each area scored it higher than others (the others did not score it at all in the Springfield sample). However, we could propose two possible reasons. First, it may reflect the increase in personal instability in the Shankill due to the breakdown of close-knit family units and the growth of individualism. Second, it may reflect a greater concern for problems associated with these needs from professional youth workers.

The third category covered 'positive education' (drugs education, sex education and health education). This scored significantly higher in the Springfield (17 per cent), where it was rated second, than in the Shankill, where it was rated last (5 per cent). This possibly reflected the professional versus religious motives and approaches of the workers (although it did not score at all in the statutory sector in the Shankill). It is more likely, however, that it was a reflection of the social problems associated with both areas. The Springfield has a much higher birth rate and population density and more serious 'health' problems (and lack of adequate health centres).

The fourth category covered 'social and recreational' facilities (cheaper leisure centres, free day centre, informal facilities). This was rated third (12 per cent) by the Springfield respondents and joint fourth (10 per cent) by the Shankill. There were no significant differences except that it was not rated by the voluntary club on the Shankill (which provided these facilities to an extent) and the church club on the Springfield (which placed an overwhelming emphasis on structural needs).

Category five covered 'youth club initiatives' (more facilities for the clubs, more discos, more activities generally, more workers, more transport). There was not, as may be expected, a significant difference here in scores. It was rated third (12 per cent) in the Shankill and fourth in the Springfield (10 per cent). It was, however, rated significantly lower (7 per cent) by the uniformed sector in the Shankill sample and was also unrated by the church group in the Springfield. It was, not surprisingly, rated higher by the statutory and voluntary sectors in both areas.

Category six consisted of 'moral developments' (character building, spiritual leadership, sense of responsibility, morality). This category only applied to the church and uniformed sectors in the Shankill where it was rated joint fourth (10 per cent) overall. It did not score at all in the Springfield and was only significantly rated (13 per cent) by the uniformed groups of the Shankill.

Category seven was also rated higher in the Shankill (8 per cent) than in the Springfield (5 per cent), although it scored low overall. It covered 'social control' (discipline, more supervision, control, more police, more uniformed organizations, respect for law and order, fewer counter-activities). It was, significantly, rated joint fourth (13 per cent) with 'moral developments' by the uniformed groups of the Shankill. It was only rated by the statutory sector (last) in the Springfield.

Category eight covered those who simply replied 'none' in response. There were none in the Springfield sample and five in the Shankill. Category nine covered those who did not respond to the question. Again, there were none from the Springfield but nine from the Shankill.

Categories eight and nine indicate something about the different types of worker involved in the survey. The 'nones' and 'no responses' only existed in the uniformed (11) and church (3) sections in the Shankill. One may expect youth workers working in one of the most deprived areas of Europe to have some conception of the needs of young people. However, the fact that 14 out of 62 (exactly a quarter of the workers, 56, in the two sectors concerned) of those workers in the Shankill had no idea what the needs of young people were, did not seem to think that they were in a position to say what they were or did not think they existed is, to put it bluntly, incredible. The church and uniformed positive respondents in the Shankill also accounted for the much lower positive response rate (using less than half of the five spaces available for needs). There appears to be a wide discrepancy between professional youth workers and church, uniformed and voluntary workers concerning the perceived needs of young people. As one Girl Guide leader put it: 'There is plenty to do in the area – leisure centres, churches etc. The majority just don't want to know.' There is thus likely to be a wide divergence in the types of youth work practised, in policy and social consequences.

Overall, the workers perceived the needs of young people in material terms. Personal needs did rate second in the Shankill but was still low considering the lower positive response rate. Besides this, if we look at the emphasis on personal development, as it is preached and practised by the youth service, a little more closely, it becomes apparent that what we are seeing is really Baden-Powell's character building.

Of the 48 youth workers in the Shankill who replied positively to the question on needs only 14 had any ideas on how they could be met. Eight said they did not know how and 26 did not respond to the question. All ten from the Springfield who replied positively to the question on needs had some ideas on how the needs could be met. However, in this case the Shankill respondents did have a lot more ideas and these were more varied. The total positive responses offered by both groups numbered 62 (Shankill 45, Springfield 17) and were divided into six general categories for the purpose of analysis. The Springfield sample did not score in three of the categories. First was category three, which covered 'better schools'. The Shankill only scored two on this, which is surprising considering the increasing criticism of educational standards from lay-people and professionals, as well as from pupils. The Shankill had, in fact, recently witnessed a major community campaign against school closures, declining standards and cut-backs in education spending, which had clearly gone unheeded by those who were supposedly sympathetic to the welfare of youth. The second was category four, which covered social and recreational initiatives (excluding youth clubs). This only scored 1 in the Shankill. The responses here seem odd considering that both samples rated such priorities as fairly high in the question on needs. It is a case of some workers believing that a need in the areas is more bats and balls but they do not know how this need can be met (which seems quite clear to us). Third was category six, which scored 5 on the Shankill and covered 'religious initiatives'. These included increasing the role of the church, more church organizations and young people coming to Christ. The response rate in this category appeared low in both areas at first glance but a number of the other strategies were suggested with the assumption that the local churches would be involved in them to one degree or another.

The highest positive score in the Springfield group and equal highest in Shankill was category one, which was 'structural changes'. This included promotion of family bonds, increased public expenditure and giving young people more say. Fifty-three per cent of the Springfield responses included these more radical strategies, compared to only 27 per cent of the positive (15 per cent of all) responses in the Shankill. The discrepancy here lay mainly with the church and uniformed sections from the Shankill, and the statutory sector in the Shankill scored slightly higher here than the Springfield. This would appear to suggest that the professional youth worker is much more radical in terms of suggesting strategies for meeting needs than church and uniformed workers. On the other hand, it could suggest a much deeper analysis in terms of ideological relations in Northern Ireland generally (in simplistic terms, the radical elements of the nationalist struggle versus the subterranean conservatism and individualism of Ulster protestantism). The wider distribution of responses over the protestant sample would tend to suggest that those who did respond positively were prepared to consider a number of different strategies within the framework of the politico-economic system of

Northern Ireland. The concentration of Springfield respondents on radical solutions (and their lower numbers of responses) perhaps reflects the more inherent hopelessness and alienation of catholic West Belfast. The only other two categories considered by the respondents in Springfield were 'local initiatives' (better match of local skills and services, community research and action, fostering local pride, employment grants, improve environment, voluntary service) and 'youth club initiatives' (full-time official, committed youth leaders, more local resources, more local youth workers, imaginative programmes, purpose-built centre, equipment). There was no significant difference here between the two areas. It seems that youth workers tend to agree on the need for youth and community provisions even if they markedly differ in their form of approach and prioritization.

On the face of it category two responses may appear to be radical in nature, but taken within the context of the rigid territorial interpretation of communities in Northern Ireland we are more likely to see a struggle developing between deprived areas for scarce resources, which in the long run would benefit no one and hinder the development of a concerted progressive effort.

We asked the respondents to indicate the extent to which the youth workers themselves thought that their particular clubs helped to meet the needs of young people. No one in the Springfield sample thought that the club helped 'a lot' and only 18 per cent in the Shankill (none of these was in the statutory sector). It appears that the uniformed groups in the Shankill are most sure of their own worth, with 29 per cent stating that they helped 'a lot', none stating 'not at all' and only 3 per cent stating 'very little'.

Over a third of the Springfield sample thought they helped 'very little' compared to 5 per cent in the Shankill. In fact nearly half (46 per cent) of the Springfield sample thought that their clubs helped 'very little' or 'not at all' to meet the needs of young people. Bearing in mind that these are the workers themselves speaking, this seems an incredible admission.

Only 8 per cent of the Shankill sample considered this to be the case. This poses a number of questions: are the needs of young people in the Springfield greater (or more complex) than in the Shankill, or are youth clubs more efficient in the Shankill, or are youth workers in the Shankill more full of their own self-importance (or less honest)? We suggest that it is a case of youth workers in the Springfield taking a more serious view of the nature and extent of social problems concerning young people in their area and the inability of peripheral strategies to alleviate such problems adequately. Perhaps the Shankill youth workers are more optimistic.

Perceived socio-economic status of participants

The workers did not have ready access to the relevent background data here so the findings are not necessarily accurate. However, there are some glaring discrepancies between the two areas. Nearly all those in the Springfield sample described the participants to be overwhelmingly lower working class (96 per cent). The only significant exception was the statutory sector, which had 10 per cent upper working class (the biggest statutory club is in Moyard, which is a marginally better off area than Ballymurphy). There were no participants from upper or middle class backgrounds in any of the clubs according to the leaders.

In comparison, the Shankill had a sprinkling of upper and middle class participants (7 per cent) in the clubs and only 48 per cent were described as lower working class as opposed to 45 per cent upper working class. This may reflect two things. Either the Shankill youth clubs attract a wider distribution of the population than the Springfield clubs or this represents the difference in socio-economic background between the two areas, with the Shankill tending towards more skilled working class backgrounds and the Upper Springfield to a more semi-skilled or unskilled working class one.

There is another significant pattern in the Shankill sample that is consistently repeated throughout the section on socio-economic indicators. There is a definite and significant correlation between type of youth club attended and socio-economic background of participants. Uniformed organizations are rated top in terms of socio-economic background of participants, followed by the non-uniformed church groups, then the voluntary sector and, lastly, the statutory clubs. This illustrates interesting characteristics, not only about the types of youth work practised but also about the social character of the area. The church influence has often been perceived as being of a conservative, 'respectable' nature, with the uniformed organizations as forms of elitist, religious, quasi-military brigades often scorned by non-participants.

This also shows, to some extent at least, that the statutory sector is catering mostly for the lower end of the class structure which is significantly excluded from the church and uniformed sectors. This supports the case for an extension of statutory youth work in the area (n.b. there was no significant difference between socio-economic indicators of participants in statutory clubs in the Shankill and Springfield).

The same pattern was repeated in terms of employment status of those over school age, with uniformed organizations having the lowest proportion of unemployed. The data again ran the same way for the variable 'employment status of head of household'.

Nearly twice the proportion of participants in the Shankill as opposed to the Springfield come from 'elsewhere'. Elsewhere usually meant the more well-to-do areas surrounding the Shankill, whereas elsewhere in the Springfield usually meant other surrounding estates, such as Turf Lodge and Beechmount. Nearly one in five of the uniformed organization members came from elsewhere.

5 FORMAL YOUTH CLUB PARTICIPANTS

Introduction

This chapter presents a description of the attitudes, activities, lifestyles and social backgrounds of young people in West Belfast who attend formal youth clubs. We interviewed 257 people in nearly all the youth clubs in the Shankill and Upper Springfield (only two uniformed groups in the Shankill declined to co-operate).

The samples of young people were chosen at random, with age and sex being controlled in proportion to the actual numbers of each. We interviewed 10 per cent of the young people present in each club, usually on the same night. In some of the smaller groups in the Shankill we increased the sample to allow for a minimum of three respondents in each club or group.

This chapter is organized in a number of sections, each of which considers issues raised by the young people themselves.

1 The types of club

School or work status

There was a significant difference between the two areas and between clubs in regard to the type of school attended. None of those in the Springfield sample attended grammar schools. There was, however, a different picture in the Shankill. Table 2 gives a breakdown for the Shankill. It is apparent that the overwhelming number of those who attend grammar schools (78 per cent) are members of uniformed organizations.

There were no uniformed organizations in the Springfield study so

Table 2   Type of club by school – Shankill

Type of club	Grammar		Secondary		Primary		Total	
	No.	%	No.	%	No.	%	No.	%
Statutory	1	4	7	7	2	8	10	7
Church	4	17	27	26	6	25	37	24
Uniformed	18	78	68	65	13	54	99	65
Voluntary	0	0	3	3	3	13	6	4
Total	23		105		24		152	

Some percentages do not sum to 100 because of rounding.

unfortunately we were unable to make assumptions about the nature of Catholic uniformed organizations or correlations between school/ occupations and type of club attended. There was a greater percentage at primary school in the Springfield sample (19 per cent) than in the Shankill (13 per cent) and this probably reflects the younger age structure of the area. Of those over school age it is difficult to draw comparisons because of the smallness of the Springfield sample in this category (though only two out of eleven had jobs and one was at college). In the Shankill sample 36 were over school age (one at college and 21 with jobs). Only one out of 18 in the uniformed organizations was registered as unemployed although four were in training projects (YTP).

Family type

We did not have a significant enough number of one-parent families in the Shankill sample to warrant analysis. However, we discovered that 12 (17 per cent) of the Springfield sample were from one-parent families. They accounted for 21 per cent (six) of the statutory club sample and 27 per cent (four) of the church club sample. They also were over-represented in the unemployed parental background group, accounting for 21 per cent of that category.

Frequency of attendance

Although nearly everyone we interviewed (only seven exceptions) attended their respective clubs at least once a week, there was a significant differ- ence between areas in the number of nights attended. Eighty-eight per cent of those in the Springfield sample attended *more* than once a week while the corresponding figure for Shankill was 35 per cent. The differ- ence here is almost certainly due to two factors:

1 The preponderance of church and uniformed groups in the Shankill that meet only once a week (the church group in the Springfield, on the other hand, operated on a full-time basis and had 94 per cent of those interviewed attending more than once a week).
2 The greater inclination towards dual membership in the Shankill (and possibly the existence of other facilities).

Whatever way we look at it the fact remains that, for formal youth club members or participants, the youth club plays a significantly more central role in the Springfield than in the Shankill.

Duration of attendance

We did not find any significant difference between the two areas in the length of time members had belonged to or attended their respective groups or clubs. However, the percentage of members in the uniformed and church groups in the Shankill who had attended for over two years tended to be much higher than in the statutory clubs (church 55 per cent; uniformed 69 per cent; statutory 27 per cent). This was probably partly because one of the two statutory clubs had just opened and there was a longer tradition of church and uniformed groups in the Shankill.

This trend surprisingly expressed itself in the Springfield as well, where 94 per cent of the church club attenders had been attending for more than two years. This was opposed to 31 per cent of the statutory club members and 48 per cent of the voluntary members. It would appear that the church has much more success in retaining its members (although one of the statutory clubs – a purpose-built project – had only been operating since 1983).

Age and sex

There were 121 males and 132 females in the sample. There tended to be a preponderance of females in the 10–12 age group (45 per cent, compared to 22 per cent for males). This was particularly the case with statutory clubs. Indeed 74 per cent of the females in statutory clubs were in this age group compared to 25 per cent of the males. Sixty-five per cent of the males were in the 13–17 age group and were fairly evenly distributed. There were only 13 males and 11 females in the 18–21 age group and two males and one female in the 22+ group.

Father's occupation

The tendency in both areas was for the father to be the head of household. We therefore took this as an indication to see if there was any correspondence between the type of club attended and parental employment status. There were significant differences here between the areas and also between the types of club attended.

Whereas 23 per cent of the fathers in the Shankill sample were unemployed, the figure for the Springfield was 61 per cent. The Springfield figure is close to the unemployment figure for the area, as is the preponderance of unskilled (25 per cent) as opposed to skilled (13 per cent) workers. The Shankill figure for unemployed fathers is significantly less than the unemployment figure for Lower Shankill (37 per cent approximately) but similar to that for the Greater Shankill area, and this may be a reflection of the geographical as well as the social position of participants. In skilled/unskilled terms the Shankill fathers reversed the Springfield trend (42 per cent skilled, 27 per cent unskilled), which is indicative of the socio-economic differentials between the two communities.

There were no significant differences between the type of club in the Springfield sample but this was not so for Shankill. Fifty per cent of the fathers in the statutory sample were unemployed (2½ times the total percentage). The figure for the church group was close to the total (25 per cent) while the figure for the uniformed sample was only 16 per cent. Of the 13 respondents whose fathers had middle class occupations 12 were in uniformed organizations. It would appear that, generally speaking, young people from the Shankill who attend church youth clubs are more likely to be better off than those who attend statutory clubs. Those who are members of uniformed organizations are likely to be even better off again.

2   Sex and attendance

Table 3 gives a breakdown of the participants in Shankill by sex and frequency. Most of those we interviewed did attend on a regular basis. There was, however, a significant difference in the Shankill sample be-

Table 3   Sex by frequency of attendance – Shankill

Sex	More than once a week	Once a week	Once or twice a month	Less than once a month	Row total
Male	48	52	1		101
Row per cent	48	52	1		54
Column per cent	74	44	33		
Female	17	66	2	2	87
Row per cent	20	76	2	2	46
Column per cent	26	56	67	100	
Column	65	118	3	2	188
total	35	63	2	1	100

tween males and females when it came to whether they attended more than once a week. Only 20 per cent of the females as opposed to 48 per cent of males attended more than once a week. This, taken in conjunction with what was said in section 1, would tend to suggest that girls in the 13 and over age group do not find youth clubs and organizations appealing enough to attend more than one evening a week.

In the Springfield, on the other hand, there was a significantly larger number of female (45) than male (20) participants. This would mean that clubs in the Upper Springfield cater mainly for females, and/or that males are attracted more to alternative activities in that particular area.

3   Occupational status

Occupational status and frequency of attendance

Our results showed that there was a higher frequency of attendance in both areas for those who had left school. In the Upper Springfield all of the ten post-school respondents attended the club more than once a week (six were unemployed). There was, of course, a tendency for this to be the case in the Upper Springfield for all the respondents anyway.

In the Shankill sample 48 per cent of the employed respondents and all the unemployed respondents attended more than once a week. In contrast the grammar school figure was 35 per cent and the secondary school figure was 30 per cent. This may be accounted for by absence of homework in the employed group, allowing them more nights to attend. In the unemployed sample it would appear that for those who did attend, either the clubs offered some sort of provision or else they simply had little else to do.

Occupational or school status and father's occupation

Type of school attended was related to father's occupational background. Twenty-eight per cent of those at grammar school were from middle class backgrounds, although they only accounted for 9 per cent of the sample. Only 14 per cent of those at grammar school were from unskilled backgrounds although they constituted 27 per cent of the sample. Only one person, or 5 per cent of those at grammar school, had fathers who were unemployed, although this group represented 23 per cent (33 persons) of the sample. Significantly, those from 'unemployed backgrounds' accounted for 58 per cent of the primary school respondents (over 2½ times their proportion in the sample).

The findings also suggest that there is a tendency for those from unemployed backgrounds to be unemployed themselves after leaving school while those from middle class or skilled backgrounds are more likely to be employed. None of those in the latter two groups over school age was unemployed whereas only 14 per cent of the employed respondents, and 75 per cent of the unemployed, came from unemployed backgrounds.

We did not have a sufficiently large sample from the Springfield over school age for worthwhile analysis and, as we have already stated, none of those of school age attended grammar schools. The only significant fact was that, as was the case with the Shankill, there was a disproportionate number of primary school respondents (77 per cent) from unemployed backgrounds (61 per cent of the sample).

Mother's occupational status by area

There were definite distinctions here as with the father's occupation, and the preponderance of Shankill mothers (52 per cent) in unskilled employment should also be noted as it bears out much of what has been said about the economic character of the area (preponderance of casual work for women), although there have been significant changes since redevelopment.

The tendency for mothers, as well as fathers, in the Springfield was to be unemployed. Seventy-four per cent of the respondents to this question in the Springfield said that their mother was unemployed, compared to 31 per cent for the Shankill (which was similar to the figure for fathers). Eighteen per cent of the Shankill women had skilled or even 'middle class' occupations while this was the case for only 3 per cent (two persons) of the Springfield sample.

Mother's occupation and type of club

The most striking feature was that 82 per cent of those who had mothers in skilled occupations belong to Shankill uniformed organizations although they only constituted 42 per cent of the sample. Indeed, only 25 per cent of the mothers of these respondents were unemployed which almost equalled the Belfast unemployed rate for men and women.

It should be noted that in general the mother's occupational status in both areas tended to be the same as – or similar to – the father's, except in Springfield where 'unskilled' working mothers as well as unemployed mothers tended to have unemployed husbands.

4 Frequency of attendance

Frequency of attendance and area

There was a significant difference between the two areas in terms of participants who attended more than once a week. This was the case with 89 per cent of the Springfield sample as opposed to 35 per cent of the Shankill sample. This was partly accounted for by the discrepancy in the Shankill between male and female attendance (see section 2). Other factors include: the fact that most of the Shankill clubs are part-time and many of these only operate once a week; the shortage of 'legitimate' alternatives in the Springfield; and the geographical isolation of the Springfield as opposed to the Shankill.

Frequency of attendance by father's occupation

We though it might be useful to consider the social class background of those who made most use of the youth clubs and organizations in the Shankill. We did not consider that the situation in the Springfield warranted this analysis as only a handful of the participants did not attend more than once a week.

The 'middle class' category was most likely to attend more than once a week: 47 per cent of the respondents in this category did so as opposed to only 21 per cent in the 'unskilled' category. This may suggest a tendency for middle class youths to associate themselves with formal youth provision (remembering also that in the Shankill there tended to be an abundance of the more 'respectable' type of organizations and groups) and perhaps an aversion to it in regard to unskilled youth. Significantly, though, the unemployed category scored second highest here; 40 per cent of them attended more than once a week. This is possibly a result of the fact that they cannot afford alternative forms of entertainment and there are fewer 'luxuries' at home.

Frequency of attendance by type of club

There were significant differences in attendance patterns for the different types of clubs. Ninety-three per cent of those attending the statutory clubs did so more than once a week. Although accounting for only 16 per cent of the sample they accounted for 30 per cent of the participants in this category. Voluntary clubs also scored high, with 76 per cent of their participants attending more than once a week. Church clubs just about held their own, with 51 per cent of their members attending more than once a week (it was, however, much higher for the full-time church club in the Springfield). The most significant finding here, which bears out what was said before about the Shankill, concerns the uniformed organizations. Only 27 per cent of their members attended more than once a week. They accounted for only 25 per cent of the respondents in this category although they constituted 46 per cent of the sample.

5 Length of attendance

Length of attendance and area

Just over half the respondents (53 per cent) had been attending between two and ten years. There was not a significant difference between the

Shankill and Springfield in this category or in the second largest, six months to two years (28 per cent). From these figures we can safely assume that our sample was fairly representative in terms of the opinions of youth club users (that is, nearly 80 per cent of them had been attending for at least six months).

Length of attendance and father's occupation

Although there did not appear to be a significant correlation in the Upper Springfield sample, there does appear to be a definite trend in the Shankill sample for those from unemployed backgrounds to be over-represented in the short-term categories (six months or less) and under-represented in the long-term categories. Although accounting for only 23 per cent of the respondents, participants from unemployed backgrounds accounted for 64 per cent of those who had been attending for one month or less and 86 per cent of those who had been attending for between one month and six months. They accounted for only 13 per cent of those who had been attending for between two and ten years and 15 per cent of those attending for more than ten years.

This may suggest that youth clubs and organizations are unable to sustain the interest of young people from unemployed backgrounds compared to those from employed backgrounds. A further investigation showed that 84 per cent of those in the 'over two years' category belonged to uniformed organizations although they constituted only 46 per cent of the sample. In comparison 42 per cent of those in the 'under six months' category belonged to statutory clubs although they formed only 16 per cent of the overall sample. This is partly due, no doubt, to the fact that the statutory clubs were a relatively recent development in our study areas, while the uniformed organizations had a long tradition in the Shankill.

6   The activities

This section will attempt to analyse the responses given to the question 'What activities do you come here most for?'

Activities and area

The most striking factor here is that the overwhelming proportion of our sample in both areas (83 per cent) attended first and foremost for sport or physical activities. These scored a massive 87 per cent in the Shankill sample and lower (70 per cent) in the Springfield. Group and social activities scored more (30 per cent) in the Springfield than in the Shankill and this probably reflects the different emphasis on ethos in the type of clubs in each area (sport and physical activities scored 94 per cent first preferences in the Shankill uniformed organizations).

Group and social activities did score better overall although the response rate was down from 100 per cent to 64 per cent. Sport and physical activities also scored high again in the Springfield sample (49 per cent) and educational and creative activities scored 39 per cent with the Shankill respondents.

Perhaps one of the most significant low responses to this question was for spiritual activities, which were hardly mentioned. This is particularly significant for the Shankill sample given the high profile given to spiritual development by the church and uniformed groups that dominate the area.

Although there were variations between different types of club it should be noted that 65 per cent of the respondents in the statutory clubs also gave sport and physical activities as their first preference activity. Group and social activities scored 33 per cent in the statutory sector first preferences, which was significantly higher than for the other clubs (the total for all four types was only 15 per cent).

Activities and sex

Sport and physical activities accounted for 92 per cent of the male respondents. They were much lower but still very significant (74 per cent) for the female respondents. Females were much more interested in group and social activities (22 per cent) than males (7 per cent).

With second preferences, group and social activities scored high (51 per cent) with the males as opposed to the females (although it was their highest second preference, with 36 per cent). Educational and creative activities scored higher for females than males in all the first three preferences.

7 Evaluation of clubs

We asked the respondents to evaluate simply what they thought of their club or group. They were given four options:

1 It's a very good club.
2 It's quite a good club.
3 It's all right as far as clubs go.
4 It's not much of a club.

Club evaluation and area

Generally speaking the Shankill sample tended to have more positive feelings towards their clubs and groups than the Springfield. This may be due to the fact that the Shankill respondents expressed fewer negative reasons for attending in the first place.

Evaluation of club and occupational status background

There were differences in the evaluation of the clubs by different social class groups. Generally, the lower the class background, the less the respondent was likely to hold positive attitudes to the clubs. For instance, 24 per cent of the unskilled working class group from the Shankill replied that it was 'all right as far as clubs go' although only 11 per cent of all the sample gave this response. In contrast 69 per cent of the middle class group replied 'it's a very good club' although only 48 per cent of the total responses were in this category.

8 Youth club friendship networks

There was a significant proportion of the respondents' friends attending the clubs. Eighty-one per cent of the Springfield sample indicated that most or all of their friends attended the club. It was also high for Shankill (57 per cent). This may be an indication that friendship networks extend beyond the club to outside activities as well and could possibly support the argument that youth club participants and non-participants are distinctive groups of young people who do not often socialize with each other, although there was a significant number (18 per cent), particularly in the Shankill (22 per cent), who replied that only some of their friends attended.

9 Participants' perceived function of clubs

The next question we asked the subjects was 'What do you think this club or organization is here for?' They were allowed up to four responses and we asked them to indicate their order of importance.

The 'social control' responses scored highest, accounting for 41 per cent of the first responses, about twice as much as the second rated 'social and recreational' facility. As was expected, the actual responses to this open-ended question came in a number of forms. We should indicate here some of the most common ones. Social control included: discipline, keep kids off the streets, avoid bad company, alternative to fighting and prevent break-ins. The Upper Springfield sample was adamant about this being the function of the clubs. Fifty-eight per cent of them thought so and this supports the way in which many community activists in the area perceived the role of the youth provision. It also scored high in the Shankill sample (35 per cent) although not as dramatically so as in the Springfield. Perhaps this is a case of social control not being quite so obvious in the Shankill, or being less needed. Or perhaps a substantial number of the respondents did not see it for what it was. 'Social and recreational facility' included such responses as: place to meet and pass time, trips, social activities, enjoyment, mess about, make friends, meet people and comradeship.

'Spiritual activity' scored third highest overall although it did not score at all in the Springfield sample. It accounted for 17 per cent of the Shankill first preferences and included: spread gospel, Christianity, learn about God and make kids Christians. Its high response rate in the Shankill clearly reflects the predominance of church clubs and quasi-religious uniformed organizations.

Only the first two named categories scored significantly in the Springfield. 'Personal development' accounted for 11 per cent of the Shankill group but a mere 1 per cent (one person) of the Springfield group. We included a wide variety of responses in this category, which makes its low ranking even more significant: so much for the Youth Service's stated primary concern with the 'social education and personal development of young people' (Youth Committee for Northern Ireland 1986: 1). The responses we coded as 'personal development' included: expand skills, widen scope, teach kids, make you more mature, education, create interest, broaden mind, prepare for life, better opportunities after school, counselling, positive thinking, positive activities and mental development.

Only one person in the entire sample rated 'reconciliation' first (bring communities together) while a handful (it ranked third in the Springfield positive responses) actually thought their club was there for 'financial reasons' (get money, school funds, charity).

In the second preferences 'social control' again scored highest. It was down overall at 33 per cent but maintained its dominance in the Springfield (53 per cent). It still scored 26 per cent of the Shankill responses although it lost out to 'social and recreational facility', which scored highest of the second preferences in the Shankill (32 per cent). 'Spiritual activity' was increased proportionately to 23 per cent of the Shankill second preferences. Personal development again figured poorly (it had 11 responses in the Shankill and two in the Springfield). Again, only one person saw 'reconciliation' as the function of the club. Responses to third and fourth functions were too few to comment on. (It should be noted that only very slightly over half of the respondents actually gave a second preference. So although, for example, the 'social and recreational' category increased its proportion of the responses significantly in the second preferences for the Shankill, its actual score, the number of responses, was down from 37 to 31.)

Perceived function and length of attendance

It was not only the 'newer' members who had 'misconceived' ideas about the clubs. With the Springfield sample there is no significant variation between attendance variables, but with the Shankill sample there are some but not where one might expect to see them. For instance, although 36 per cent of the sample gave 'social control' as the first function, the proportion of those in the two to ten years category giving this response was 41 per cent. 'Personal development', which accounted for 11 per cent of the responses in the Shankill group, accounted for 21 per cent of those in the one month or less category.

Another interesting factor to emerge here is that the proportion giving 'spiritual activity' as a first response (17 per cent) increases significantly with length of attendance (3 per cent for one to six months, 16 per cent for six months to two years, 81 per cent for over two years). The church and uniformed groups must be getting their message across to those who stay on long enough.

Perceived function of club by age and sex

'Social control' was much more prevalent for the males (51 per cent) than for the females (30 per cent). In the male sample its significance increased with age whereas with females it remained static (this was especially true for the Shankill). It is also significant that 'personal development' was only really perceived as a function by females, especially the younger they were, and young males. Females saw the clubs much more in terms of their social and recreational functions than males (27 per cent compared to 15 per cent).

Perceived function and occupational status background

We did not discover significant differences between social class and occupational status group. We should, however, mention that the Shankill middle class group tended to see 'social control' as less of a function (24 per cent) than the other groups, especially the unskilled (44 per cent). They also tended to emphasize the spiritual function (39 per cent against an overall response rate of 21 per cent). We should note that the small group of unemployed young people in the Shankill saw 'social control' as the primary function (75 per cent against an overall rate of 35 per cent). The unemployed young people tended to opt more for the spiritual function (28 per cent against 17 per cent overall rate) and this may confirm some commonly held folk myths about the area that the good living ('Christian types') are only like that because 'it gets them on'.

Desired function

We asked the respondents what they thought the clubs and organizations should be there for. Just over 40 per cent did not know or did not respond. The positive responses tended to comply with what they thought the clubs and organizations were there for. The only significant difference was in the 'social control' category where the first responses were down from 41 per cent to 19 per cent (a decline that was reflected fairly evenly in both areas).

10 Dislike of youth clubs

We asked the young people to tell us what they liked least about attending clubs. The most significant factor was the proportion of those who said 'nothing' or 'do not know', or gave no response (over 50 per cent). Discipline, however, did rank highest (14 per cent) of the rest. Lack of discipline, significantly, came second (9 per cent), accounting for 24 per cent of the Springfield sample (3 per cent Shankill). There was no significant response about resources, whether physical (facilities, equipment), programme (boring, not enough to do) or human (not enough people, not enough boys/girls). 'Discipline' ranked much higher for males (22 per cent) than females (8 per cent), while with 'lack of discipline' it was the other way round (males 6 per cent, females 10 per cent).

The 'nothing' and 'do not know' responses were much higher for females (55 per cent) than males (43 per cent), which may indicate that females were more content with formal youth provision than males (it may, of course, mean that they were less inclined to 'complain'). Those from unskilled working class backgrounds complained most about the 'discipline' in clubs (31 per cent Shankill, 29 per cent Springfield).

11 Levels of influence by participants in club and organization programmes

We asked the participants to state whether they had any say in the organization of activities. They were evenly divided between yes and no overall. However, there was a significant difference between the two areas. The yes rate for the Shankill was 61 per cent while 37 per cent said no. For the Springfield sample yes responses accounted for only 18 per cent of the sample while no responses were a massive 79 per cent. This distinction expressed itself most clearly in the different types of club. The large yes response of the Shankill was a reflection of the predominance of uniformed organizations in the area. Members of such groups usually receive more responsibility for the organization of the activities as they achieve 'promotion' (with a mixture of 'ability' and 'seniority'). Uniformed organizations accounted for 70 per cent of the yes responses. Church and voluntary clubs were about level (35 per cent and 36 per cent yes responses respectively).

We next asked the young people whether they would like to have more say in the organization of the activities. There was a fairly even split between yes (43 per cent) and no (46 per cent) responses overall. However, 58 per cent of the Springfield sample would have liked to have more say compared to 38 per cent of the Shankill sample. This suggests a desire for those who do not have any say to have some. There was also a much more significant yes response from those in the Shankill sample who came from unskilled backgrounds (53 per cent) as opposed to skilled (33 per cent) and middle class (23 per cent) backgrounds.

Males (47 per cent) were more inclined than females (39 per cent) to desire more say. However, the no responses were evenly distributed (47 per cent of males, 46 per cent of females). This is because 14 per cent of the female sample said they did not know.

12 The non-participants

We invited the participants in the youth clubs and organizations to suggest why they thought other young people did not use youth clubs or organisations. There was a wide variation of responses, which we coded under 11 separate headings for analysis. The most common reason given was what we coded as the non-participants' 'social perception of participants', which accounted for 22 per cent of the responses. This included such responses as: they think we're sissies, snobs, goody goodies, different, too quiet, weird, stupid, against their image and because their friends don't come, they would feel left out.

What emerges from this is that there does appear to be a perceived distinction between participants and non-participants in terms of their respective social images. 'They would not fit in with the lads' was another response in this category, which epitomizes much of this distinction. Clearly, some participants felt that if non-participants were to start attending the club they would be ridiculed or ostracized by their peers and many of the forms this ridicule would take are demonstrated by the list of responses. They would not wish to be called weird, snob or goody goody by their peers. 'They think we're all fruits' was how one scout described why he thought others did not join the movement. There does appear to be a distinction in terms of social values and behaviour drawn by participants between non-participants and themselves, and to a large extent it focuses on a 'respectable/rough' dichotomy. The other kids were not interested in the youth club or organization because it represented what was good and respectable about society. This is supported by reference to another category, which accounted for 9 per cent of the responses and was coded as 'undesirable personality traits in non-users'. Included here were such as: they lack the will-power to attend regularly, which was an actual response from a uniformed organization member. Other actual responses included: they're bad thinkers, they don't want to better themselves, they can't be bothered, they don't want to learn, they're hateful, they're disgusting. All of these responses tell us at least as much about the respondents' self-perception as about the actual personality of those they are attempting to describe. Clearly, the youth club and organization members see themselves as having will-power, good thinking, wanting to better themselves, interesting and so on. One Boys' Brigade member gave the response, 'their masculinity's lacking', which seems to suggest that some members of that organization thought it made them 'better men' (consider the emphasis on sports and drill in their programme).

An examination of other responses futher supports this analysis. Eight per cent (11 per cent in the Springfield) of the respondents thought that restrictions would stop others attending (wouldn't get on with the officers, it's too strict, not like uniform, not allowed high shoes, no smoking, being thrown out). Six per cent (9 per cent of the Shankill sample) of the respondents, all from the Shankill, gave 'ethos' as a reason for non-attendance, and this referred to the specifically religious ethos of many of the Shankill church and uniformed groups. The responses included: don't like Christian element and didn't like cursing in front of the leaders. Anti-social activities accounted for 3 per cent of the overall responses but 7 per cent of the Springfield's. This included hooding, petty crime and bad company.

The distinctions made by participants between non-participants and themselves are crucial for an understanding of the social values and perceptions of youth club participants. They also reflect, to a large extent, the distinctions made by adults in working class West Belfast about each other and about young people. Providing youth clubs is often perceived as the panacea for social ills by community conscious and 'respectable' adults.

There were, of course, many other reasons given by participants for why others did not use clubs. 'Other organized activities' accounted for 12 per cent of the responses and included discos and other organizations. Ten per cent thought that aspects of the 'programme' (don't like football, don't like snooker, lack of activities, over too late, not good enough) put people off. Other informal activities accounted for 8 per cent of the responses (11 per cent Shankill, 2 per cent Springfield). These included: playing in the street, sitting at home, chasing girls and chasing boys.

There was a greater tendency for the Shankill respondents to accredit non-participants with 'undesirable personality traits', than for the Springfield respondents. This may be a product of the 'character-building' role of the church and uniformed groups there (particularly the latter). A further examination of the Shankill respondents revealed that 59 per cent of those who gave 'social conception' as a response to this question came from skilled working class backgrounds, although they constituted only 41 per cent of the sample. On the other hand, only 9 per cent of the respondents in this category came from unskilled backgrounds, although they formed 26 per cent of the sample. This group also accounted for a significant proportion (41 per cent) of the 'ethos' responses. In the Springfield sample the major distinctions also came in 'social conception' responses. Forty-one per cent of the unskilled group gave this response compared to only 16 per cent of the unemployed group.

The only significant difference between males and females was in the two categories 'social perception' (19 per cent males, 25 per cent females) and 'other formal activities' (11 per cent males, 6 per cent females). It seemed the males were more inclined to look at the non-participants by giving other activities as a reason for not attending whereas the females looked at it in terms of how the non-participants saw them (the participants).

13   Non-club activities

For comparison we asked the respondents how they spent their free time when not participating in club activities.

The most striking feature to emerge is the predominance of 'informal activities', which account for 37 per cent of the first preferences (a massive 55 per cent for the Springfield sample) and 31 per cent of the second preferences (the response rate for second preferences was 75 per cent). This category was similar to the 'informal activities' category in the previous section, although it also included responses such as visiting relations, watching TV and baby sitting. The second ranked category was 'sport and physical activities' and this was the first preferred activity of 28 per cent of the Shankill and 16 per cent of the Springfield sample. It covered a wide variety of sports, especially snooker, weight training, cycling for males, aerobics and gymwork for females and swimming for both. We also had some golfers, runners, karate enthusiasts, horse riders, canoeists and motor cyclists. BMX riders also figured prominently.

The third highest ranked category was 'general hobbies', which received 10 per cent of the first preferences and 15 per cent of the second preferences. These included activities such as the Duke of Edinburgh Award, reading, computers, playing guitar, drawing, music, models, fiddle making, photography, visiting museums, war games, collecting coins, knitting, playing machines and cars.

The fourth ranked category was 'other clubs or recreation facilities', which also accounted for 10 per cent of the first preferences but fewer, 8 per cent, of the seconds. This included: going to the leisure centre or the family centre, cadets and going to the park. Some of the respondents indicated that they were involved in the organization or supervision of other clubs or organizations (as a Brownie leader for instance). We had no responses from the Springfield at all for 'church activities' and 'school work' and no first preferences for 'general social outings' (going into town, going to football, cinemas, concerts, parties, trips). Response rates for all these categories were also low from the Shankill. Only a handful admitted to 'courting' and 'anti-social activities' (drinking, fighting, throwing at Brits, rioting, stealing cars and 'rapping' doors).

Non-club activities by sex and age

Further analysis showed that females (42 per cent first preferences) were more likely than males (31 per cent) to participate in 'informal activities'. This was especially true of girls in the 10–12 age group (54 per cent) and males in the 18–21 age group (15 per cent). 'Sport and physical activities' were more popular with males (35 per cent) than females (16 per cent). They were more popular with females in the 13–17 age group (24 per cent).

Non-club activities by type of club

There appeared to be a definite correlation between the type of club attended by participants and some of the non-club activities they were likely to prefer.

Fifteen per cent of the church group were more likely to be involved in 'other clubs or recreational facilities' compared to only 5 per cent of the voluntary respondents. Thirty per cent of the uniformed organization members preferred 'sport and physical' activities, compared to only 17 per cent of the statutory group. They were also much more interested in 'general hobbies' (15 per cent) than all the other groups (next was statutory groups with 7 per cent). The same can be said about 'general social outings'. Uniformed organization members were much less likely to be engaged in 'informal activities' (25 per cent) than other groups. Fifty-nine per cent of the statutory sample, on the other hand, gave responses in this category.

School and non-club activities

Participants from the Shankill who attended secondary schools were much more likely (29 per cent) to engage in 'informal activities' than those at grammar schools (13 per cent).

14 The needs of young people as perceived by youth club participants

We asked the participants what they thought were the three main needs of young people in their relative areas. However, only 38 per cent gave more than one and only a few more than two.

Perceived needs of area

From the responses there are two important points to stress. First, there does not appear to be a significant difference between the two areas. Second, social and recreational facilities were perceived as being the most pressing need by the respondents. The first point shows that young people in the two areas have much in common in terms of priorities in life. The second point raised two further points.

First, it appears that young people tend to see social and recreational provisions as the answer to their problems, although it is obvious from both communities that what is required is a much more widespread campaign of social and economic revitalization. Remember though that we are talking about youth club participants and it appears that they have a much more optimistic assessment of their needs than non-users. Such an assessment of need is probably also a reflection of the lack of meaningful social and political education programmes. Second, it seems surprising bearing in mind the existing provision of such facilities, especially in the Shankill. Does this suggest that projects such as the leisure centre are not sufficiently meeting local need? This was in fact claimed by a number of the community workers we talked to.

The responses themselves, in this category, were very wide ranging, including: parks, BMX tracks, a rally park, community centres, more clubs, a leisure centre, more discos, pubs, slot machines, a day centre, a permanent fair, summer schemes, more activities at school and more sports.

Some of the respondents in a church club gave responses of 'more leisure and recreational' facilities. The club was about three hundred yards from the Shankill Leisure Centre, about two hundred yards from the Hammer Youth Resource Centre, the Hammer Community Complex and a statutory youth club and less than a hundred yards from another statutory club. We should point out that the 'no information' category made up 24 per cent in the Shankill but did not appear in the Springfield.

With the Shankill group we found that the rate of 'jobs and money' responses actually increased with social class scale. It was 3 per cent for unemployed, 7 per cent unskilled, 10 per cent skilled and 23 per cent middle class. 'Environmental' received 12 per cent of the responses from the unemployed group (this category included: more houses, transport, space, cleaning up and safer roads).

The highest rate of negative responses (don't know, none, nothing) was found in the unemployed group in the Shankill (30 per cent). The lowest rate of 'social and recreational' responses came from the unskilled group in the Springfield sample (41 per cent). The same group scored highest of the Springfield sample in the 'jobs and money' (17 per cent) and 'environmental' (23 per cent) categories.

Perceived needs by type of club

There were some significant differences between the various types of club. The lowest rate of 'social and recreational' responses came from the statutory sector (32 per cent). The response was about 50 per cent for all the other categories. The statutory sector accounted for the highest response rate (15 per cent) in the 'jobs and money' category (mean 9 per cent) and the 'environment' category (20 per cent). The next highest was the church group (6 per cent). These factors may suggest that statutory club participants are more likely to be more aware of the real needs in their areas than those at other clubs. They also scored lowest (15 per cent) in the negative category (mean 24 per cent), which may suggest more positive thinking.

The responses (or lack of them) in this section would tend to suggest that for the young people of the Shankill and Springfield there has been a definite shift in aspirational emphasis away from the things that contribute to the abstract quality of life towards a preoccupation with mass entertainment (as reflected in the demand for ready-made social and recreational facilities even when these are already available).

15 The perceived needs and formal youth provision

This section considers the responses to the next question in our survey: 'How many of the needs of young people does this club meet?' There were no significant differences between areas. Significantly though, 20 per cent of the youth club participants we interviewed did not think their particular club on organization met any of the needs of young people. This was the case for 25 per cent of the statutory sample compared to 18 per cent of the uniformed sample. Females, in general, tended to feel more that clubs met most of the needs (32 per cent) than did males (22 per cent).

16 Sexual equality in club

The next question asked respondents if they thought males and females were treated equally in their own clubs.

There appeared to be a much more significant problem or perceived problem in the Springfield clubs than in the Shankill clubs, with over a third (34 per cent) of the respondents in the Springfield sample claiming sexual inequality in youth clubs. The problem is probably overcome, to an extent, in the Shankill by the existence of single-sex organizations like the Boys' Brigade and Girls' Brigade. Further analysis showed that girls (16 per cent) were more likely to suffer from feelings of sexual inequality in clubs than boys (12 per cent) and that this was especially true of girls in the 10–12 age group (22 per cent).

17 School and work

This section considers some questions regarding school and job satisfaction, career expectations and perceived drawbacks in career expectations. We must state here that the findings, on the whole, present an extremely optimistic picture that is completely at odds with the actual situations of *all* young people in both areas.

Occupational and school satisfaction

The respondents were asked: 'What do you think of your job, training project or school?' The 'all right' responses were surprisingly high at 82 per cent overall, considering the widespread criticism of schools in both areas. This may suggest that youth club participants tend to have a more positive attitude to school than non-participants (our conversations with non-participants certainly bear this out). This may indicate that youth clubs and organizations are, to some extent at least, extensions of school and therefore not likely to attract young people who dislike school.

The 'hopeless' responses were much higher in the Springfield (18 per cent) than in the Shankill (7 per cent). Another 8 per cent of the Springfield sample also described their schools (jobs are almost non-existent there) as 'not so good'. This would tend to suggest a higher standard in schools in the Shankill and/or a higher degree of conformity in the Shankill sample. This may be supported by an analysis of respondents by club.

Only 4 per cent of the uniformed organization members from the Shankill gave 'hopeless' responses compared to 22 per cent of the voluntary sample and 13 per cent of the statutory and 12 per cent of the church clubs sample overall. This would also support the contention that voluntary clubs are more inclined to provide for young people who have less positive attitudes to school.

Career ambitions

We asked the respondents who were not in employment what sort of a job they would like, if any.

The first noticeable characteristic was that there was a large proportion of responses in the professional category. Although higher professional was more common in the Shankill (7 per cent compared to 2 per cent), lower professional was much higher in the Springfield (37 per cent compared to 26 per cent). White collar and office work was also higher in the Springfield (16 per cent) than the Shankill (7 per cent) sample.

Surprisingly, again, skilled manual scored higher in the Springfield (34 per cent) than Shankill (24 per cent). Semi-skilled or unskilled was slightly higher in the Shankill (9 per cent) than Springfield (7 per cent). We had no takers for the police or armed forces category in the Springfield sample (or at least they did not say, which would be understandable) whereas 7 per cent of the Shankill sample expressed an interest in these. Overall the figures would suggest that the Shankill respondents' ambitions were much more attuned to reality. Remember that almost all the Springfield sample came from unskilled or unemployed backgrounds.

Interestingly, in the Shankill group it was with the skilled working class respondents that the most ambitious are to be found. They provided 64 per cent of those aspiring to higher professional careers despite constituting only 40 per cent of the sample, and they also accounted for 56 per cent of those aspiring to white collar or office work. They were the main group in the police or armed forces category too, accounting for 60 per cent of the responses.

The major tendencies for unskilled background respondents were to get semi-skilled or unskilled jobs (10 per cent of them), lower professional (26 per cent) or, most significantly, skilled jobs (28 per cent of them). The unemployed group scored similarly, with 41 per cent of them seeking lower professional jobs and 25 per cent seeking skilled jobs.

In the Shankill the major class distinction in terms of career aspiration tended to be between the skilled working class and the unskilled and unemployed classes. There tended to be a distinct gap there. With the Springfield sample, however, the gap was most noticeable between the unskilled group and the unemployed group. There was a definite tendency for those from unskilled backgrounds to aspire to white collar and office work. They accounted for 36 per cent of the respondents in that category although constituting only 24 per cent of the sample. Unlike their counterparts in the Shankill they did not have a desire for skilled jobs, which accounted for only 17 per cent of the sample. The only significant trend for the unemployed group was towards skilled work, where they accounted for 70 per cent of the responses (they constituted 62 per cent of the sample).

Part of these processes may be explained by different attitudes about work in the two areas; for instance, the long tradition and status in the Shankill of skilled manual work or the lack of access to it in the Springfield (with white collar and office work providing a possible alternative in terms of status). A further explanation, however, can be given in terms of sex if we consider the greater number of females in the Springfield sample. Thirty-eight per cent of all females preferred lower professional careers compared to 18 per cent of the males. It would appear from this that girls tend to be significantly more ambitious than boys (although it may well be that boys simply attach more status to manual work). Girls also accounted for all but one (96 per cent) of the respondents in the white collar category. Seventy-two per cent of the skilled manual respondents were male (40 per cent of the male sample) although there was a significant female response rate here (14 per cent of them). Females tended more than males towards semi-skilled or unskilled work (12 per cent of them against only 4 per cent of males).

Perceived prospects of finding work

We asked the respondents what they though their prospects were of finding their preferred or similar work.

Most of the respondents in both areas were optimistic about career ambitions. Forty per cent of the Springfield sample noted their chances as good or very good, which is remarkable considering the unemployment situation in the area; 34 per cent thought their prospects were average; 6

per cent of all the respondents rated their chances as very low or nil. This would tend to suggest a picture of optimism in regard to the position of youth in both areas. However, we would stress here that all this does is underline the fact that participants in formal youth provision do not give a representative picture of young people in general.

Generally, males were more confident then females about attaining their desired career. Fourteen per cent of the males rated their chances as very good compared to 7 per cent of the females; 23 per cent of the males rated their chances as good compared to 17 per cent of the females. Females were more inclined to give average in response (47 per cent compared to 36 per cent for males).

Obstacles to career prospects

We asked the respondents what, if anything, they thought might hinder their chances of attaining their desired careers. There were no really significant differences between the two areas. Sub-standard education (31 per cent) was the most common response to the question, which is surprising considering the low response given to education in the needs question. Shortage of jobs was next (23 per cent). Twenty-three per cent thought that nothing would hinder their prospects or they did not know of anything. 'Personal and physical limitations' (which included responses such as not good enough, personality, not working hard enough, size, not enough brains and speech) only scored slightly significantly in the Springfield sample (12 per cent), which may suggest a higher level of self-confidence in the Shankill sample.

Categories such as residence, police record, being female and religion were not rated to a significant degree, which may seem surprising to some given the perceived nature of the two areas (bad localities, high crime rate, sectarian ghettoes, to name a few of the terms sometimes used to describe them). Being female probably scored low because the females tended to aspire to female-dominated occupations rather than because of the lack of sex discrimination in employment patterns.

Further investigation showed that the 'nothing/do not know' responses were much more common for those from skilled working class back-grounds (33 per cent Shankill, 33 per cent Springfield) than for those from unskilled backgrounds (23 per cent Shankill, 13 per cent Springfield).

In the Springfield sample 31 per cent of the unemployed group gave shortage of jobs as the major hindrance compared to 13 per cent of the unskilled group. The unskilled group tended more towards sub-standard education (44 per cent) than the unemployed group (29 per cent). The unskilled group in the Shankill also rated sub-standard education highest (31 per cent). Shortage of jobs ranked high for the skilled working class groups in both the Shankill (24 per cent) and the Springfield (33 per cent), which may reflect an awareness, possibly learned from their fathers, that skilled jobs were drying up in West Belfast. Personal and physical limitations, significantly, had high rates of response from the unskilled background respondents in both the Shankill (13 per cent) and the Springfield (19 per cent).

18 Friends in the area

The respondents were asked how many of their friends came from the same area. The Springfield sample had a greater proportion of 'most or all' responses (80 per cent) than the Shankill (56 per cent). This would tend to reflect the greater physical isolation of the Upper Springfield as well, we would suggest, as the different forms of youth clubs and organizations in the two areas. In a breakdown of responses according to type of clubs we found that only 52 per cent of the uniformed organization respondents were in this category. This would reflect the greater social and geographical mobility of those in such groups. On the contrary, 94 per cent of the voluntary club respondents stated that most or all of their friends came from the relevant study area. This would tend to suggest that the voluntary (secular) sector provided for participants who identified most readily with the local area in which the club was based (the rates were 61 per cent in the statutory and 66 per cent in the church sectors).

19 Fashions and tastes

We asked the subjects which, if any, fashion trend or group they belonged to. The overwhelming majority stated 'none' (76 per cent) or gave no response (12 per cent). This would appear to contradict those who tend towards the conception that youth, as distinct from everyone else, follow definite patterns in fashion and style or that they usually belong to specific recognizable sub-cultural groups, like mods or punks (our findings with 'unattached' youth were also similar).

When they were asked to state their musical preferences a similar picture emerged. The overwhelming majority (84 per cent) preferred 'general pop and rock' music and there was no significant response for any of the other categories.

20 Visiting the city centre

We asked the respondents how often they visited the city centre in an effort to ascertain, to some degree, their habits regarding leaving their own locality and/or socializing with those from different backgrounds. In simplistic terms we were measuring the extent of 'ghettoization'. The Shankill sample was much more likely to visit the centre more often (it is, of course, much closer). There was a staggering proportion from the

Springfield (22 per cent) who visited it very rarely or never. Another 33 per cent only visited occasionally. Thirty-eight per cent of the Shankill sample visited quite often, while another 28 per cent visited frequently.

There were a number of other factors to be considered, however. In the Upper Springfield, for instance, 72 per cent of those who had been attending clubs for between six months and two years visited either frequently or quite often, compared to only 39 per cent of the long-term members (over two years). This may suggest, simply, that long-term members are more likely to be more locally orientated instinctively or it may mean that long-term membership stifles the inclination to look outside one's area – that it institutionalizes the individual, in a sense, towards parochialism. Further investigation showed that those in the 10–12 age group (56 per cent) in the Upper Springfield were more likely to visit the city centre than those in the 13–17 group (39 per cent). This may be because the younger people accompany their parents or other adults for business or shopping and social purposes.

Occupational class background was a crucial variable in this question. Sixty-two per cent of the Shankill's middle class respondents visited quite often. Those in voluntary clubs are much more likely never or very rarely to visit the city centre (25 per cent) which supports what was said in section 18 about such clubs tending to attract more locally orientated individuals.

21   Authority

The following three sub-sections examine how young people assessed the police, army and local paramilitary organizations. We asked them to say whether they thought each was: (1) very good; (2) good; (3) all right; (4) bad; (5) very bad.

There was a high rate of 'don't know/no response' in the Springfield sample as a result of local 'advice' not to continue with these questions because of local sensitivities. Unfortunately we were not then able to assess accurately the degree of support given to the security forces and paramilitary organizations by youth club participants in the Upper Springfield. We had already asked the question in one voluntary club in Ballymurphy and we include the responses in order to give some indication with regard to the attitudes of voluntary youth club participants. We also had a problem here with the fact that the responses were intended to be mutually exclusive and some of the respondents insisted on replying to more than one category. For instance, some of them thought that the army was sometimes good and sometimes bad. We were forced to treat such responses as 'don't know' in order to simplify analysis, although we would like to note that they did indicate a degree of flexibility in attitudes to authority.

The police

There was a high degree of support in the Shankill sample, with only 15 per cent expressing negative attitudes. We should stress that the survey was carried out just before the signing of the Anglo-Irish Agreement in 1985, which resulted in a series of serious street confrontations between large numbers of youths and the RUC in the Shankill in early 1986. Relations with the police had deteriorated in the Shankill before the Agreement, however, and there had been a spate of serious rioting in 1984, mainly against the supergrass system. We would suggest that the high level of support expressed in the survey reveals the particular ethos of the groups concerned; that is, the high degree of emphasis placed on respect for law and order by, in particular, uniformed organizations.

It should be noted that no one in the Springfield sample described the police as very good or good, although the responses were fairly evenly divided between those who thought they were all right and those who did not. This is surprising for an area that is usually presented as one where alienation from the police is total.

With the Shankill group we found that none of those who had been attending clubs or organizations for more than ten years expressed negative attitudes to the police. However, it would be inconclusive to state that length of membership or attendance is likely to promote positive attitudes to the police as the next group – those in the two to ten year category – accounted for 70 per cent of the bad and 72 per cent of the very bad responses although they constituted only 54 per cent of the sample. There were no significant differences on this variable within the small Springfield sample.

There was a definite correlation between class background and attitude to the police in the Shankill (and possibly also in the Springfield). None of those expressing negative attitudes towards the police in the Shankill had fathers in the middle class category. Only 3 per cent of the skilled working class group said they were bad compared to 10 per cent of the unskilled and 9 per cent of the unemployed groups. Five per cent of the skilled group said they were very bad compared to 13 per cent of the unskilled and 6 per cent of the unemployed group. It is difficult to draw any conclusions from the Springfield sample because the response rate was so low. However, 75 per cent of the bad responses and 83 per cent of the very bad responses came from the unemployed group, who constituted 61 per cent of the sample.

Negative attitudes towards the police were more common for males than females. Seventy-one per cent of the bad responses and 67 per cent of the very bad responses came from the males, who constituted 48 per cent of the sample. The difference would be even greater if we allow for the fact that most of the Ballymurphy respondents, in this case, were female (15 of the 19).

There was a tendency for the uniformed organization respondents to express positive attitudes to the police. Only 10 per cent of them expressed negative attitudes, compared to 17 per cent of the church groups. The response rate for the statutory group was too low for meaningful analysis because of the absence of the Springfield responses.

There appears to be a positive correlation between type of school attended and attitudes to the police. No one attending a grammar school, from the Shankill, expressed negative attitudes towards the police, compared to 14 per cent of the secondary school sample. Thirty per cent of the grammar school respondents said they were very good compared to only 11 per cent of the secondary school respondents, and for the good category it was 44 per cent compared to 27 per cent respectively. One's employment situation is also likely to affect one's attitude to the police. Seventy-five per cent of the unemployed respondents from the Shankill expressed negative attitudes compared to 29 per cent of the employed respondents.

The army

Overall, attitudes to the army tended to be more favourable than those to the police. Fifty-eight per cent of those who responded from the Springfield thought that the army was all right. Only 3 per cent of the Shankill sample expressed negative attitudes (compared to 15 per cent for the police). This may reflect the much lower profile of the army in the Shankill in recent years and the fact that the police have been to the forefront in the various confrontations. The army may be more acceptable in Ballymurphy because people there see them as being less partial than the predominantly protestant and locally recruited RUC.

Again, there appeared to be a correlation between class background and attitudes. Thirty-one per cent of the middle class group on the Shankill said that the army was very good compared to 20, 15 and 13 per cent of the skilled, unskilled and unemployed groups respectively. In the good responses the corresponding figures were 54, 37, 28 and 38 per cent. Eighty-two per cent of the all right responses in Ballymurphy came from the unemployed group (who constituted 61 per cent of the sample).

Only one respondent from the uniformed organizations expressed negative attitudes towards the army (bad). The same was true for the statutory respondents but there were only 13 of them.

As with the police, those in grammar schools tended to have more favourable attitudes to the army. Twenty-six per cent of the grammar school respondents said they were very good compared to 16 per cent of the secondary school respondents. With good responses the figures were 44 and 39 per cent respectively.

The paramilitary organizations

There was a high overall 'all right' response, which would tend to suggest a certain amount of flexibility in attitudes to paramilitaries. Whichever way we look at it there was a substantial proportion of respondents (in the

Shankill at least) who thought that both the British Army and the local paramilitary organizations were all right. There was a higher rate of negative responses among the Shankill sample, 47 per cent, compared to the Springfield, 21 per cent (we are referring here to those who actually responded).

Only 8 per cent (one person) of the middle class group from the Shankill thought that paramilitaries were good or very good compared to 10, 18 and 17 per cent of the skilled, unskilled and unemployed groups respectively. Sixty-nine per cent of them thought that paramilitaries were bad or very bad compared to 42, 46 and 42 per cent of the other class groups in descending order.

Females expressed slightly more favourable attitudes to paramilitary organizations than males. Forty-four per cent of the females thought they were good, very good or all right compared to 41 per cent of the males, while only 27 per cent of them said they were bad or very bad compared to 41 per cent of males.

Sixty-one per cent of those at grammar school in the Shankill sample expressed negative feelings about paramilitary organizations compared to 39 per cent of those from secondary schools. Nearly half the Shankill participants thought that paramilitaries were all right or better compared to less than a quarter on the Springfield.

22 National identity

There has been much debate about the nature of national identity in Northern Ireland. Many observers have attempted to explain the continuing political crisis in terms of separate ethnic identities in which one, if not the key, concept is that of 'national aspiration' or 'nationality'. Explanations of the conflict in purely national terms (unionists versus nationalists) do, however, tend to be over-simplistic. Such analyses ignore many of the core elements in the dispute (social and economic deprivation, oppression, ideological social relations). Indeed many commentators, and even some members of the republican movement, have frequently stated that the 'armed struggle' is a civil rights campaign expressed in terms of national liberation.

It is frequently assumed that protestants hold a British identity and believe that removing the border in Ireland would make the situation in Northern Ireland worse, and that catholics hold an Irish identity and believe the opposite. We decided to put the question of nationality and the border to the respondents in order to test this assumption as well as to attempt to locate various factors that may influence attitudes about such issues among youth club participants.

Nationality

Sixty per cent of the Shankill sample considered themselves British compared to only 4 per cent of the Springfield sample. Seventy-seven per cent of the Springfield sample considered themselves Irish compared to only 5 per cent of the Shankill sample. Sixteen per cent of the Shankill sample considered themselves of Ulster nationality and this response was exclusive to the Shankill ('Ulster nationalism' has frequently been associated with reactionary loyalist politics and paramilitary organizations and is therefore unlikely to appeal to catholics who, generally speaking, do not perceive the six county state of Northern Ireland as constituting the nine county province of Ulster anyway). Northern Irish, however, did receive some measure of identification from both sets of respondents: 11 per cent of the Shankill sample described themselves as such and 9 per cent of those from the Springfield.

There were several variations in responses according to age. British accounted for 41 per cent of the Shankill's 10–12 age group and 84 per cent of the 18–21 age group. Northern Irish accounted for 16 per cent of the 10–12 group, 9 per cent of the 13–17 group and none of the 18–21 group. Ulster accounted for 18 per cent of the 10–12 group, 15 per cent of the 13–17 group and 16 per cent of the 18–21 group. Most of those who considered themselves Irish were also in the 10–12 group (12 per cent compared to 3 per cent of the 13–17 group and none of the rest). What all these figures appear to indicate is that for young people from the Shankill an ethnic identification in terms of being British (instead of Ulster, Northern Irish or Irish) is something that is learned from the secondary education stage up. To support this further it should be noted that most of the 'none of these' and 'do not knows' belonged to the 10–12 age group.

A similar pattern emerges in the Springfield sample with regard to Irish identity. In the 10–12 age group 8 per cent considered themselves British and 12 per cent Northern Irish compared to 3 and 8 per cent in the 13–17 age group and none of the over-17s. Sixty-eight per cent of the 10–12 group did consider themselves Irish, but this was compared to 82 per cent in the 13–17 group and all but one of the six over-17s in the sample (who did not know). Most of the 'do not knows' also belonged to the young group (12 per cent of the group).

There was also a correlation between type of school and national identity. Seventy-eight per cent of the grammar school pupils from the Shankill considered themselves British compared to 56 per cent of those at secondary school (39 per cent primary). Only 9 per cent of grammar school respondents considered themselves Ulster compared to 15 per cent of those at secondary schools (26 per cent primary). Nine per cent of the grammar school sample considered themselves Northern Irish compared to 13 per cent of the secondary school pupils (13 per cent primary). No one in the grammar school category considered him or herself Irish compared to 7 per cent of the secondary school pupils (4 per cent primary). All of this would tend to support the concept of 'protestant' grammar schools as the bastions of 'respectable unionism, (emphasizing the union with Great Britain rather than a distinctive Northern Irish identity).

The border

We next asked the respondents what effect they thought removing the border would have on the problems of Northern Ireland (assuming that it would then be included in an all-Ireland state, independent from Britain).

The first factor to note is the large response from the Springfield group (29 per cent) in the 'make them worse' category. Twenty-three per cent did think it would solve some of them but only 9 per cent thought it would solve all or most of them. Thirty-five per cent said they did not know or gave no response. These figures would tend to suggest that the association with an Irish identity is not necessarily an expression of, or desire for, Irish unification. It at least tells us that the respondents were conscious of the problems involved in unification. Only one-third of the Springfield sample, in effect, expressed views supporting the assumption that the removal of the border would solve some, most or all of the Province's problems. This may appear surprising in an area that is widely regarded as a republican stronghold. We would contend that it merely illustrates the complexities inherent to nationalist or republican ideology in West Belfast. The expression of Irishness is a symbol that re-affirms a social reality located within the area. It is the result of a peculiar *ethnic* identification that includes a resistance to the practices, symbols and effects (oppression, occupation, deprivation, etc.) of the British or 'Orange' state.

On the other hand, a significant proportion of the Shankill sample (17 per cent) admitted that removing the border would solve some of the problems (they may, of course, also believe that it would make others worse). We did not, however, get a response for the opposite, solving most or all the problems (4 per cent), anywhere near the Springfield response for making them worse. These figures do, to some degree, indicate a tacit acceptance, at least, of partition in catholic West Belfast. Of course we are speaking about youth club participants who may, therefore, be reflecting the 'more respectable' opinions in the area (republicans would admit that the British presence in the six counties is bolstered by a significant proportion of the catholic population – the constitutional nationalists, the castle catholics, the Uncle Toms, the collaborators, or whatever they may wish to name them). The simple fact of the situation is that the statutory (state) and the church (which republicans view as being in cahoots with the state) youth clubs are likely to promote the appropriate ethos. They are, in effect, an extension of the school system. Indeed, further analysis indicated that there was a definite correlation between length of attendance/membership of a club and the border issue. Only 18 per cent of the two to ten year participants believed that removing the border would solve all, most or some of the problems compared to 43 per cent of the six months to two years group and 56 per cent of the under six months group. The longer-term groups also accounted for 96 per cent of the 'do not knows/no response', although constituting only 48 per cent of the sample. Only three of the respondents had been involved in the clubs for more than ten years but they all thought that removing the border would make problems worse.

In the Shankill sample there was a significant difference between the age groups in the responses. Generally, responses tended to become less favourable to the effects of Irish unification with age. Seventy-one per cent of the 'solve all or most of' responses in the area were in the 10–12 age range, which constituted 33 per cent of the sample. The corresponding figures for the 13–17 age group were 14 per cent and 56 per cent respectively. Fifty-seven per cent of the 13–17 group gave 'make them worse' responses compared to 46 per cent of the 10–12 group. For 'solve none of them' the figures were 11 and 3 per cent respectively.

There were also class distinctions in the responses in the Shankill sample. Sixty per cent of the skilled working class group gave 'make them worse' responses compared to 49 per cent of the unskilled group, 47 per cent of the unemployed group, and 31 per cent of the middle class group. Such figures would support the thesis that it is skilled workers or the 'labour aristocracy' that are the backbone of the Ulster Unionist resistance to Irish nationalism.

In the Springfield sample 41 per cent of the unskilled group gave 'make them worse' responses compared to 24 per cent of the unemployed group. This would lend weight to the theory that Irish nationalism is strongest in those sections of the Catholic population (such as the unemployed) who have little or no stake in the Northern Ireland state. These factors to a degree illustrate the economics of nationalism and partition.

In the Shankill sample there were some differences according to type of school attended. Only 9 per cent of the grammar school respondents gave 'solve some' responses compared to 22 per cent of the secondary group. Three per cent of the latter also gave 'most' or 'all' responses. On the other hand, 22 per cent of the grammar respondents gave 'solve none' responses compared to only 6 per cent of the secondary respondents.

23 Politics

This section attempts to describe the political affiliations of youth club participants in West Belfast. However, as with the questions on authority, we were inhibited by the lack of co-operation in regard to these particular questions in the Springfield. We did, however, include the responses from the one club (voluntary) that had already been interviewed before we were advised to withdraw the two questions.

Political party affiliation

For the reason stated above there was a high proportion of 'no responses' in the Springfield sample. However, the percentage of 'none/don't know' and 'no responses' in the Shankill sample was also extremely high (76 per cent). Indeed there was a much higher positive response rate in the Springfield club that had been 'allowed' to be interviewed. It should be noted that 11 of the 13 positive respondents opted for Sinn Fein as the preferred party. However, we should consider here that the interviews were carried out in one of the secular voluntary clubs. We suspect the responses may have been significantly different in the church and statutory clubs.

With the Shankill sample the Democratic Unionist Party (DUP) had almost double the Official Unionist percentage of the responses, which may indicate a growing militancy among the young or could be a reflection of the dominance of 'religious' clubs and organizations in the Shankill (bearing in mind the DUP's close connection with evangelical fundamentalism). Further analysis showed that father's occupational status appeared to be positively correlated with political affiliation in the Shankill sample. Only 18 per cent of the Official Unionist supporters belonged to the unskilled class and none of them belonged to the unemployed class, compared to 50 and 21 per cent respectively for the DUP supporters.

Type of club and political affiliation were also positively correlated. Sixty-two per cent of the Official Unionist supporters belonged to uniformed organizations and 34 per cent to church clubs. The figures for the DUP supporters were 29 and 68 per cent respectively, which would again emphasize the close identification that the uniformed organizations foster with the 'respectable' side of unionism.

Type of school attended also appeared likely to influence political affilia- tion. Twenty-five per cent of the Official Unionist supporters attended grammar schools compared to only 5 per cent of the DUP supporters. Employment status gave a similar picture. Twenty-five per cent of the Official Unionist supporters were employed and none unemployed compared to 14 per cent and 19 per cent respectively for the DUP.

Politicians

We asked the respondents to name their favourite politicians. Again there was a high rate of 'none' and 'no response' in both the Shankill and the Springfield. It should be noted that there was no significant support for the Official Unionist politicians (Powell and Molyneaux) in the Shankill. They accounted for only 2 per cent of the sample (Neil Kinnock scored as many). The overwhelming support of those who did respond positively went to the two 'firebrand' politicians, Ian Paisley (11 per cent) and George Seawright (9 per cent).

Again it appears that there would have been a much higher positive response rate in the Springfield sample if we had been allowed to continue with the question, which may suggest a much higher political conscious- ness among young people in the Springfield. It may, however, merely mean that young people in the Shankill are more disillusioned with politics and politicians. Of those who did respond positively in the Springfield sample all 12 opted for Sinn Fein politicians (Gerry Adams 8, Sean Keenan 4).

Overall, in the political questions, females were more likely to give negative responses (80 per cent) than males (72 per cent). Most of Seawright's supporters (82 per cent of them) were males, as were Paisley's (65 per cent) to a lesser degree. Kinnock was more popular (four positive responses) than Seawright (three positive responses) among young females in the Shankill sample. It should also be noted that only 33 per cent of the positive respondents in the Shankill sample were female.

Most of Seawright's supporters came from the unskilled (55 per cent) and unemployed (36 per cent) social class categories in terms of father's occupation. Most of Paisley's (58 per cent) came from the skilled category while the unskilled and unemployed categories accounted for 21 and 5 per cent of his support respectively. Fifteen per cent of the church club respondents in the Shankill supported Seawright compared to 5 per cent of the uniformed organization respondents. The only four Molyneaux/ Powell supporters belonged to uniformed groups as did three of the four Kinnock and two of the three Thatcher supporters. Paisley's support was evenly split between the church (11 per cent) and uniformed (10 per cent) groups.

Although the response rate was low (27 per cent) overall for the Shankill sample it was much higher (52 per cent) for those in full-time employment. Twenty-four per cent of them preferred Seawright, Molyneaux/ Powell came second (14 per cent) and Paisley came third (10 per cent). Of the 14 respondents on YTPs or registered as unemployed only four responded positively and they all preferred Seawright.

The most significant factor to emerge in this section is that the respondents in general were not really interested in politics in the party political and/or personality sense and that they were indecisive in their views. Those who were, however, tended towards the more militant parties (DUP, Sinn Fein) and personalities (Paisley, Seawright, Adams).

24   Church attendance

It is significant that in the Springfield sample 81 per cent attended church at least once a week. This would seem to refute claims made by many local people and even some priests that secularization was rampant. It may, of course, merely illustrate that youth club participants are more likely to be disposed towards church attendance than non-participants. A similar pattern emerged in the Shankill sample, where 52 per cent of the participants attended at least once a week despite claims from some clerics and lay people that young people no longer attended church.

Significantly, a higher proportion (14 per cent) in the Shankill attended church more than once a week than in the Springfield (12 per cent). There was a much higher proportion of those who never attended (34 per cent) in the Shankill sample than the Springfield (12 per cent).

Further analysis showed that there was a definite tendency in the Shankill for religious observance to be related to class factors. For instance, 85 per cent of those whose fathers were in skilled working class occupations attended at least once a week compared to 46 per cent of those whose fathers were in unskilled occupations and 36 per cent of those whose fathers were unemployed. Fifty-eight per cent of those whose fathers were unemployed attended never or less than once a month compared to 46 per cent of those whose fathers had middle class occupations. A similar trend did not occur in the Springfield sample.

There was a positive correlation between sex and church attendance. Seventy-four per cent of the females attended at least once a week compared to 44 per cent of the males; 42 per cent of the males never attended compared to only 15 per cent of the females.

Church attendance could also be linked to the type of club attended, although those who went to church clubs tended to be those *least* likely to be frequent church attenders. Those who attended church at least once a week included 68 per cent of those who attended statutory clubs, 65 per cent of those who attended uniformed organizations and 56 per cent of those who attended voluntary clubs. However, the percentage for those from church clubs was only 48 per cent.

Only 19 per cent of those who belonged to uniformed organizations never attended (church attendance was, however, obligatory for most of these organizations on certain occasions but enforced to varying degrees depending on the disposition of the officers). Twenty-eight per cent of statutory club participants and 28 per cent of those from voluntary clubs never attended. The percentage, however, for those from church clubs who never attended was 45 per cent. This trend may, of course, be explained by the claim that the programmes of such clubs are designed to attract the unconverted and *then* gradually, and unwittingly to the participants, to inculcate a religious ethos. Certainly, many of them did have a latent religious function.

There were some comparisons to be drawn between church attendance and school and occupational status of the respondents. None of the small (eight) unemployed group from the Shankill attended church at least once a week (seven of them never) compared to 22 per cent of those at grammar schools. Only 8 per cent of those at primary schools in the Upper Springfield sample attended less than once a week or never compared to 21 per cent at secondary schools. This may indicate a slackening in religious practice as parental pressure lessens.

25 The 'other sort'

This section examines a wide range of views held by youth club participants in relation to people of the 'opposite' religious background and their willingness to mix or socialize with each other.

Relations

We asked the participants how many relations they had of the opposite religion. As could only be expected, the overwhelming majority (78 per cent) had none and another 17 per cent had a few.

Oddly enough, those from single-parent families tended to be more likely to have relations of the opposite religion. Exactly 33 per cent of participants from such families had relatives of the opposite religion compared to only 16 per cent in the Shankill and 20 per cent in the Springfield of two-parent families. This may be a reflection of a higher level of marital break-up in 'mixed' marriages.

Friends

We asked the respondents to indicate how many of their friends were of the opposite religion. Most of them (59 per cent) had none. However, this was higher (66 per cent) for the Springfield than the Shankill (56 per cent), which may be an indication of the greater isolation of the Upper Springfield. Almost all the rest (34 per cent) had only a few friends of the opposite religion.

Further analysis showed that the participants were more likely to make friends of the opposite religion as they grew older. In the Shankill sample 71 per cent of those in the 10–12 age group had none compared to 51 and 39 per cent in the 13–17 and 18–21 age groups respectively. The corresponding figures for the Springfield were 80, 62 and 40 per cent.

There appeared to be a correlation between having friends of the opposite religion and father's occupation in the Shankill sample. Only 31 per cent of those with fathers in middle class occupations had no friends of the opposite religion compared to 48 and 77 per cent for those with fathers in skilled manual occupations and unskilled occupations respectively. In the Upper Springfield sample the difference tended to be between those with fathers in skilled manual occupations (33 per cent) and those in the unskilled (71 per cent) or unemployed (73 per cent) groups.

Those in uniformed organizations (50 per cent) were least likely to have no friends of the opposite religion whereas those in voluntary clubs (72 per cent) were most likely. The rates for statutory and church clubs were 69 and 61 per cent respectively.

School attended was another significant variable here. Only 26 per cent of those at grammar schools from the Shankill had no friends of the opposite religion compared to 64 per cent of those at secondary schools. Only 29 per cent of those in employment had none compared to 71 per cent of those who were unemployed.

Seventy per cent of those from two-parent families in the Springfield sample had no friends of the opposite religion compared to 50 per cent of those from single-parent families.

Integrated clubs

There was an overall majority (53 per cent) in favour of integrated youth clubs, although the Shankill sample (48 per cent) was more in favour of exclusively protestant clubs than the Springfield sample was in favour of catholic clubs (38 per cent).

There was a significant increase in the proportion of participants favouring integrated clubs as they grew older. In the Shankill sample, 40 per cent of the 10–12 age group favoured integrated clubs compared to 53 and 68 per cent for the 13–17 and 18–21 groups respectively. The corresponding figures for the Springfield were 44, 63 and 100 per cent.

There was also a positive correlation between social class background and choice of club. In the Shankill sample 39 per cent of the respondents with fathers in middle class occupations were not prepared to attend integrated clubs compared to 42, 49 and 55 per cent of those with fathers with skilled manual, unskilled manual and unemployed backgrounds respectively. In the Springfield sample, 22 per cent of those from skilled manual backgrounds favoured catholic only clubs compared to 41 per cent each for those from unskilled and unemployed backgrounds.

Mixed areas

We asked the respondents to state their preferences with regard to residing in mixed or catholic/protestant only areas. Only about a third (35 per cent) would live in a mixed area if given the choice. It should be noted that although the Springfield sample was more inclined than the Shankill sample to attend integrated clubs, the process was reversed when it came to living in mixed areas. Sixty-eight per cent of the Springfield sample preferred to live in catholic only areas, whereas 61 per cent of the Shankill sample preferred protestant only areas. The discrepancy may be accounted for by the fact that catholics are more likely to be subjected to random sectarian attacks than protestants in Belfast.

There was a positive correlation between age and willingness to live in mixed areas. In the Shankill sample 31 per cent of those in the 10–12 age group were prepared to live in a mixed area compared to 33 and 68 per cent for those in the 13–17 and 18–21 age groups respectively. The corresponding figures for the Springfield were even more significant: 16, 32 and 100 per cent respectively.

In the Shankill sample 54 per cent of those with fathers in middle class occupations were prepared to live in mixed areas compared to 37, 28 and 30 per cent respectively for those with fathers in skilled manual, unskilled and unemployed positions. There was not a significant similar trend in the Springfield sample.

Overall, females (40 per cent) were more prepared than males (31 per cent) to live in mixed areas. Forty-one per cent of those in uniformed organizations were prepared to live in 'mixed' areas compared to 39 per cent, 28 per cent and 23 per cent of those in church, voluntary and statutory clubs respectively.

Socializing

There was a large majority (63 per cent) who never or very rarely socialized with those of the opposite religion. Only 7 per cent socialized frequently and 8 per cent quite often. There were no significant differences between the two areas on this question. There was, however, age and social class correlations with this variable.

In the Shankill sample 73 per cent of those in the 10–12 age range socialized never or very rarely compared to 62 and 47 per cent for the 13–17 and 18–21 age groups respectively. Thirty-seven per cent of those in the 18–21 age range socialized frequently or quite often compared to only 14 and 8 per cent for those in the 13–17 and 10–12 age groups respectively. Not one of those in the 10–12 age group socialized frequently or quite often with those of the opposite religion. Twenty per cent of the 18–21 group and 21 per cent of the 13–17 group socialized frequently or quite often. It should, of course, be borne in mind that the opportunity to socialise, particularly outside one's own locality, avails itself much more as one grows older.

In the Shankill sample only 39 per cent of those from middle class backgrounds socialized never or very rarely with those of the opposite religion compared to 58, 77 and 89 per cent of those from skilled, unskilled and unemployed backgrounds respectively. Twenty-three per cent of those from middle class backgrounds socialized frequently or quite often with those of the opposite religion compared to 20, 8 and 6 per cent of those from skilled, unskilled and unemployed backgrounds respectively. In the Upper Springfield sample 44 per cent of those from skilled backgrounds socialized with those of the opposite religion never or very rarely compared to 65 and 67 per cent respectively of those from unskilled and unemployed backgrounds. Thirty-three per cent of those from skilled backgrounds compared to only 12 per cent and 10 per cent respectively of those from unskilled and unemployed backgrounds socialized with those of the opposite religion frequently or quite often.

Attitudes to increased mixing

We asked the respondents whether young people of both religions should mix socially more than they do. Sixty-two per cent overall were in favour of this with only 26 per cent against. The response rates were similar for both areas. Males were overall more against increased mixing (31 per cent) than females (21 per cent). Uniformed organization members (69 per cent) were most in favour while voluntary club members (47 per cent) were least in favour.

Although, in the Shankill sample, respondents from secondary schools had far fewer friends of the opposite religion than those from grammar schools, 61 per cent of them did think that young people should socialize more compared to 65 per cent of those from grammar schools. Clearly, the reason they do not mix as much already must be found in other social indicators, such as lack of opportunity, rather than in lack of inclination.

Courtship

We asked whether the respondents would be prepared to 'go out' with someone of the opposite religion.

There was a majority against (53 per cent) and only 27 were prepared to do so. There were, however, 7 per cent 'maybe' responses and 13 per cent said they did not know (some said it depended on what they 'looked like' or 'how much money they had'!). There was a significant difference between the two areas in that 41 per cent of the Springfield sample were prepared to go out with a protestant compared to only 22 per cent of the Shankill sample prepared to go out with a catholic. Perhaps it should be stated that for a number of reasons that we need not go into here it is dangerous in the Northern Ireland situation for a protestant to court a catholic and vice versa.

Attitudes to courting those of the opposite religion did not appear to improve by youth club attendance. In the Shankill sample 51 per cent of those who had been members between six months and two years replied no compared to 59 per cent of those in the two to ten years category. The discrepancy was even more marked in the Springfield sample. While 24 per cent in the six months to two years category replied no, the corresponding proportion in the two to ten years category was 49 per cent. The corresponding figures for 'yes' responses were 57 and 39 per cent.

While the male 'no' responses remained fairly constant (mean 52 per cent) for all age groups, the 'yes' responses appeared to increase with age. While only 27 per cent replied yes in the 10–12 age group, 32 and 39 per cent replied yes in the 13–17 and 18–21 age groups respectively. There was a corresponding decrease in 'no' responses from 63 per cent down through 49 per cent to 36 per cent. Of course, such tendencies may be explained by the fact that younger people are less likely to be interested in members of the opposite sex, and that interest increases progressively throughout the teens. There was no significant correlation between social class background and courting members of the opposite religion in either the Shankill or Upper Springfield. Males (32 per cent) were slightly more willing to court females of the opposite religion than the other way round (24 per cent).

Although members of uniformed organizations were the most willing to socialize, live with and have friends of the opposite religion they drew the line at courtship. Only 23 per cent of them said yes compared to 33, 31 and 29 per cent of statutory, voluntary and church club members respectively. They also headed the list (57 per cent) of the 'no' respondents.

Perceived differences in the 'other sort'

We asked the respondents whether they thought that people of the 'opposite' religion were different from them.

The majority (62 per cent) thought that they were 'basically the same' and the response was almost identical for both areas. Slightly more (13 per cent) of the Springfield sample than of the Shankill sample (8 per cent) thought that they were very different. Thirty-one per cent of the Shankill sample thought that they were a bit different compared to 24 per cent of the Springfield sample.

There was no indication from the results that length of attendance at youth clubs in any way altered perceptions of differences in those of the opposite religion, which would tend to refute the idea that formal youth provision helps promote mutual understanding in a diverse community. We found no significant correlation between social class background and perceived degree of differentiation, which would tend to refute the ideas that prejudice is increased as one descends the social class scale. There was also no positive correlation between sex and perceived degree of difference.

Those in uniformed organizations (65 per cent) were most inclined to consider those of the opposite religion as basically the same while those in voluntary clubs were least inclined (50 per cent; mean 62 per cent). Uniformed organization members were also less likely to consider those of the opposite religion as very different (6 per cent). Thirteen per cent of those in statutory clubs thought they were very different (mean 9 per cent).

There was no significant difference in the Shankill sample between grammar (70 per cent) and secondary (62 per cent) schools in regarding those of the opposite religion as being basically the same or in regarding them as very different (4 and 6 per cent respectively). Those in employment (71 per cent) were, however, more likely to regard young people of the opposite religion as basically the same than those who were unemployed (57 per cent). The corresponding figures for those who thought they were very different were 14 and 29 per cent respectively. This would support the argument that spiralling unemployment accentuates sectarianism in the Province.

26 The troubles

We asked the participants why they thought the troubles in Northern Ireland had lasted so long. This was an open question and the responses were coded for analysis after collection.

The most prominent reasons given related to 'segregation' (22 per cent) and this was common to both the Shankill (21 per cent) and the Springfield (24 per cent). Answers referred to: two traditions, people living apart, ignorance, and so on.

A close second in the Springfield sample (18 per cent) were responses that could best be coded under 'British presence' and/or 'security forces' (army, RUC, Brits, British power). These were hardly seen in the Shankill sample (2 per cent).

The Shankill sample (12 per cent) was more inclined to blame the troubles on 'trouble-makers' (paramilitaries, psychopaths, gangsters). Such differences in response for the second highest categories clearly reflect the socio-political realities of the two communities. This would include the prevalence of the nationalist campaign (some would say 'war') in catholic West Belfast against the British presence or at least against the more openly repressive state apparatuses. The protestant areas of West Belfast, on the other hand, have traditionally been associated more (or at least substantial elements within them) with a concern for 'law and order' (as it is within their interests to maintain the status quo).

Only 5 per cent of the Shankill sample blamed catholics directly while only 3 per cent of the Springfield sample blamed protestants. This would tend to illustrate the implicitness of sectarianism in Belfast. Six per cent of the Shankill sample did, however, blame republicans and/or the IRA.

Only 1 per cent of the Shankill sample and 3 per cent of the Springfield sample gave responses relating to nationality, while only 6 per cent of the Shankill sample and 4 per cent of the Springfield sample blamed religion in general. Five per cent of the Shankill sample and 7 per cent of the Springfield sample blamed older people or politicians in general.

Perhaps the most significant finding was that only 2 per cent of the Shankill sample and none of the Springfield sample blamed 'social and economic conditions'. This is a clear indication of how the troubles and their effects (segregation, concern with law and order, dislike of the security forces) have served to direct the attention of people away from their real problems by concealing or structurally excluding from thought the actual conditions of existence. The troubles re-affirm and reproduce ideological definitions of reality in everyday life.

27 The difficulties facing youth today

We asked the respondents to indicate, in order of importance, what they thought were the major difficulties facing young people at the time.

'Inequality' (unemployment, lack of money, taxing dole, Thatcher's policies, exploitation) came first, with 38 per cent of the first preferences overall (50 per cent of the Springfield sample). 'Restraints' (not enough say, voting age, lack of freedom of expression, criticism, lack of involvement) came second with 22 per cent of the first responses, although it was only third (12 per cent) behind 'intolerance' (14 per cent) in the Springfield. 'Intolerance' (lack of co-operation, segregation, racism, making trouble, different backgrounds) was third overall with 13 per cent of the first responses. 'Interpersonal relationships' (broken families, lacking parental care, generation gap, sex, deciding about marriage) was fourth overall, with 9 per cent of the first preferences.

None of the other categories scored significantly here. When we consider what they included it becomes evident that what young people see as being their major problems are far removed from what are regarded as major youth problems in popular folk mythology. Only 1 per cent of them thought that 'lack of social facilities' was the most major difficulty. Only 1 per cent thought it was alcohol or drug abuse. Remember we are considering the views of the more 'conformist' of the young population.

Only 1 per cent were concerned primarily with education and 2 per cent with war/violence. Yet when we come to consider views of unattached youths these topics are often to the fore, along with the 'Northern Ireland problem', which only received 4 per cent of the first responses here.

'Inequality' also scored highest in the second choice responses (43 per cent) followed by 'lack of social facilities' (17 per cent) and 'restraints' (14 per cent). Over a third, however, of the sample did not give a second response. Only about a third of the sample gave a third choice response, and 'inequality' and 'lack of social facilities' tied with 25 per cent each of the responses.

Further analysis of first responses showed that males in the 18–21 age group were much more concerned (15 per cent, mean 8 per cent) about interpersonal relationships, as were females in the same age range (20 per cent, mean 11 per cent). Females in this age range were also much more concerned about restraints (30 per cent, mean 12 per cent) than their male counterparts (8 per cent, mean 33 per cent), who did not seem to have many qualms about this. Females in the 13–17 age group were most concerned with inequality (53 per cent, mean 42 per cent). Males in general, however, were more concerned about restraints (33 per cent) than females (12 per cent). Females were more concerned about inequality (42 per cent) than males (33 per cent).

Those in statutory clubs (21 per cent) were most concerned about intolerance, while those in church clubs (5 per cent) were least concerned. Voluntary club members were concerned least about restraints (9 per cent), while those in uniformed organizations were most concerned (26 per cent) about them.

6 YOUTH AND YOUTH SUB-CULTURE IN THE SHANKILL

The context

Chapters 4 and 5 have indicated the nature and extent of youth provision in the study areas and given a comprehensive analysis of the attitudes, motives, background and expectations of those working or participating in formal youth provision. This chapter and Chapter 7 will consider the position of those young people who do not participate in youth clubs or organizations, frequently referred to in youth work terminology as 'unattached' or 'unclubables'. Such terms do, of course, imply that 'non-participants' are particular types (note the prefixes) of non-conformist individuals (as we have seen, some of the descriptions of them imply much worse). We must emphasize here what has been stated earlier, that when we talk about non-participants we are talking about the majority (at least two-thirds) of the young people in the community.

We intend to show that our examination of participants and non-participants in formal youth provision in West Belfast presented us with much more than an explanation of why some young people are attracted to organized youth clubs and some are not. The analysis presented is also intended to consider the tensions and implications of a complex 'web' of social relations that have a particular form and content representing the underlying social structure of West Belfast. The 'culture' of working class youth in Shankill and Ballymurphy encapsulates the social, economic and political characters of the two communities, which may also be seen in terms of a peculiar ethnic national identification.

While the youth service claims to offer 'personal development, social education, recreation and reconciliation', our investigations have revealed that most young people who do attend clubs do so first and foremost for games and physical activities. Our investigations have further revealed that youth clubs are basically in the business of 'social control' (the participants were clearly aware of this) – getting the kids off the streets. Personal development, social education and so on are the official terms for the different means of achieving what is, in effect, character building (conformity).

When we proceed to consider the position of the non-participants it becomes apparent that they are not uncontrollables, unattached, unclubables, undesirables, anti-social or hoods. Their culture is an expression of their social location in the parent culture and we must see it in terms of its relation to the wider class cultural networks of which they form a distinctive part. Their culture includes divergent forms of social activities as well as complex sets of attitudes and ideas that articulate divergent experiences in relation to national identity, social and economic upheaval and deprivation. The same could be said of the working class in West Belfast in general. Indeed, it has been argued convincingly (P. Cohen 1972) that youth cultural styles and practices represent, in their different ways, an attempt to retrieve some of the socially cohesive elements destroyed in parent culture in order to sustain a sense of community and collective identity in a situation where traditional structures and sentiments of communality have been eroded by urban redevelopment and industrial decline. Such an argument is particularly relevant in the Northern Ireland context and, as with Bell's (n.d.) analysis, we will argue that young people in Belfast are more than passive initiates into political and cultural practices. Rather, as we shall see, they play an active part in the reproduction of 'sectarian' ideologies.

The culture of working class youth in West Belfast does include a variety of negative manifestations of behaviour that are associated with the failure (of society) to provide or allow for many of the basic desirable objectives in life, such as peace, a healthy environment, relevant education, meaningful relationships, secure jobs and real democracy. There were, however, widely divergent attitudes and social status between the groups of young people as well as within them.

We must also consider one of the largest, though often ignored, sections of the youth population: those who don't participate in easily recognizable groups or activities (corner gang, drinking club, flute band, sports team) but who spend most of their spare time in informal activities at home (watching television, playing records, visiting friends or relations) or participating in adult or parent activities (going out with a parent, helping with the housework). This 'hidden' culture has largely been ignored by commentators, who have subsequently failed to give an accurate overview of youth activities and attitudes.

Working class youth from the Shankill and Springfield inhabit, like their parents, a distinctive structural and cultural milieu defined by territory, objects, relations, and institutional and social practices. As stated in Chapter 2, it is in terms of kinship, friendship networks, the informal culture of the neighbourhood and the practices articulated around them that the young are already located in and by the parent culture. They mediate it to the subordinate culture and thus permeate it. We shall examine how youth in West Belfast experience, and react to, the key institutions and agencies of public social control – the schools, work (or lack of it), leisure (and youth clubs), the security forces and religion. The response of youth to such institutions is a working class response to institutions and should be analysed as such rather than in terms of 'generation gap'. The so-called generation gap was not an important issue (if it was one at all) in the study areas. The responses of the youth of West Belfast to particular institutions are based on similar values to those held by their parents. We are not arguing that distinctive youthful values, activities, styles and so on are unimportant or that tensions in the family do not exist. There have been tremendous tensions in family life but such changes have arisen out of changes in the structure of working class communities. Urban redevelopment and the destruction of local economies have clearly left their mark. This has, among other things, led to an erosion of the more informal agents of social control. This process has, however, been the product of bourgeois attempts to promote a greater emphasis on 'individual freedom' (for the motives for this de-velopment see Chapter 1). This concept, however, involves a negative view of freedom and it back-fired as the restructuring of the British and Irish economies created large industrial wastelands with previously unparalleled unemployment rates. Freedom is not an apt description of being in a position to organize one's own time through being on the dole.

Family ties have remained quite strong in the Shankill despite the upheaval in recent years. We encountered some ridicule (most of it good-hearted) of parents but little or no animosity in our discussions. Indeed parents were usually regarded with affection and respect (although this was not always explicit).

Finally, we should reconsider what was said in Chapters 4 and 5, which consisted of an analysis of youth workers and participants in formal youth provision. A comparison is necessary if we are successfully to account for the unwillingness of non-participants to take part in formal activities. In order to do this it is imperative that we understand their culture – and we mean culture in the broadest sense of the concept. A comprehensive explanation of the form and content of such culture should, we hope, provide us with an answer to the 'million dollar' question: why some people are not interested in formal youth provision. As we have seen, both youth workers and youth club users do, generally speaking, perceive the unattached as morally, ideologically and behaviourally different from participants or at least as possessing moral, ideological and behavioural characteristics that are incompatible with the aims, activities and objectives of formal youth provision. This chapter and Chapter 7 will consider the validity of this proposition and its implications, if valid, for youth (and social) policy and, indeed, society in general.

The subjects

In the Shankill sample a series of informal (some semi-structured, some unstructured) discussions with various groups of young people in various settings was conducted over a period of several months. Some of the groups met regularly (once a week at least) for ten to twelve weeks. Others were unwilling or unable to co-operate for more than two or three sessions. In the latter case this was sometimes unfortunate as participation in the discussions tended to increase with familiarity. However, it should be noted that young people, in the 16–19 age range especially, do tend to be very expressive, generally speaking, in the company of their peers. Ideally it is better if an initiation period of two or four sessions can be managed. This was particularly useful when we came to tape the discussions. At first some of the participants in the discussions were reluctant to use, or were shy of, the tape recorder. Others were inclined initially to exaggerate their reactions because of the presence of the microphone. It was possible to overcome both sets of problems as the researcher, and the equipment, became more acceptable and less conspicuous. The settings aided the process enormously. The discussions took place in allocated rooms in school, work, YTPs and drop-in centres. In the first three especially the level of co-operation was high because the subjects were excused class, work or instruction in order to participate in the discussions. This made the researcher extremely popular (which says a lot about the respondents' attitude to their work, school and YTP) and created a relaxed, hospitable (generally speaking) atmosphere. Owing to the relative importance of religion to a large section of the Shankill population we include a group of young Christians. The discussions lasted between one and two hours. Sometimes there were only three people present (including the researcher) and sometimes as many as eight (which we felt was too many). The median was five or six, which tended to be the most efficient number for our purposes. On occasions when the subjects talked freely with each other, the researcher tended to allow the conversation to flow with little or no comment. On other occasions the researcher was required to probe to a greater or lesser extent in order to maximize response. On occasions the researcher played the role of 'devil's advocate'. Some of the discussions were more structured around particular subject headings with the researcher using cues (photographs, tape recordings of people speaking on the pertinent issue) to initiate or sustain discussion.

Forty-five young people between the ages of 15 and 22 (except for two who were older) participated in the discussions. There were eight different groups situated in six different locations. There were 30 males and 15 females in all. Four of the groups were exclusively male, two exclusively female and two mixed. (One of the male groups was also combined with one of the female groups on several occasions.)

We have attempted to present what follows under 'subject' headings. However, it should be stated that these are very general, given the often spontaneous flow of conversation from one topic to another and the complexity of the respondents' relationships with peers, work, school, authority, family, community and so on. We hope, however, that this will not impede upon the central concern – an analysis of the culture of working class youth located within the parent culture and the effects of its encounters with, and attitudes to, the dominant culture.

Gender, family and social life

One of the most commonly held assumptions about the changes in community life in the Shankill in recent years has been that 'family life is breaking down'. Certainly there have been widespread changes, particularly a greater abundance of nuclear as opposed to extended family units (although it is still common to have three generations of a family living in the same street). Moral priorities and obligations have also undergone a radical transformation and a combination of industrial decline and the growth of the welfare state has served to challenge traditional roles within marriage. There has also been a move away from traditional family outings and activities towards a greater emphasis on individualism and the pursuit of consumer goods. From the views of some young people it would certainly seem that family life had changed and that this was necessary and inevitable. For instance, financial restrictions or the pursuit of goods have led to changes in attitude to family size:

> MALE (18): There's less money. There's a fella down the street with a family of nine and he gets about one hundred pounds to keep them. It just about does. There's two of them working and it still isn't enough.

Attitudes to parental authority also appear to be negative, in some cases at least.

> FEMALE (17): Your parents tell you not to do things but you do it anyway . . . the more you're not allowed to do, the more you do it.

There is, however, a certain amount of flexibility concerned. Some females, for instance, complained more of their fathers being strict whereas males tended to regard them as all right in this respect, an indication that certain types of behaviour which would be deemed as unacceptable for females would be tolerated or even approved of in males. There was a general tendency for the mother to be in charge of managing the home, and in such cases they were also more concerned with discipline:

> FEMALE (17): My mother's stricter but my Da's softer . . . could you picture our das going out to get the messages and pay the electric bills and things like that . . . you'd only get one in ten would do it.

There is a definite awareness, learned from the parents, that times were harder for the older generation, but an inability to perceive any significance in this for their own lives:

NG: Do you ever hear your parents talk about when they were young?
FEMALE (17): [They say] 'we'd no money'.
MALE (18): 'it wasn't fifty pence until you were twenty-one'.
MALE (17): That's what's wrong, they keep going back to the past. We don't want to know about the past, only the future.

Although being critical of parents on such issues as their talk of the past and discipline, in the latter case at least, most of the above group of young people agreed that they themselves would not tolerate disobedience:

FEMALE (18): I would be strict if I had kids. I'd break their fuckin' backs for them. I wish my ma had done that on me.

Attitudes, of course, differ significantly not only between groups of young people but also between individuals. The last group of young people discussed were mainly secular in outlook, relatively independent and socialized quite frequently in the city centre. They were employed under a community project (Action for Community Enterprise (ACE)). The next group was interviewed in a church social centre in the Shankill. While having their own distinctive 'Christian' beliefs about love and marriage, they tended to share some views with others on the consequences of familial disintegration. They blamed participation by young people in acts of violence on negative parental influence.

BILL (18): I think the parental role has an awful lot of play in it . . . There is an awful lot of families about the area where if you picture a big skinhead coming in . . . the impression is he will probably hit the da.

The family unit was perceived by this group as being the major determinant of social life. The breakdown of family life was not attributed to transformations in social structure. The negative changes in social structure were attributed to the disintegration of family units.

DON (23): Sadly, these days, so many parents are looking after themselves and letting their children look after themselves. Then it comes back to the family unit which is the whole basis of society. Society is made up of family units and the family unit is falling apart.

Family life, to the above respondents, was undergoing a dramatic transformation due to a disinclination to take marriage seriously:

DON (23): Marriage . . . is taken so lightly in the sense that somebody's married . . . they don't like their husband or wife after six months . . . it's easy to get a divorce even though his wife may be pregnant. To a large extent it's just a piece of paper.

BILL (18): There's an awful lot of people who aren't married but living with their boyfriend and they've probably got three or four youngsters around them.

Child rearing is still viewed as being mainly the female responsibility and Bill drew attention to the problems involved with young women becoming involved in child rearing while still young.

BILL: A young girl who is 21 and is living with a guy who's in his thirties and he was married before and he has kids who are in secondary school and she never had a day's work in her life. She didn't know what it was like to work and she was looking after the kids in the house and making his supper and things like that and he was out working and she was only 21 . . . There's quite a lot of that in the area . . . In another ten years time that girl won't know whether she's coming or going. She probably doesn't know whether she's coming or going now . . . People's attitude has changed over the last ten years. That fella is probably living with that girl and going out with somebody else.

DON: There was a part [in the newspaper] where a girl said she didn't mind who her husband slept with. That puts marriage up the left. Two people being very nice to each other and saying it doesn't matter who he goes out with. It shows you the state the world's in that the whole laws of marriage has fallen an awful lot.

BILL: The laws of marriage has probably stemmed from the Bible as well and a lot of people are not really going to think of the Bible or God and it's just a vow they make to a judge or minister. It doesn't mean anything to them . . . I think it's a reflection of society generally.

In religious families, at least, traditional attitudes about the family and marriage still hold strong. Indeed there tends to be very little to distinguish the attitudes of the young from those of the parent culture. Such attitudes about morality and marriage are also strikingly similar to the position of Catholic theology. This point has not gone unnoticed:

BILL: That's one thing I would respect the Catholic Church for is their stand against divorce. They are really strong against it . . . A lot of the Protestant churches today have taken the easy way out . . . People go head over heels not thinking . . . then four days later they are getting divorced.

Such views on 'quickie' marriages are not exclusive to Christians. There tended to be a significant voice of opinion against marrying young among more secular sections of the population. This was particularly marked in the children of parents who had been married young in the 1960s and had found it a struggle at first. Lily (17), who 'never went to church', was quick to criticize it:

> LILY: I think people are stupid getting married young. My ma says she's been married eighteen years.

Lily and her sister Martha (16) were close to their parents and rarely ventured out without their mother except to work in a local YTP. It is still quite common to find girls of this age group in the Shankill in similar positions. Parental ties in a sense have strengthened as a result of the removal of pressure on young females to marry: 'you don't have to get married now', rather than the reverse.

There was a general belief among the young people in the ACE project that many parents were spoiling their kids through supplying too many consumer goods while neglecting them personally.

> JANE (18): I think they would rather go to a disco or hang around street corners and write on walls. Kids get bored with things dead easy.
>
> NICOLA (17): They've got too much now. They just expect too much.
>
> NED (18): I think parents try to spoil them because they found it too hard in their day and they don't want their kids to be brought up like that.

The last sentiment is one that is constantly expressed by parents in the Shankill (and elsewhere, we should imagine) as 'we want our kids to have all the things that we never had'. However, it seems that even the kids in many cases have realised the implications of 'getting all the things'.

> NICOLA: You can't win in the long run if parents spoil their kids and don't have a steady hand on them. Then when they get outside they run wild. If they are at school they're going to run wild and smoke and cheek the teachers. If they do get away with it in the house they think they can do anything outside.

When it came to 'treatment' in the home, parents were stricter to girls and more protective towards them.

> NICOLA: No matter how old you are you're still his [her father's] little girl.

Preferential treatment combined with the greater tendency to be protective towards girls may well explain why girls tend to stay at home more than boys.

> PAUL (17): I think that parents think that fellas grow up quicker and are able to fend for themselves, say, out on the street.

Children featured in the discussions, particularly of females, and often the topic was interwoven with that of 'morality' – a morality that was not far removed from traditional theology although the participants were not practising any form of religion. There was a deep concern with the problems that may arise from child bearing.

> LILY: It must be awful for parents with a child born with a deformity. Like it would need more attention an' all. Then the other kids would feel left out. But abortion's just murder like.
>
> MARTHA: Like them kids have nothin' in front of them.
>
> DEE (17): What would you do if ye had a baby an' the doctor told ye it was gonna suffer for three or four years and then die?
>
> LILY: Well like if it was gonna suffer then put it out of it's misery but if it wasn't gonna suffer that's three or four years I'd have it.
>
> MARTHA: Our aunt Linda had a wee Mongol (Down's Syndrome) and they found a whole lot of other things wrong wi it an' all. The wee boy only lived ten hours. Its arms were all twisted an' all. It only had one kidney.
>
> LILY: But she said if it wasn't sufferin' she would still have had it and cared for it.
>
> MARTHA: But his [Linda's husband Mark's] Ma was saying like ti him, 'there must be something wrong wi' her, ye shouldn't a married 'er'.
>
> LILY: The child was really sufferin'. Its heart an' all went. They had it on a machine. They had the machine turned off. It only lived on an hour after they turned it off.
>
> MARTHA: Sometimes it comes from the generations but like wi Mark and Linda it wasn't that.
>
> LILY: The doctor said that it was a fifty/fifty chance of it happenin' again. But she still wants one and would keep it even if it was like that one.

The above conversations should serve to illustrate that although many aspects of family life have been changed dramatically, the crucial factors determining relationships between parents and children (love, responsibility, care, etc.) have remained stable. It is also significant that the mother in the above case, who suffered terribly, was blamed for the misfortune by her mother-in-law. There was no question of the male being responsible. The problems associated with family life, we should stress, are not the result of a psychological transformation peculiar to the present generations. They are a product of recent upheavals in social structure, as outlined in Chapter 1. People are not 'all goin' mad', as we frequently heard from elderly members of the community. They are, however, encountering serious problems of adjustment.

Social life and social problems

This section will examine the major problems, as perceived by the young people themselves, that have arisen through the transformations in social structure. One male (18) in attempting to distinguish the major difference in social relations between the present and the past quipped, 'It's a look after number one society'. We shall attempt to discover the extent to which this is the case and its implications for the quality of life through focusing on the major social problems that confront young people and their attempts to compensate through interpersonal relationships and social life (in the broadest sense of the term). Finally we shall examine the fears that, at the time, dominated a generation faced with impending uncertainty, despite their youth, in a world that was seemingly preoccupied with diverting the resources of civilization into the mass production of the means of mutual destruction.

Childhood

It is not only elderly people who reminisce sentimentally about the past. It is quite common for young people in their late teens and early twenties to do so too. Relatively young members of the community also often spoke nostalgically of the old days in the Shankill. As one commentator in his late thirties described it:

> I don't feel that young people nowadays have a better time than I did. I had a great time when I was young . . . there was always plenty of work to do. In one yard we had pigs and in the other we had horses and in the other yard we had scrap and the other we had horses and carts and so on. I had a paper run in the morning and a paper run in the afternoon and the *Telegraphs* at night . . . and that run went from me to my brother and my other brother. We were always kept busy and I think that is part of the problem with a lot of young people today. They are just handed things and . . . expect a lot of things as well.

This commentator was referring to Mid-Shankill in the early 1960s before redevelopment, when the area consisted of rows of closely packed and often overcrowded terraced houses. Formal leisure provision was negligible and professional youth work non-existent. Yet the above comments are sincerely shared by those who spent their childhood in the Shankill then. We asked some of the young people how they felt about the Shankill ten years ago. Their comments, surprisingly, were very similar to those of the older people when recalling the past:

NOEL (17): I would like to go back to them days. I remember years ago we never had a inside bath. We had a big iron tub and you used to get a bath in the kitchen.

MARTHA (16): Do you remember the outside toilet? It was freezing. Broom Street still has its toilets outside.

NED (19): We had giders [home-made go-karts].

JANE (19): Remember all the games kids played when we were

younger? That game where you had a hoop which you had to put round your leg with a ball on a string and you jumped over it. Also hoola-hoops and two ball.

BRENDA (21): They don't play hoola-hoops any more. They're all too wise now. They don't even play marbles.

The above comments would tend to suggest that everyone, not just the elderly people, believes that social life has deteriorated and that this is somehow due to the disappearance of informal entertainments that required very little outlay but an element of imagination and effort. The commentators in the above passage were discussing the Shankill in the year 1976 (they were prompted by being provided with photographs of the period), when the redevelopment programme was exhibiting its worst side-effects and the troubles were at a height. In contrast we asked another group who worked in the ACE project and who regarded themselves as rakers ('rakers' is a term used by those who like to 'rake about' to describe themselves; a rake is a general term for a variety of activities such as 'horse-play, takin' the piss, disruptive behaviour' and being boisterous) what the important things were in their lives now and for the future:

OSSIE (19): Nothing, I don't know.

JOHN (21): Money and happiness. No. Money can't buy everything.

SHARKEY: It can buy you a prostitute down the Albert Clock . . . No mon', no fun, simple as that.

TOMMY (20): No fun if you have no money.

NG: What comes after money?

SHARKEY: Drink, sex, drugs.

NG: Do you need money to get things or is it just for the sake of having money? What if you had more money?

JOHN: I wouldn't drink so much.

SHARKEY: Sure you'd be full every day. He would have a contract with Smirnoff or something to supply him a bottle of vodka every day.

TOMMY: Na, the middle class is wiser wi their money.

JOHN: They buy fuckin' cars an' all.

The most striking difference between the two groups was in the sense of hopelessness and dependency on money expressed in the latter. Money was perceived as the ultimate goal in life – the solution to all their ills, boredom, lack of status. It was the springboard for an enjoyable social life. Yet it was a mean form of existence, socially, that the respondents (Sharkey was not an exception) craved for – prostitutes, drink, drugs. Social life was not seen in terms of creating and sustaining rewarding personal relationships, access to 'culture' and the provision of comfortable recreational facilities. However, John (who was the most thoughtful and intelligent in the group) had grasped the significance of all this: 'the middle class is wiser with its money . . . money can' buy everything.' Yet the process by which the situation had arrived whereby young working class people preferred the individualistic, introverted, hedonistic and ultimately self-destructive pastimes of getting drunk, having sex with prostitutes and taking drugs was what Brenda (in the previous group) was referring to when she said 'they don't play hoola-hoops anymore. They're all too wise now.'

Work

Work was not perceived by most of the young people we spoke to as a desired end in itself. Rather it was regarded as a means of attaining money. This is understandable considering the nature of the few jobs that were available. Not having a job meant not having money. Greg (22) had a police record and had just been released from remand, having been detained, on the uncorroborated evidence of a supergrass, for 18 months:

> GREG: Not much chance a me gettin' a job wi' me record. Buildin' sites maybe like.

Bill, the Christian from the drop-in centre, had just started a temporary job, having been unemployed for two years. His attitude to work was no exception to that of the secular respondents in our study:

> BILL: I would have done my own garden or painting [when unemployed] . . . Regarding a voluntary job . . . to be perfectly honest I wouldn't have done it because I would have had the attitude I was working for nothing.

Don, his friend, agreed with this sentiment:

> DON: It's called the cult of the wage packet . . . it's not real work unless you get your wage packet at the end of a week.

The YTPs are regarded simply as another way of making some money (although this is viewed as negligible). Each week the participants in the discussions openly declared how pleased they were at seeing the researcher because it got them 'off the job' for an hour or two. Noel (16), who lived in Mid-Shankill, regarded all the supervisors in the YTP as 'bastards'. Alice (16) from Woodvale hated it all and was 'always bored'. The pay was treated with contempt:

> MARTHA: We're getting a one pound raise soon.
> NOEL: That wouldn't get you a shit on a railway. All you could get is a bottle of lemonade and it's away. You couldn't even get a packet of Durex.

Unemployment

The chance of school leavers finding a job within two years of leaving school in the Shankill, at the time of our research, was one in five. A large

proportion of the rest found themselves in YTPs. Some of those who
found work were actually only working temporarily, some of them on
ACE schemes for one year. Most of those employed in ACE schemes
viewed their chances of finding work afterwards as slim.

> JANE: We go on the dole for a year until we qualify for ACE again
> and hopefully they'll take us back.

One particular community project, which employed young ACE workers,
was the only place in the Upper Shankill/Springfield area that was taking
people on. It is widely regarded that YTPs and ACE schemes are merely
different methods of 'tinkering' with unemployment figures. Dee was
asked, in the YTP, if he classed himself as unemployed. He replied, 'No.
Because when Maggie Thatcher gives out her figures at the end of the
month we are not on them.'

All of those who had experienced unemployment in the discussions
(nearly everybody) complained of similar problems to a greater or lesser
degree:

> BILL (THE CHRISTIAN): I had two periods of unemployment. I didn't
> really know what to do with myself to be honest. I had no money
> to go to the leisure centre. I tried to keep an interest about the
> house or the garden or I was out looking for work. Boredom did
> set in . . . to the degree you could very easily crack up. Maybe
> that's why there is a lot of people doing what they do . . . I think if
> you're unemployed for a long time you become complacent [and
> say] 'why should I look for a job, I'm not going to get one
> anyway'. Maybe that's why I stayed out half the night hanging
> around street corners. I'd say 'I'll never get a job' so I'll lie in bed all
> day.

For the Christian group there were underlying spiritual motives for
working as well as the practical ones such as earning a wage and having
something to do. As Bill's friend, Don, explained:

> DON: I think man was made to work. Taking it back to the Bible it
> says in the Old Testament that you go out and toil in the land and
> work with your hands. Basically, for me, man was made to work
> in order to eat and if you don't have a job there is something
> missing!
> BILL: When we were at school we used to have ideas . . . But when
> we left school and found there was over three and a half million
> people unemployed it knocked the heart out of you.

There was a lack of understanding, generally, as to the causes of
unemployment and its consequences. One of the boys in the secondary
school thought that 'people on the dole shouldn't get paid' because it
meant that people like him (when he got a job) 'would be working to keep
them'. We attempted (without much success) to discuss the causes of
unemployment with the people on the community ACE scheme.

NG: Why do you think there are so many people out of work about this area?

NED: Because they're all lazy bastards. There's jobs if you look for them.

In fact it was impossible to initiate meaningful discussions on unemployment (and other social problems) from the position of a class analysis of society, as the participants in the discussions were vague about what class meant. Their position in fact tallied with the observation made by Jenkins (1983) that the perception of the 'kids' of Rathcoole (a sprawling working class protestant estate to the north of Belfast) about their deprived situation was one in which the vocabulary of social inequality and a consciousness of class injustice were absent. They experienced the inequalities of opportunity almost entirely in terms of individual failure and their common-sense thinking about their social position was dominated by a trenchant individualism which, Jenkins argued, functioned both to legitimize the very meritocracy that freezes them out of life's material rewards and to encourage fatalism about such structures of inequality and, indeed, about their deteriorating life chances in general.

As Bert, one of the fifth-form male school leavers put it, 'Nobody will employ us. We're all thick. Binmen are smarter than us.' None of the fifth formers, whom we talked to in the two months leading up to their leaving, had any qualifications. One or two of them thought that they may have had a chance to be accepted for a YTP, which they regarded as 'just like school only more money'. We asked the others what they would like to do if given the opportunity and how much they would expect to be paid if successful. Ian was well spoken and mannered, dressed neatly and tidy, was thoughtful and exhibited a level of intelligence that did not seem to belong in the 'lowest' stream. He would have liked to get into printing where, he had been told, he could earn £106 a week. William wanted to join the army. He was enthusiastic about the idea, exhibited initiative and considered himself adaptable. He had learned that soldiers would earn £100 or more a week. Barry, who was a talented artist, wanted to be a signwriter and thought that he could earn £150 per week. George, hyperactive and outspoken, said he could be a 'paint-stripper' and earn £160 a week. Sammy, quietly spoken, amenable and unassuming, 'wouldn't expect anything' but when pressed thought that he 'wouldn't mind a job just labouring' in a factory earning about £100 a week. None of them on the face of it were really asking for a lot out of life but they were denied even that.

Courtship

Relationships between the sexes in the 16–18 age range are, as is the case in most places, complex in the Shankill. It is quite common for 'feelings' to be suppressed by both males and females by the adoption of a whole range of crude, and unsentimental, terminology and behaviour towards members of the opposite sex. This process of concealment of one's 'true' emotions is an attempt by the individual to ensure that a caring or sentimental nature will not be mistaken for weakness. It also serves, in many cases, to hide a latent shyness. In short it is often an expression of emotional insecurity that is characteristic of teenagers the world over and has provided the inspiration for a multitude of million-selling popular songs since Buddy Holly. Working class male culture has always exhibited a 'macho' image and such is the case in areas like the Shankill, where traditional mores about sexual roles remain strong despite the advent of sexual revolution, male unemployment and increasing independence for females. There has, however, always been what can best be described as a 'hardness' in women in areas like the Shankill, which is to a large extent a defensive mechanism against the worst excesses of the men. It is common therefore, in verbal exchanges at least, for the females to give as good as they get. Such exchanges, taken out of context, would suggest to the observer that the antagonists were bitter enemies. This is often not the case. Consider the following exchange, which took place in the YTP, in the Upper Shankill between Noel and Alice (16):

NOEL [TO ALICE]: Ye fuckin' whore bag!
ALICE: I'll knock ye fuckin' out.
NOEL: Ye fuckin' stink. What're ye goin' red for. [Slaps Alice on the head. She punches him on the arm.] I'm fuckin' off outta here. Couldn't stand that scum beg. Cheerio!
ALICE: [arrogantly] Cheerio, fuckin' whore master! [Noel leaves the room, banging the door aggressively.]
LILY: It's as well we know yis like.

Such exchanges were quite commonplace between Alice (who tended on the whole to be of a retiring nature) and Noel (who tended to be over-active). They were quite good friends and the exchange can only really be understood by reference to Lily's remark at the end. 'It's as well we know yis like.'

'Real romance', which is not often experienced directly (as in the case, say, where a female rarely ventures out without her mother) is often experienced second hand. Consider Martha (16), who like so many young females of her age spent most of her time at home with her family. She never went out with boys, was 'quiet' but intelligent. She spent much of her spare time reading girls' magazines, such as *Jackie*.

MARTHA: I like the stories. All the love stories an' all. I've no love life a mi own like so a might as well read about somebody else . . . an' the people writin' in about their problems.

Local males were quick to point out that there were distinct differences between what they called 'trendy' females and local ones, as well as between catholic and protestant females. Ian, the school leaver, said he would love to go to Queen's (University) because of all the 'big rides' that went there. Barry was quick to respond that they were all 'la-di-dah' while William added, 'they smoke dope over there'. Clearly 'smoking dope', being polite and promiscuity were not things they associated with, or wished to associate with, local girls. While it was frowned upon for local girls to go with other males it was all right for the males to go with other girls. Similarly, many of the males did not believe in taking their girlfriends 'drinking' although they would 'chase' other females who were in the bars. Juke, for instance, was no mean drinker and 'went steady'.

NG: Do you take your girlfriend when you go out drinking?
JUKE (18): No. Fuck, are you joking? Go down ti her house and sit.
BILL (18): You have ti leave the girl in the house so yi can come on with another one.

Girlfriends were a constant source of banter among the males:

JUKE: What age is your girl Bill? Fifteen? Jail bait.

Courtship mores were strong with young people in the Shankill. Attitudes though, at times, appeared to be somewhat confused. One of the most sensitive areas of discussion is courtship with members of the 'opposite religion', which is generally disapproved of to a greater or lesser extent. Wally, for instance, accused the girls from the Shankill of being 'fenian lovers' but boasted many catholic girls among his list of conquests. The following discussion took place in the Lower Shankill YTP:

WALLY: See all the girls on the Shankill, they're all fenian lovers. See the catholic girls like, they're alright. I buck the whole lot of them an' all.
ALEC (17): You buck fuckin' nothin' . . . Ye fuckin' bastard.
BRENDA: I can well believe it.

In the present climate, in Belfast, it is dangerous (sometimes fatal) to court across the religious divide. We asked the fifth-form boys if they would go out with catholic girls.

WILLIAM: Aye. If it was somebody like Samantha Fox [laughs].
IAN: It would be a fuckin' knee-cap job.

Sex in general was rarely discussed seriously. Usually it was mentioned as a source of amusement or diversion and, one would assume anyway, grossly exaggerated. In the Upper Shankill YTP an alarm went off one day in the middle of our discussions:

MARTHA: What the fuck was that? The bomb or something.
NG: What would you do if it was the bomb and you only had four minutes left? [laughter]
NOEL: [looking at Martha] I'd ride you if you'd ride me. Two

minutes each way. I would. I'd go out and ride all round mi. I'd fuckin' do it if it had ti be me granny [Martha laughs].

DEE: I'm glad I'm not your fuckin' granny.

Leisure

Courtship and social life in general do of course co-exist. The components of social life for the young people of the Shankill vary from group to group and individual to individual. Generally though, there is a clear distinction between the social lives of those who participate in youth provision and those who do not. In the latter group there tended to be a relative lack of interest in formal social events and organized hobbies and pastimes. Many of them did participate in informal activities in the home and on the street, as did many of the youth club participants when not attending their club or organization. However, there is an inclination for the non-participants to be more involved in what may be termed by some as negative behaviour: excessive drinking, belonging to 'blood and thunder' bands, fighting and so on. Such activities have, in fact, been traditionally associated with the 'less respectable' or rough sections of the working class. Indeed, it could be argued that such activity was a physical manifestation of their identification with traditional working class values and their rejection of the more bourgeois values associated with formal youth provision. As we shall see, a similar pattern emerges in attitudes to school and work. They also tended to be more prone to bouts of boredom when such activities were unavailable (through lack of money, lack of rivals or being 'out of season'). A surprising number of them do visit the city centre for outings, mainly discos, but for some it is not primarily for dancing.

PAULINE (17): We were down the Abercorn, saw Mark and Kate in there. He had his hand up her skirt and her buttons were all opened. Me and Maggie were out till five in the mornin'.

NG: Dancing?

PAULINE: Fighting.

NIGEL: Sure you're always fuckin' fightin'.

NG: Smithey, what were you doing?

SMITHEY: Fuck all. Just sat in.

PAULINE: We yer Ma.

SMITHEY: Aye, just me and mi ma.

PAULINE: Ah! Fuckin' wee mammy's boy! [laughter]

NIGEL: You laugh at everything.

PAULINE: Ah fuck off you, yi fuckin' cunt. See if you were my son I'd fuckin' kill ye!

NIGEL: If you were my daughter I'd a had ye drowned at birth.

The above discussion serves to illustrate some of the attitudes of different individuals to various forms of social life. Smithey is an introverted skinhead who was also known as 'Evo-stik'. His social outings were limited to the Thursday night gathering in a derelict building with a few friends, some beer and cider and, often, a bag of glue. He was often the brunt of Pauline's ridicule, and she considered him an 'eejit' (a fool). Pauline, who was hyperactive and extrovert, tended to class most people who were not like herself as inferior in some way or another (dickheads, eejits, fenian lovers, fuckin' cunts, bastards). She herself was classed 'educationally subnormal', had received psychiatric attention, and exhibited violent tendencies (she had been sacked twice from YTPs that we knew of – on one occasion for stabbing another trainee). Nigel also took a lot of Pauline's ridicule. She saw him as being a 'snob'. He was not a snob. He was intelligent and articulate and he preferred to socialize outside the area. This was not because he resented the people or activities but because he resented paramilitary involvement in providing many social facilities (he also resented people like Pauline and clubs like 'The Loyalist').

Not all the groups we talked with were as hostile to each other about their preferred leisure and social activities, although there was some friendly banter as with the ACE project group.

> Ossie: The best thing in life now is sitting down to a good film with twenty fags.
> Tommy: No it's not. That only gives you square eyes and cancer.
> John: You want to go out and enjoy yourself.

When Ossie did go out it was usually with John, when the two of them would 'get pissed' and 'ride up and down the road at eighty miles an hour' (on John's motorbike).

John and Ossie often complained about there not being enough excitement in their lives and that more conventional activities (as in youth clubs) were boring. Sharkey also considered clubs boring and stupid. His major pastime was not quite as dangerous as John's. He played football for 'Shankill Young Men' (in the Churches League). 'Best team in the league', he called them (they probably were), to which John usually quipped, 'only team in the league'.

Ossie had a reputation, when he did go out, of starting rows. John wrecked the bike (and himself) shortly after this discussion in a crash (Ossie was fortunately not with him on that occasion). Sharkey was a joker. A talented soccer player, he was not keen on the fitness side. He liked to drink when he could afford it and frequently 'took the piss' out of the supervisors in his project. He was sacked from the job during the series of discussions for 'continually giving cheek' (he frequently told the supervisors to 'fuck off and do it yourself' when told to do something he was averse to).

Drinking was the favourite pastime of most of the those we spoke to in the ACE project. Friday was the main drinking night and quite often the participants spent so much of their pay on drink that they were broke for the rest of the week afterwards. The following conversation took place on the Monday after a typical weekend and there was not, initially anyway, a lot being said as most of the participants were hungover.

NG: What did you all do on Friday night?

JUKE: Not very many can remember that.

JOHN: Who was sober? Put it like that we were all at this party they were all talking about.

NG: The one in the Community Centre.

NED: Aye. Now you know why there's no fuckin' youth club. There was a big fight.

NG: Where's Ossie?

JOHN: Down in the Mater [hospital].

NG: Would you say your social life revolves around drinking?

BILL: No, drinkin' and screwin'.

NG: Do you intend to get drunk every time you go out?

NED: It just happens naturally. We never go out for just one or two.

The most significant aspect of social life here is that it is confined almost exclusively to the weekends. The rest of the week was usually associated with boredom and putting in the time until the following weekend 'booze-up'. The work (on a community project) was treated merely as a means of obtaining money for the weekend. Quite a few of this group visited the city centre regularly for a night out, although most of them had reservations.

Some of those we spoke to had reservations about having to walk past Unity Flats (a catholic area between the Shankill and the city centre) late at night if they happened to miss the bus or taxi home. Their fears were justified in that it was one of the most notorious flash-points in Belfast. Others were wary about the places they visited in town. Even the city centre places of entertainment were labelled according to real or imagined sectarian affiliation.

Jane preferred socialising in the city centre because it meant 'your family wouldn't see you drinking'. Bill visited a disco in town regularly and preferred the town to local clubs and pubs. There often discussions on the relative dangers of such a policy:

BILL: I go to the disco in Cornmarket.

NED: Sure you have all them fuckin' provos gettin' in.

JUKE: If you go into Cornmarket ye get a beatin'.

The prices in the city centre also served to discourage many of the respondents from socializing there. Drinks in a club in the Shankill are about 20–30 per cent cheaper than in a pub in town. Although the entrance charge to the unlicensed clubs and discos was high, a 'bring your own bottle' policy meant relatively cheap drinks (at off-licence prices), which suited the 'big drinkers'. Indeed this prompted a successful campaign at the time (headed by licensed club and pub interests and concerned religious and political groups) to prevent alcohol being allowed in clubs that were not licensed to sell it. There had been a rapid growth of such places in the city centre and they were blamed for an apparent increase in excessive drinking by young people. Fighting and boredom were closely related. Boredom affected the behaviour patterns of most of the group. For example, there was Closie, who often 'sat in' in the discussions. He was small, 17 and quiet (almost timid) by nature:

> JUKE: Like a Closie there. When he gets fed up he wants to fight. He thinks he's Rambo with a pair of knickers on.

Occasionally the group went to a party in one of their friend's houses or flats. Such events were usually impromptu affairs organized after the pubs and clubs had closed. Fortunes at such events could be mixed:

> SHARKEY: I went up ti Ray's Saturday. Bumped into a couple a strangers we about twenty tins a fuckin' Bass Export in their bag.
>
> ALAN: Last time I went ti one a them do's some big bloke came up to me and said 'I'm gonna kick your bollocks outta ye outside'. You wanna see the size a him I just burst out laughin'. A don't know why like. Just burst out laughin' and later he comes up ti me and apologizes and shakes my hand.
>
> SHARKEY: Fuckin' Geordie UDA man, spent fuck-all all night [Geordie was an older man who sometimes 'hung around' with members of the group]. I ended up dancin' we fuckin' oul dolls. Fuckin' kept trailin' me off the settee. I was fuckin' near gurnin' . . . Geordie was sittin' there preachin' about . . . makin' a civil disobedience after the workers' strike. . . . We were in the Pony Club before it down the Hammar. It's our local. All the oul dolls sit in the corner and sing songs.

Not all social life for the young unattached focused on clubs and pubs. There were others, like Angela, who was 'never worried' about social facilities because she would 'never go out anyway'. Then there was the Christian element.

> SAMMY: Before I became a Christian I would have been more involved in going to clubs through the week in that my social life then obviously was revolving around a pub or place I would go to meet sort of specific friends every night whereas now it would be the Mission and Christianity. So it's two different sort of maybe types of people or whatever, you know, two ways of living.

Another important aspect of social life in the Shankill is the various musical (mainly fife and drum or accordion) marching bands. The bands fall into two categories. First, there are 'respectable' brass and/or woodwind bands, some of which have international reputations for their musical achievements. Others, which are more associated with 'rough' elements, are the so-called 'blood and thunder' or 'kick the Pope' bands. The latter are usually flute bands and are associated with militant loyalism.

We shall not discuss the sociological significance of the bands here. Suffice it to say at this stage that they do provide an important social function with perhaps two practice nights a week and a parade at the weekends (usually during the summer 'marching season'). Recently the bands have adopted the practice of including colour parties, which carry the flags of one or other of the major paramilitary organizations.

Sam is in two bands (Shankill Star and Springmartin). He has described the experience as 'brilliant. You get to show them uns off over there [points to the Falls]. Awk you get a good oul crack.' Sam viewed the role of the bands as being both a 'show of strength' and 'just something to do and get drunk'. He didn't think they represented part of his heritage, 'just something for the orangemen to walk behind'.

Not all of the group were enthusiastic about the bands. Barbara, who described her father as 'band mad', said 'they give me a headache'. Ossie, on the other hand, was quick to respond: 'I love the oul twelfth and the bands. It's brilliant.' Sam stressed the 'recreational' aspects of the band he was a member of: 'Look at the exercise you get out of it. You know, all the walking an' all . . . learn to be a musician an' all'.

> BARBARA: The band comes to my Ma's house every year from Scotland and I hate it. You have to feed about sixteen of them so you have. It's all right [meaning for the men] it's me Ma that does all the cookin'.
> SAM: The band left from our house last Easter Tuesday an' the' almost ate the house outta house an' home. They ate everything. Everything that was in their way was away. And then up the street yi know the way the' leave early mornin'. Half the street was still in bed an' I got the band ti play like fuck down the street and all the oul dolls were out the windie shoutin' at them an' all. The two bass drums. It was wild. I love it too . . . gettin' the oul dolls outta their beds.

Barbara was a fan of heavy metal music yet one of the complaints she had about the 'blood and thunder' bands was that she couldn't stand the noise.

The Twelfth celebration is probably the biggest social event in the loyalist calendar. However, its political significance is not rigidly adhered to (the entire festival anyway is clouded in mythology and contradiction) especially by the young. The fact that William Prince of Orange had the Pope's blessing (and catholic forces in his command) is ignored. Formally, the Orange Order position is that the 'Twelfth' is a ritualistic re-affirming of the 'principles' of the 1688 'Glorious Revolution', which among other things, was supposed to guarantee 'liberty and freedom of religion and law'. In reality it has come to symbolize the more triumphalist aspects of the Orange and unionist tradition. The content of its informal rituals and practices (songs and bonfires) is decidedly and often crudely anti-catholic. The 'kick the Pope' bands are aptly named. However, for the majority of participants the festival is a social event. Popular music is relayed by loudspeakers on to the streets, there is an abundance of house parties, there are discos in the clubs. Even Barbara used to take part. Sam, who was an enthusiastic bandsman, was primarily interested in the 'drinking', the 'mates in the band' and a fair degree of (relatively harmless) mischief – 'gettin' all the oul dolls outta bed'.

It is events like the 'Twelfth' that appeal to young people in the 16+ category and that youth clubs can never really facilitate. Most formal provision was, in fact, seen by the 16+ unattached young people as being irrelevant to their needs. The implications of having nothing to do are likely to be serious. We asked one of the group in the ACE scheme why they thought there were no sectarian riots in upper class areas:

> JOHN: The reason why there is none of that up the Malone Road is because they've got the money and they take themselves off at nights.
>
> NED: If you've no money where can you go out . . . Most of the places now you've got ti pay in. Unless you go ti a bar but then you're just gonna sit and watch everyone. So why not just go out and petrol bomb somebody . . . Say you go to a disco, you have ti pay in . . . so if you've no fuckin' money yi can't go ti the disco and if you've no job you've no money.

Money

In a society where 'success' is defined in terms of material wealth, and access to material wealth depends on one's capacity for making money, then limitations (through unemployment or low pay) upon the availability of the latter cause not only serious material problems, but psychological problems as well, for those who are denied the means of acquiring it. Access to money, for some people, becomes the 'solution' to everything. Work is unimportant except as a means of obtaining money. Luxury and sex are the most desired ends and money is the means for providing these. The following conversation was recorded in a YTP in the Lower Shankill:

> WALLY (16): Money can buy everything.
>
> PAULINE (17): Fuckin' right it can.
>
> WALLY: I'd buy a yacht and sail around the world. There'd be plenty of girls on it.
>
> PAULINE: Plenty of fellas on it. One for every night of the week. A don't want a job.
>
> DOROTHY: Aye that'd be you down the big clock [laughs: she is referring to the Albert Clock, where reputedly prostitutes solicit their clients]. [Screaming, shouting, laughing.]

The participants in this particular YTP regarded it as work rather than a training project and it was poorly paid work too. They considered themselves better off, financially, at school and on the dole. Shortage of money has different implications but nevertheless they are probably even more serious as one grows older. Billy is 25 and has three young children:

> BILLY: There's one a them wee community halls over there. I've never bin . . . The kids go but they have ti pay like. I thought it should be free. Yi don't mind them payin' in like but they've ti pay for things inside. Where's the parents gettin' the money from?

Billy lives in the Lower Shankill estate and is unemployed. The question he posed poses another question. How is deprivation alleviated by providing certain facilities if they are not available to the most deprived sections of the community because of their deprivation?

Shortage of money is something that is seen as the result of deliberate and malicious policies, although it is not clear how the situation actually arises. Subsequently the solution appears to be quite straightforward.

> LILY: I'll tell ye somethin'. If it was me was MP I'd give people grants an' all. What's money? Sure all the' have t' do is make it in a machine then hand it out ti everybody.

Failure to attain the means to success (money) not only leads to physical problems, such as limitations to activities. It seriously undermines self-esteem. There are well defined ways to behave and not to behave according to one's position in the 'money-go-round'. Anyone from the Shankill was perceived as being at the very bottom and expected to behave accordingly. Dee (17) had unwittingly spoken to some people (including Lily) in the third person one day. Lily recounted this to Martha (her sister), who quipped:

> MARTHA: Who ti fuck's he think he is. He's from fuckin' here like. Not England or the Malone Road. From Belfast like. The Shankill.

Youth and leisure facilities and political education

One of the most surprising revelations to emerge from the research was the general dissatisfaction with youth and leisure and recreational provision. This was true of both those who participated in formal youth clubs or organizations and those who did not. Yet the Shankill, in particular, has experienced extensive developments in these areas in recent years. The leisure centre remains grossly under-used by local people and many of the youth clubs and organizations are short of members. We attempted to discover what it was that prevented the non-participants from becoming involved in formal youth programmes or attending clubs and what their attitudes were to leisure and recreational provision in the area. We should recall here that out work with the youth club and organization participants revealed that they had fairly definite opinions regarding the non-attendance of the non-participants and that such opinions were informed to a large extent by what may best be described as their perception of the 'behaviour patterns' (such as apathy or negative behaviour) and 'social image' (being hard men, not one of the lads etc.) of those who did not attend clubs, what they thought the area needed in terms of leisure and recreational facilities and how they perceived available leisure provision.

The fifth-form school leavers thought that their final year of school had been by far the best and that this was the result of a reduction of restraints on them, increased informality and a greater diversity of activities to choose from. This may suggest a lesson for all those involved in working with young people (particularly in the 16+ age bracket).

They also agreed that there was not enough excitement in their lives and that a riot was the best thing for providing this. Youth clubs, they maintained, didn't 'really meet the needs of young people . . . just snooker and things . . . They should get old cars an' all and fix them up.' We asked them why they thought so many young people did not attend youth clubs. They agreed that the main reasons were: 'lack of excitement', 'not knowing the people . . . some of the people don't want to know', 'not open long enough' (some close at nine o'clock), 'age limits' and 'organizers . . . some youth workers are all right but some are like "peelers", too strict'. They also thought they would be victimized if 'they didn't like the look of you'. Most of them thought youth workers should be more concerned with allowing them to enjoy themselves rather than just keeping young people off the streets.

The girls in the ACE project agreed that most nights they just sat in each others' houses playing records. They also spent some evenings doing housework. Friday nights were an exception, when they went to a disco – if they had the money or if there was a youth club controlled by them (and the boys). They were confident that the latter would work and that there would be no trouble.

The group from the Upper Shankill YTP could not be convinced that the Shankill was adequately provided with leisure and recreational facilities. In fact, they firmly believed that what they did receive was sub-standard and unusable:

LILY: The Shankill's got one fuckin' leisure centre and it's filthy.

There appears to be a distinct lack of communication somewhere when a winning leisure centre can be perceived in such terms by members of the local population it is supposed to serve. Perhaps that is part of the problem, that the centre does not do enough outreach work and publicity (at least to counter incorrect negative impressions such as those contained in the discussion). Some young people, of course, would not really be interested in any formal youth club unless (as Pauline from the Lower Shankill put it) 'it had a bar in it' or (as Wally from the Lower Shankill put it) 'it had a stripper in it'. Both the latter had assimilated at an early age

(16) a fair degree of the more escapist and negative aspects of their adult cultures. Wally's father rarely came home at nights. Pauline's mother and sister (we were told) were 'on the game'. Nigel used to belong to a youth club, but 'the were all Christians. We went til Ballygally once. About one shop, that was fuckin' it.' Ballygally would be an extremely pleasant place for anyone who wanted to spend a quiet weekend on the Antrim coast but it obviously fell far short of meeting Nigel's desire for excitement.

There was a definite lack of social facilities for girls and there was also some dislike of church-organized activities (remember that the churches accounted for most youth provision in the Shankill). We asked at the Mission drop-in centre why they thought some people they knew would not use it.

GEORGE: Because they're Christians.

BILL: Sometimes I forget ti mind me language.

The lack of 'girl's activities' was highlighted by Gina (20), a Christian who worked in the centre:

GINA: There's nothin' really in it for girls, only sit an' watch TV, maybe have a chat with somebody. There's no activities for girls . . . Another girl used to have this group of girls who used to come in with their kids and that and we used to have a wee Wednesday afternoon chat but then when she left it all fell away . . . but mostly girls are always busy in the house if they're not out working. They have got kids to look after, you know. Things like that.

There tends to be a vicious circle operating in regard to girls and young women and participation in youth clubs. Girls (we are speaking here about the 16+ age category) do not tend to use clubs because there are not enough other girls in their age group attending. The reason why other girls in their age group are not attending is because there are not any specific activities for them, and the reason for this is that they are not provided because it is assumed that girls have other things to do (meaning in the home and/or with the kids). This circle needs to be broken if progress in providing meaningful programmes for females is to be made.

Many people, of course, never felt a need even to consider attending a club. They were satisfied simply occupying themselves with the business of growing to maturity in other, less formal and more traditional ways:

FROGGIE (18): I always have something to do. Like go to my girl's house.

Froggie did not attend a youth club because he did not feel any particular desire to do so. The same may be said about countless others whose alternatives did not pose a problem to anyone and who did not hold any ill-feeling towards club members or think that they were in any way different. John thought that clubs were an extension of the school system 'only with less control' and that their primary function was to 'keep people off the streets and give them something to do'. He thought that those who enjoyed being on the streets and already had something to do would not, therefore, be interested in attending a youth club. John thought he would be too old to join a youth club anyway. He was 19. When asked if he thought youth clubs met any of the needs of young people he replied bluntly: 'Playin' fuckin' snooker? What need does that meet?' There were five other people in the room at the time (Juke, Pete, Sharkey, Barbara and Nicola) and they all appeared to be in agreement with that statement.

In the group from the Upper/Mid-Shankill four out of six spent most of their weekends 'sitting in' because there was nowhere to go (including all three of the girls). They all agreed that there were no facilities or meaningful activities in the area for people of their age group (16–18) and this may be supported by reference to the age ranges of the youth club participants. They thought that places closed too early: 'The leisure centre closes at half nine. What are you supposed to do between half nine and half eleven?' Noel added that it was all right for those who wanted to go to the pub but not for those who were non-drinkers. The females thought the leisure centre should open later and hold discos (they said it used to do that).

We asked the people in the ACE project why they thought that not so many young people were joining uniformed organizations. Jane replied that it was 'all the goody goody ones that go to places like that now in this generation'. This remark clearly tallied with reasons given by many of the formal participants for why the non-participants would not join their club or organization. Jane and some of the others in the project had a desire to set up their own club and organize it themselves. They frequently discussed the pros and cons. Ned was sceptical about the feasibility of having a club without youth workers:

NED: They [the participants] would start wrecking the place.
JANE: It might get out of hand but you'd have to remember it's our youth club so you'd have to keep it under control.
NED: You get some clowns breaking a leg off a chair or writing on the walls.
NICOLA: Everyone does that but then it gets a bit borin' after a while. So then everybody just goes against whoever that is.
NED: The place would be already wrecked. It only takes one maniac to shut it down.
NICOLA: Then that's up to the people not to let it happen. Why should they wreck it?
NED: Because they're bored.
JANE: If they're bored in the house do they get a knife and rip their ma's good settee? Why should people do it if they don't do it at home?
NED: Why wreck a phone box? Why write on the walls? It's the

excitement of doin' something that's against the law. Boredom plays a part as well.

JANE: I think it has got to do with attention.

NICOLA: You would look at it as if it was your own house. You're not going to ask friends round and light matches and burn your house.

Jane and Nicola thought that a club organized by the girls (with some help from the boys) would offset the male-orientated prejudice usually associated with traditional forms of youth work. Their club, they envisaged, would not have a television or snooker table (or things like that) but would function primarily as a place 'to relax and *discuss* things'. What they were proposing was a novel and potentially effective exercise in social education. One community activist proposed for youth work:

That it's seen as an educational thing . . . developing young people . . . in the fullest sense . . . and catering to all their needs . . . and within that I think there's the idea that the whole sexism of what is provided needs looking at and this obviously doesn't mean cookery for girls instead of pool. What I mean is the whole thing needs turning on its head so that the girls are taken totally into account in educational terms, the whole thing about sexism confronted and what girls should be doing and boys should be doing.

What the girls were advocating came close to what this commentator was advocating. It could also serve as an experiment in real responsibility being diverted to the participants at the local level. It would certainly be much more democratic than the mere token representation of the Youth Forums. Those in the 16–18 age group frequently complained that they did not have any real say in their lives and that there were far too many restrictions placed upon them. It is the crucial age in terms of responsibility as adolescents reach the physical, mental and social stage of adulthood of their lives but are not officially recognized as such until they become 18. 'You can't even vote until you're 18' one of the school leavers said, which was an expression of their feelings of powerlessness as well as, perhaps, a poignant reminder of their estimation of the worthlessness of the right to vote in a politically stagnant (and powerless) society: 'It doesn't matter who you vote for, *they* always get in.'

School

It has often been argued that formal youth provision is merely an extension of the formal education system. Indeed, the statutory Youth Service in Northern Ireland is controlled and administered by the Department of Education and the various Education and Library Boards. Given the nature of the criticisms of formal youth provision and the generally negative attitudes towards it by those we spoke to, one would expect similar responses regarding school. As we shall see, this was the case and this further supports the assumption made earlier (in Chapter 5) that there does appear to be a definite cultural division between sections of working class (and socially aspiring) young people (as there undoubtedly is in the parent culture as well), which can best be described in terms of rough/ respectable, non-conformist/conformist or non-participation/participation dichotomies (many of the participants in formal youth provision viewed the dichotomy in terms of negative and positive thinking).

There did appear to be, to various degrees, a definite resistance to the authority of the school. Most of the non-participants exhibited this to one degree or another. Wally, who considered himself 'a hard man', boasted that he had 'given them (the teachers) a hard time'. Pauline had also been a problem pupil (one of her ex-teachers informed us that she was 'nuts'):

> PAULINE: See me an' fuckin' school. I fuckin' hated it. The' thought I was fuckin' nuts . . . the' got this man in ti see mi . . . Know one a them there psychiatrists . . . He gimme these fuckin' tests. 'What colour is glass?' and 'What colour's fuckin' grass?' [laughter]. Fuck sake!

Pauline was somewhat of an exceptional case in terms of resistance. More often apathy was the rule as one of the fifth formers confirmed, when asked what classes he was attending: 'Most people don't do anything.' Sharkey viewed what he had learned at school as absurd and banal and had been obviously confused by the experience:

> SHARKEY: We read chicken lickin' and coconuts fallin' from the tree and the wee man thought the world was ending. That's what we learned at school . . . chicken lickin' and mickin' pickin', looster the rooster. And the fox ate them in the end.

Noel conceded that he had a good time at school but qualified this with 'that's when a was there . . . to tell the truth . . . a was never there'. Dee said that he had 'learned how ti count an' read an' that was it'. Martha described her school as 'a mad house' while Lily admitted that she 'mitched as well' and 'got into trouble over it'. 'School', she added, 'didn't do me any good.' Some of them did manage to pass some examinations before leaving (Wilbur said that he had passed seven CSEs).

School was viewed as irrelevant by those who had left a number of years previously as well:

> BILL: I didn't like it . . . ev'rything th' said went in one ear and out the other.
> ALBERT: I got three CSEs but like I got mi job without them.
> NG: Why do you think people send you to school?
> BILL: Ti keep you off the streets for a lotta years.

The latter statement seems to have a certain ring to it will regard to other forms of youth provision.

Teachers, to many of those participating in the discussions, were classed in the same league as policemen. Juke expressed his dislike of teachers in forceful terms: 'the only good teacher is a fuckin' dead one.' Sharkey had often fought with the teachers and, when the opportunity afforded itself, he would 'smoke, drink, sniff glue, pish up the fuckin' walls and shite in the buckets'. John, who had some O levels, said that 'they didn't do me any good'. None of the rest in the ACE project group had any GCEs. Ned believed that 'all they can do is get you a binman's job. Binmen are smarter than some of us.' Being a 'binman' (refuse collector) was regarded as one of the most undesirable jobs by those in the group and they regarded it as 'dirty' and menial. Their attitude to 'binmen' being 'smarter than us' is an indication of their own lack of self-esteem.

The resistance to school life and discipline had several forms, ranging from 'going on the beak' and 'pissin' in the corridors' to violent attacks on teachers and even strikes:

JOHN: We went on strike and just tied the school gates up with ties. Fuckin' right wi did.

Sharkey and John both enjoyed school because of the raking they did. They were experts at diverting the teacher away from the lesson to a subject they found more interesting:

SHARKEY: History wasn't bad because yer man once ye started him talkin' 'bout films you never done history. He just kep' talkin' about films.

TOMMY: And you know oul TB if you were talkin' 'bout fuckin' Linfield. He always goes on about Linfield [soccer club].

While teachers such as those just mentioned would be tolerated, others were regarded with particular disdain.

SHARKEY: See that fuckin' teacher that was in 1MC, oul C. . . . I'll tell ye what I would fuckin' do ti her. . . . She wouldn't let yi go ti the toilet until yi kicked a fuckin' hole in the wall.

Others were regarded as 'soft touches'. One of the lads had been caught red-handed excreting on the floor of the classroom in front of the teacher's desk:

NG: Did they throw him out . . . or anything?

JOHN: No, no. She [the teacher] was a fuckin' oul soft touch.

SHARKEY: We used ti throw books at her.

JOHN: She cracked up but she never done anything about it. She knew not to or we'd break the windies.

Part of the resistance culture involved fighting with the rival (Catholic) school's pupils:

SHARKEY: We used ti go up ti St Gabriel's . . . an' get our chips up there an' on the way down the fuckin' wee fenians lookin' at yi, a few kicks ti the head an' run. The oul headmaster came down ti our school.

JOHN: They got us ev'ry Wednesday comin' down in the buses. The bus driver wouldn't stop ti let us out.

SHARKEY: We chucked the seats outta the back windie an' ev'rything.

JOHN: The' near broke my fuckin' head when the' smashed the windie wi' fuckin' bricks.

Prefects were regarded as being different from the other boys in the secondary school. This was another example of the cultural dichotomy between sections of working class people. Prefects were more likely to be socially mobile, belong to youth clubs, possess more 'liberal' views regarding catholics and be more enthusiatic about education. The boys in the lower stream fifth-form class had definite ideas about prefects:

IAN: They think they're like peelers. They think they can go around telling us what ti do.

WILLIAM: Aye, but they're afraid e' us. We'd knock their shites in. Sure they're poofters.

BARRY: They're a load of dickheads.

IAN: They've got brains. They're all in A1. We're in B2 . . . They sit in the classes and there's not a word from them.

The perceptions here of the prefects were similar to how the youth club members thought the unattached perceived them in our survey. Prefects 'respected' and conformed to the rules and regulations of the school. The boys in lower streams rejected the discipline imposed by the school. Some openly resisted it. One of the Christians we spoke to recalled one particular incident, which he considered to be representative of the general acts of 'resistance' practised by the boys:

DON: The teacher had an awful job . . . they'd [the pupils] let down the car tyres . . . I remember a guy . . . got everyone to get bits of paper and put them into a desk and put a match to it in front of the classroom and sat and laughed at it burning. He was suspended for two weeks. He done it because he didn't like school and *wanted* to be suspended.

This is an example of one of the rakers actually achieving a temporary victory over the school in that his adopted strategy (burning the desk) achieved its desired goal (suspension). Most of those employed in the ACE project had similar experiences at school. The most common strategy for getting out of school was to forge an excuse note from a parent. This was a widespread practice. Most of the school curriculum was viewed as irrelevant and a waste of time, as were qualifications. Sex education was one exception although most of the males, such as Ned, thought that, 'it's more t' do wi'them [the females] in case the' get knocked up the duff'. The females, on the other hand, agreed that there should be more sex education for males, who tended to hold, in general, what can best be described as chauvinistic views on sexual activity, roles and responsibility.

There is little, if any, evidence to suggest that 'education' in itself is rejected by the working class communities in West Belfast. Indeed education in general would appear to be highly regarded by the parent culture. However, all the evidence suggests that most working class young people do, to a greater or lesser extent, resist something in the school system. Any teacher in West Belfast would confirm that the school is a 'battleground', with the pupils' weapons ranging from apathy through indiscipline to truancy and violence. In terms of ideology the school is always the loser. The use of repressive power by the school reinforces the pupil's experience of education as an imposition. Failure confirms the reality that school is irrelevant, a waste of time. The attitudes of working class young people to school must be understood as a response to the problem posed by a framework of bourgeois institutions from a working class experience of those institutions. The school is one of the major arenas where the apparent contradiction of working class participation in a bourgeois institution takes place. Despite having experienced resistance to the institution themselves, the parents nevertheless comply willingly with the demands of the school on their children. This contradiction in working class culture exhibits itself in all the major institutions of society. The whole issue has been debated for over a century by the various strands of left-wing politics. Working class and left-wing organizations have campaigned for over a century for the extension of formal state education, while the 'ultra-leftist' organizations have campaigned for its abolition.

Religion

Religious belief among the young of the Shankill can generally be classified under three categories. First, there are the 'Christians', who are regular church attenders and are usually regarded as being 'good living'. Good living is a label applied to the Christians by others and refers to an 'ideal type' of individual in terms of attitudes and practices. It is not always the case that the recipients of the label are regarded by the ascribers as being of a generally high moral character. As we shall see, the reverse is often the case. Second, there are 'believers', those who believe in some form of religion, ranging from a casual belief in Christianity to reincarnation. They are not, however, regular practitioners, if they practice at all. Third, there are the 'non-believers', who do not claim to adhere to any form of religion. The last group tend to view adherents of the other two categories with ridicule, contempt or scepticism. Dee belonged to this group and was forceful and convinced in his arguments. Lily adhered to the second category:

LILY: Do you believe in God?
DEE: No. It's a load of bollicks.

LILY: It's been proven that there was a Jesus.
DEE: Aye! Some cunt *called* Jesus.

Most of the fifth formers belonged to the second group. They believed in God but did not practise any religion. They did, however, have definite views about heaven and hell, and catholicism as opposed to protestantism.

NG: Do you think there is much difference between protestantism and catholicism?
WILLIAM: Yes, they [the catholics] go to hell and protestants and Christians go to heaven.
GEORGE: Nah, protestants who aren't Christians go ti hell we the taigs.

Religious practice in the Shankill has experienced an enormous decline over the past 20 years. Twenty years ago it was rare to see kids playing football on a Sunday, either in the street or in the park. Now it is commonplace. Indeed, many churches have been forced to close owing to declining congregations, through either secularization or migration. Lord Soper once referred to Belfast as a 'city of religious night-clubs' and the Shankill was fairly typical, with almost every protestant denomination being represented and a vast array of street-corner mission halls and street preachers. Many of the more 'socially aspiring' families who moved out of the area either voluntarily through social mobility or forcibly through redevelopment were also more likely to be practising protestants. Many of them still return to the area on a Sunday to worship in their original church and are quite active in church societies and youth groups (as we illustrated in our findings). In a sense this has further removed some of the churches from their role in identifying with the local community:

IAN: On a Sunday there's a church round our way full of people who don't really belong in our area.

Membership of a church (affiliation to be more accurate) is usually retained by most of the believers for particular occasions such as weddings.

IAN: A lotta people still like ti get married in church even if the' don't go ... That's why the' go ti church a few weeks before the wedding.

Perhaps the most extensive and representative conversation on religion between a believer and non-believer occurred during one of the sessions in the Upper/Mid-Shankill YTP between Lily and Dee:

DEE: I just can't believe in it. It doesn't make sense. You say ti somebody an' they say 'Well, how did you get here?' ... How did God get there?
LILY: God's a spirit. He's always bin there.
DEE: Well tell me how women came about.
LILY: Women came from man.

DEE: Hold on. Adam and Eve had two sons so that means one a them must a stuffed his fuckin' ma.

LILY: But then it wasn't incest.

DEE: Awk that's all a lotta ballicks. Then people say the' believe in God, right? Well, then why is there so much fuckin' hatred, wars and what have yea in the world? An' the' say because they ate the fuckin' apple and God's payin' them back just because he ate a fuckin' apple. Awk it's all a lotta shit. Do yea believe yea go til heaven when yea die?

LILY: There's people don't go til heaven an' there's people that do.

DEE: Yea die an' the fuckin' worms eat yea, that's all.

LILY: Have you ever bin ti church in your life?

DEE: Aye, but a got chucked out of it . . . Do yea know there's Christians killin' ev'ryday wi'guns. Christians are a pack of dickheads . . . they look down on ev'rybody else. They've got all this money an' the' wouldn't give it ti anybody else. They're not true Christians. I knew a couple a people who were Christians an' they ended up killing each other. Meta was a Christian but she doesn't believe God now because her brother was a Christian an' he went that fuckin' mad he killed himself. She went to the _____ church in _____. Ev'ry penny she put inti that an' said it was goin' ti do this and goin' ti do that. Fuckin' minister was rippin' her off for fuck sake . . . it's a load of balls. There's things was said in the Bible, things that were goin' ti happen an' none of it even did sure. It said in the Old Testament that the world was goin' ti blow up ages an' ages ago . . . an' it never happened. So how do you explain that?

LILY: How do you know it never happened? For a first thing that there was written down in Hebrew . . . The nuclear bomb will blow up the whole world.

NOEL (who had not hitherto been much interested in the conversation): No way. It says in the Bible 'Yella man shall rule the world'. You know who yella man is? Fuckin' chinkies. They will rule the world. Chinkies haven't got no big bombs compared to the Americans and the Russians . . . Aye, an' it says the trouble will start out in the East. And it says the world could end with a fuckin' plague. You know what the plague could be? Fuckin' AIDS . . . it's started already.

DEE: Everybody all over the world believes in somethin' different . . . Egyptians had idols. Indians had idols and everybody had something different. Different things all through the years. . . . Somebody believed in it at the start then it's just been passed down. It's just been changed from the idols down the ages to spirits . . . I had an argument with Kate the other day . . . She says whenever the world ends He takes yea up. Why when the world ends? Why does he not take yea up now?

There was an inclination for the believer and non-believer to portray the good living Christians as 'no better than anybody else'. Often this was expressed by projecting some of the 'worst' characteristics (drinking, womanizing, gambling etc.) of 'immoral' behaviour as perceived by the good living back on to them. Leading public figures were the most common subjects for this ritual which functioned to re-affirm the participants' desire to present themselves as being 'no worse' than anyone else. They may describe themselves as non-believers, pagans, just prods – but they justified, indeed lauded, their secular status by claiming that at least they were not hypocrites, unlike many that they termed so-called Christians. 'Sure they're all in it for what they can get,' Dee claimed.

The fact that different churches and different clerics within the same churches, who were held to be experts on religion and God, could not agree on matters pertaining to morality, faith, God, heaven, hell and so on served to convince non-believers of their non-belief:

DEE: Sure you look at fuckin' churches. Every minister says different things. He tells people his beliefs and then they believe him so they tell other people theirs. Just the way the taigs believe in the Virgin Mary. They have idols. They have fuckin' statues of the Virgin Mary an' all. You know somethin' the taigs worship the Virgin Mary. They don't worship God. They put the Virgin Mary before God. They pray ti her an' she's meant ti give him [God] the orders and he fuckin' does it.

For those such as Dee the fact that everybody was worshipping different things in different ways dispelled the 'myth' of one God, which therefore rendered most, if not all, of the wordly religions incoherent and logical absurdities. 'So when I go that's me dead,' he maintained.

Lily's approach to religion was a pragmatic and functional one. She retorted to Dee's last statement: 'If you had kids would you want them ti believe you?' To which Dee replied: 'That's up ti them. They can believe in whatever they want.' When asked by Lily what he would want to come back as if there was such a thing as reincarnation, Dee replied, in total earnest, 'a Dobermann' (these are the most feared dogs on the Shankill and are the most popular with the 'hard men' as a status and power symbol).

Dee had an abundance of contempt for Christians.

DEE: I have always had thoughts that Christians could be leadin' us ti death. They're worse than God [this should not be taken as an indication of Dee's belief in the actual existence of God – he is referring to the concept]. See anybody fuckin' preachin' ti yea, it really gets up your nose. It only starts ti worry yea, tellin yea you're gonna die, you're gonna go ti hell an' all this here. Tellin' yea all the bad fuckin' things.

Lily had learned her views on religion from her mother. They were flexible, and were fairly widespread among the non-participating protestants of the Shankill:

LILY: My ma always says ti me that she doesn't really believe in Christianity. She believes that if you believe in God that's you. You're goin' ti heaven . . . The only thing I don't agree with is wee kids bein' born an' then dyin' straight away not even livin' their life. But then I believe in reincarnation. I think God put them wee kids, Ethiopians an' all, there ti see if we would help them and we did help.

DEE: In what way did you contribute?

LILY: I put a couple a quid by each week by Live Aid an' all. Me an' me ma done it. That's what I believe. I think that's why all them starvin' kids are. Ti see if the other part of the world would help them an' the' all did.

DEE: Can yea explain why there's so much fuckin' hatred an' all? How nuclear bombs came about? If you had a chance ti bring peace inti the world . . . say yea left it for a few years . . . there would be trouble again startin' up. That's because God has made people's minds corrupt.

LILY: That's not God. It's themselves listenin' ti people that are talkin' a load of shit through their friggin' arses. I can laugh at some Christians. They say 'I'm a true Christian'. But if the' see a poor man they'd walk on by him. I've seen them doin' it.

DEE: I knew a couple of fellas. The' were in jail an' ev'rything an' then the' went ti church an' met Christians and the' were all for it an' the' were preachin' ti me an' all saying 'Aye, yea want ti go. Yea want ti get saved. The Lord does this an' the Lord does that.' See six months later? The' were in jail again. Drinkin', fuckin', thievin', doin' robberies all the time . . . the' went back on it.

Dee, as do most people from the Shankill in the course of their lives, had more than one encounter with an attempt to 'have him saved'. Lily had several encounters. She described one to us:

LILY: See the mission down Tennant Street . . . the oul woman in there would have yea down on yer knees in the street. She's a Bible thumper. She comes out ti yer house an' all . . . she was tryin' ti get my Ma saved . . . She started sayin' to me 'You're goin' ti go through hell whenever yi die but if yea get saved nigh God will prevent all that.' I just told her ti fuck off 'cause shi was gettin' up my nose. Sure my Uncle John's saved Monday, Tuesday, Wednesday, Thursday and then Friday, Saturday and Sunday he's plastered ev'ry week.

Lily had been taught about God from an early age but was 'never pushed about it':

LILY: I remember from a was no age we were made ti say our prayers ev'rynight an' a still do say mi prayers ev'ry single night.

She was, however, aware of the many contradictions in scripture that served to prevent her from being reconciled to Christianity:

> LILY: I had an argument with Caroline yesterday and Kate today over this. And again this mornin' wi' Caroline. The same last night with me Ma. I was sayin' it was incest [the children of Adam and Eve]. Then here's her [her mother]: 'Aye but it wasn't incest in them days'. Here's me: 'How the hell wasn't it?' and she said: 'Ah Lily fuck up you're annoyin'.'
>
> DEE: Then yea have the Ten Commandments. Don't commit adultery, this, that, an' the other . . . and the' fuckin' must a committed adultery and what have yea. That's why we're all called brothers an' sisters. Because he [Cain or Abel] fuckin' stuffed his ma an' then he stuffed his sister . . . What proof is there . . . of God apart from the Bible?

There was usually an identification with a particular church or denomination and this would depend upon where one had been baptized or parental affiliation, even if the person involved did not attend church or practise Christianity.

> DEE [TO LILY]: What are ye then?
>
> LILY: A don't know. St Michael's Church, Shankill Road. That's as far as a know . . . Is it Church a Ireland?

Often denominational allegiance was based upon aspects of a particular church's practices that appealed to the young people. As in so many other aspects of social life it was excitement that appeared to be the most appealing:

> NOEL: I'm Pentecostal . . . but the Church a God are good too . . . they have a band an' all playin'. Playin' fuckin' tambourines an' all an' a big nigger . . . I'm tellin' ye. The only best people believe in our religion is niggers. See the way they have their funerals. I would love ti get buried like that.

Funerals were particularly regarded as important events and despite their youth most of those we spoke to had definite views on the subject:

> LILY: Oh, I'd love ti have a paramilitary funeral.
>
> DEE: Sure what's it ti you. Sure yi can't see it.

Funerals, of course, are much more common events for young people in areas like the Shankill as many of them or their friends, neighbours and kin are involved in paramilitary organizations. Many more are often innocent victims from 'punishment' shootings or 'mistakes' by the organizations or, on occasions, the security forces.

Religious rituals are also a means of re-affirming an ethnic identification even when the meaning of the ritual has been totally lost to those participating. As Barbara was quick to point out: 'My da doesn't believe in God but he believes in getting kids baptized.' Such rituals become problematic in 'mixed marriage' situations where one partner is protestant and the other a catholic. Such situations arise more frequently in Belfast, despite segregation and obvious dangers, than outsiders would expect. Such marriages are often open to a great deal of stress. They are often the victims of sectarian attacks and so finding a safe place to live is a serious problem. Then there is the problem of raising children in a divided society where the decisions such as where the child will be baptized will affect the rest of the child's life (even if he or she later disregards the label). 'Mixed marriages' and their children are often the targets of humorous jibes. There is at least one song about it:

> It is the greatest mix up that you have ever seen.
> My father he was orange and my mother she was green.

Despite the complexities involved in 'mixed marriages' almost everyone spoken to knew of at least one such couple quite well. Stewarty thought that such marriages could have positive effects in places like Belfast:

STEWARTY: I know a certain person you know that's married to a catholic and they've kids but they're not you know gonna say the kids are catholics or protestants until they grow up and then let them you know make their own choice for themselves that they want ti be. It's fair like.

SAM: You would be sittin' there you know when the Pope comes on the TV. They would be sittin' there sayin' 'Look at that oul cunt. Baldy oul bastard.' And when Paisley comes on they would say 'Look at that there, you grey haired fucker.' You wouldn't know what the' were at. Sure the' wouldn't. You wouldn't know who was who. They wouldn't be brought up you know to fight with each other. You know, fight with catholics an' fight with protestants. Riots an' all.

Facing up to the peculiar contradictions inherent in Belfast 'mixed marriage' situations can be an awesome task. The situation is exacerbated by the shortage of integrated schools, segregated housing, attitudes of the churches and family, and community pressure (often hostility). This is in spite of the fact that religion itself is not now a powerful force and religious practices and beliefs tend to be much less important now than in the past. Even secular mixed marriages (where one or both partners are not believers) face the same problems as religious ones. A 'taig' is still a 'taig' to militant loyalists even if he or she no longer attends mass. Similarly, many catholics regard anyone who is not a catholic as a 'prod', even if they have never been to church in their life. It is an ethnic identification that is the crucial variable.

The Christians

We asked some of the Christians we spoke to in the church group what it meant to be a Christian and the implications for their social life. For a Christian, social life and religion are inseparable.

SAMMY: I think the . . . mission has more to offer me as a Christian as well as in social activities . . . You can't really split the both of them.

Christians may belong to any denomination or none. There is only one precondition:

SAMMY: There are Christians in all the different types of churches. It doesn't matter what church you go to as long as you have sort of accepted Jesus to be Saviour . . . Some churches may disagree on small theological points or whatever . . . the basic concept is still there. We all belong to one family . . . If a Roman Catholic becomes a Christian then they are a Christian you know and they are not necessarily a Roman Catholic and I think a lot of people sort of get it mixed up in a sense that you are a Presbyterian first.

A few ex-catholics were members of the Christians group but for all intents and purposes they had become protestants (they attended protestant churches, practised evangelical religion and held fundementalist views). There is no group comparable to the Christians in the catholic community (where it is essentially assumed that all catholics are Christians). Being a member of the Christian group in the Shankill involves much more than a casual identification with a particular church. A Christian is expected to live a different lifestyle from others. They are 'good living'. Smoking, drinking, cursing and sex are definitely out. Regular church or meeting attendance is essential. One should be 'born again'. Social life revolves around the churches and one's friendship networks are normally limited to other Christians. The Christians are in fact a form of sub-culture. Converting unbelievers is a priority activity, usually carried out in drop-in centres, youth clubs and open air meetings, where people are called to 'dedicate themselves'.

Being a Christian also influenced attitudes to work and working with other Christians was preferable to working with non-Christians:

MALE (20): I'm very fortunate in a sense that my boss is a Christian and his boss is a Christian . . . A Christian boss is quite strict . . . he's more strict . . . he would adopt the same attitude as I have . . . he would be working for God as well as his boss. I think he respects you when you do your best in any sort of job. You can do no more.

Such attitudes to work were one of the characteristics that divided the non-Christians from the Christians. Christians were, on the whole, also more likely to have favourable attitudes to school and youth clubs. Despite their preoccupation with religious dogma they were more likely to *express* more tolerant attitudes to catholics. The next section will consider attitudes that the people we spoke to held about the 'other sort'.

The 'other sort'

West Belfast is a divided community. Catholics and protestants have little everyday contact with each other and hence knowledge of 'the other sort' is restricted by exclusive rituals and differential socialization patterns. Generally speaking, protestants and catholics live in different areas, attend different schools and churches, work apart, and read their own news-papers. Recreation is often varied and usually segregated. This section is concerned with the common 'folk' knowledge held by young working class protestants about catholics and catholicism. It will be stressed that such attitudes held by the young are firmly placed within the local adult culture. We shall explore how a collective sense of ethnic identity and dif-ference is continually expressed and re-affirmed in the discursive practices of the young. This discourse, as we shall see, is closely integrated with the practices of everyday life and given valency in the political and territorial anxieties of the present conflict. Central to the process of sectarian political socialization is the initiation of the individual into a sense of ethnic identity and difference – a collective sense of a mutually exclusive protestant and catholic historical identity and expressed ethnicity learnt via a discourse of myths and symbols. Bell (n.d.) has suggested that one of the major sites where this integration of the spheres of the mythical and the mundane occurs is in the expressive world of urban working class youth sub-culture.

Although religion is unimportant in the theological sense to most working class young people on the Shankill it is important as a means of *ethnic* identification. The 'Protestantism' of secular and non-Christian elements is not of the variety normally associated with the Christians and the religious zealots of Ulster (evangelical fundamentalism, puritanism, work ethic, temperance, 'respectability'). It is a crude mixture of selective theological dogma, anti-catholicism and pragmatic loyalism. One popular loyalist song espouses the simplified objectives of such protestantism:

> No Pope in Rome, No Chapel to sadden my eye,
> No nuns and no priests and no rosary beads,
> Ev'ryday is the Twelfth of July . . .

Another song describes this ethnic identification even more harshly:

> We are the Shankill Derry,
> Fuck the Pope and the Virgin Mary!
> We are the Shankill Derry,
> Shankill rules the Falls!

One of the most commonly held assumptions about catholics is that almost all of them are in favour of an immediate and unconditional united Ireland separate from Britain. Such views were common even in the 'mixed' YTP in the Upper Shankill and the solution to the problem was seen as no more complex or liberal than anywhere else.

DEE: Taigs say fuckin' united Ireland an' all 'll solve the problems. They oughta go out an' shoot all the bastards. That would solve the fuckin' problem.

Political affiliation in the same group was also determined by ethnic identification rather than policy or personality.

NOEL: Sure yer man [politician] he's another fuckin' one. All talk an' no fuckin' action. Fuck 'im. Hardly anybody wanted ti fuckin' vote for 'im but it's better ti vote for a prod than a fuckin' taig.

We asked some of the non-Christians attending the Mission drop-in centre in the Lower Shankill if they would be prepared to attend a community centre that was 'integrated'.

GREG: I wouldn't go. We went ti that centre once [an outdoor pursuit centre]. Like there was both there at the same time but the' just didn't seem ti get on.

Bill indicated that he did not dislike all catholics: 'Some are all right... Paisley and Adams are keepin' people apart.' His caution about 'mixing' with the other sort was, he perceived, an effect of the political situation in Belfast. He did not consider it was the other way around. Indeed, Bill appeared to be clearly conscious of the underlying problems in Northern Ireland. His analysis was unsophisticated but accurate all the same:

BILL: I think the important thing is that people go about the same way livin' everyday like wi' everyday things. Unemployment's more important than politics but people think it's politics that's important.

He added that the troubles would end if 'they gave them [the under-privileged] more money'. Greg, on the other hand, had clearly been embittered by experience and enforced segregation:

GREG: I don't think it [integration] would do any good at all. I just hate them. That's all [pauses]. It's sixteen years like. I don't mind them shootin' at the army or killin' peelers like. But shootin' the likes of the UDR and ordinary prods like. They're the ones that's sufferin'.

Most of those we spoke to did admit that there were similar problems facing catholics and protestants. Ian, the fifth former, observed that 'there's poor housing on the Falls as well as the Shankill.' Billy, in the same class, thought that, 'the catholics and prods in Ulster have more in common with each other than they have with Britain and Southern Ireland'. Ken, from the Lower Shankill YTP, was aware of the social determinants of sectarianism:

KEN: It depends what area they're from. The ones on the Falls an' all and the ones on the Malone Road.

NG: Why do you think there's a difference?
KEN: Because the Malone Road is all upper class and the Falls an' all
is working class.

Wally, on the other hand, thought that they were 'all the same no matter
where you go', to which Pauline added 'Aye, they're all bigoted rebel
bastards'. Most of those in the Lower Shankill YTP believed that the
protestants were misrepresented by commentators and politicians from
Great Britain:

ALEX: He [Ken Livingstone] would go up the Falls and look at all
their houses an' all. He wouldn't go round to the people that's no
money in the Shankill or Glencairn . . . He just sees the head of the
Orange [Order] an' they're not poor bastards . . . you know what
I'm sayin'? He would go up and he would see their point of view
an' all. But he wouldn't turn round to the protestants and say
right what's your point of view. He would take the taigs' side
first.

Some loyalist politicians, particularly George Seawright (who was
assassinated by republicans in 1988), were highly regarded for seeing
through 'all that nonsense' and 'having none of it':

ALEX: Mr George Seawright, best politician in the world. Like he
says burn the bastards. That's it, burn every one of them.

Not everyone agreed with such drastic measures:

SMITHEY: Just build a big wall. One big wall and that's it. And move
them all down there so they don't get our dole money.

'Dole money' was a particularly sensitive subject when it came to
catholics. The Lower Shankill trainees considered it a 'nerve' for catholics
to criticize the British state yet take dole money from it. This was especially
galling because the catholics tended to receive more (because of larger
families and more unemployment generally) and they would receive
substantially less in the Republic (or a united Ireland).

The size of the catholic families was interpreted as a deliberate strategy
to achieve a united Ireland. First, the state would be ruined by the scale of
dole money payments. Second, they would eventually outnumber the
protestants and therefore outvote or overwhelm them:

ALEX: They're goin' ti rise up an' they're goin' ti take us over.

Catholics here were perceived as being different from protestants and
practised what were regarded as peculiar habits:

BEVERLY: The' [catholics] go ev'ry night ti church an' all an' don't do
this, don't do that. Don't use the pill. Don't have sex after one
o'clock in the mornin'. Even their habits on eatin' like. The' eat fish
on a Friday, know that?

The non-Christian and unbelieving people in this group (all of them) were fairly representative of the protestant (in the secular sense) and loyalist youth sub-culture:

> ALEX: I hate Christians. It says in the fuckin' thing [UVF motto] 'For God and Ulster'. Ulster's not a God, it's for the protestant people. What's God got ti do with it?'

The claims that protestants had gained social and economic privileges were described as 'a lot a oul fuck' by Dee. None of those in the group thought that protestants were any better off than catholics. The ritual burning of census forms in places like Ballymurphy was further confirmation to Noel and Dee that the 'taigs' were up to something: 'that's so as we won't know how many of them there are'. There was a real and, at times, obsessive fear of the potential (or real) numerical power of catholics:

> NOEL: West Belfast is 80 per cent catholic. They could wipe the Shankill Road off the tiles.

The proposed solutions to such 'perceived threats' from catholics were often simple and drastic. As one of the males in the ACE projects said: 'Wipe Ballymurphy off the face of the map.' He said that he hated the place and that this was because of 'the way I was brought up'. He went on: 'You can like them [catholics] because some of the ones that work in here are dead on but you wouldn't want to turn your back on them in case they stab you.' This person's responses actually illustrate the complexity of the nature of sectarian attitudes and behaviour. When probed further he admitted that his attitudes were influenced 'by the ones you'd been hanging about with. They don't like them and you go with the crowd.' When questioned on his own the same respondent admitted that 'There is catholics go into the protestant areas and I wouldn't let anyone touch them because if we were in the same position I would expect them to do the same for us.' This is one example (there were others) of people having deep and loyal friendships with catholics yet at the same time holding blatantly anti-catholic sectarian attitudes.

Most of those working on the ACE project thought that there were ways of telling the difference between catholics and protestants through physical appearance and speech or habits (see also Burton 1978: 37–67):

> WILL: Catholics are dirty lookin'. The' don't wash.
> JOHN: No, there is no difference unless the' speak and you hear the way the' use their aitches. That's the only way you can really tell.
> NED: They're dirty lookin'. The men don't shave. Their eyes are further apart. The' can see 'round corners.
> JUKE: They're breedin' like rabbits.

Very few of those in the groups thought that all catholics were the same (i.e. 'bad'). Some, however, did have definite views although it would be difficult to assess the extent to which they would put such views into practice:

NG: What would you do if you were dying and a catholic doctor saved you?

Bob (18): I'd kill miself.

Sharkey, on the other hand, believed that 'there are some good ones and some bad ones and the' aren't all out ti get you.' Ned, while conceding that 'there's different ones', was quick to point out that many catholics were hypocritical and therefore not to be trusted: 'Sure the' go ti chapel an' get blessed and they're probably just after killin' somebody.'

There were misconceptions about Catholicism to a greater or lesser degree in nearly all of those we spoke to. This was not entirely due to lack of knowledge about the Catholic religion; it was also often the result of a total lack of knowledge of the basic premises of Christianity – Protestant and Catholic. The Virgin Mary, for instance, was perceived as an exclusively catholic figure and subjected to ridicule accordingly: 'She was a prostitute' according to some of the girls in the Lower Shankill YTP group. Geordie, the fifth former, thought that because 'catholics worshipped the Virgin Mary', this confirmed his belief that 'taig girls are all whores'.

In the course of one of the sessions in the Upper Shankill YTP the participants were shown some photographs of a republican parade. Noel immediately noted that 'they're all fenians'. Lily, however, thought that 'they don't look like fenians' to which Noel retorted, 'you know a taig when you smell [sic] one'. Lily, when informed that they were in fact 'fenians', looked disappointed and commented, 'I just thought they'd be different'. Her friend Alice, who had been uncommitted in her judgement, said she 'wasn't sure' but had noticed 'their wee beady eyes'. Noel claimed that he knew what they were because the bagpipes were 'green, white and gold' (it was a black and white photograph) and that they were 'wearing hats like the IRA wear' (black berets).

It is a curious feature of protestant and catholic ideology in that each consider themselves to be the sole inheritors of 'truth' and that the other side are either deluded or brainwashed. Nationalist dogma frequently asserts that protestants have been deluded into adopting loyalism as a political philosophy against their best interests by the British and Orange 'propaganda machine'. Similarly, protestants assert that catholics have been deluded by the 'false religion of Catholicism'. Lily believed that catholics had been 'brainwashed by them fuckin' oul priests'. Noel thought they had been 'brainwashed by the provos as well'. Such arguments are, of course, quite common in most societies where there are deep divisions. Such patronizing explanations are more peculiar to the 'libertarian' holders of anti-catholic (or anti-protestant) attitudes ('It's not that I dislike catholics as catholics. Some of my best friends are catholics. But I hate the way they've been brainwashed by the catholic church').

Quite often, the amenability to 'brainwashing' is presented explicitly as 'proof' that catholics are intellectually inferior to protestants. Catholic schools, for instance, are perceived as being major agents in the brainwashing process:

STEWARTY: In their schools all the oul fuckin' nuns and priests drill it inti them. There's no fuckin' about.

SAM: They're fuckin' dunces! Dickheads! They get taught stricter an' all in their schools but they're thicker than us you know, mathematics ways an' all. Fuckin' dunces, haven't an ounce.

TOMMY: Catholics are better educated than we are but that's because there's more discipline in their schools.

JOHN: They do what they're told. We tell the teachers ti fuck off. They don't. They sit down an' do what they're meant ti do. That's how they're educated.

It was for such reasons that the fifth formers tended to agree that catholics shouldn't be allowed to teach in protestant schools.

GEORDIE: We'd have none a that oul fuck. I'll spit at the nuns for good luck . . . pish on them.

It was also a common criticism of catholics that they were always complaining and 'never happy no matter what they got'.

JUKE: Sure look at the fuckin' catholics. The' wanted the British Army in an' now the' want them out.

JOHN: Now they're killin' them.

SHARKEY: The' just wanted target practice [laughter].

Sharkey was always quick to make light of serious conversation. His attitude to life tended to be basic. 'Having a laugh' was important and he frequently 'took the piss'. He was first to 'have a good rake' when the opportunity presented itself but oddly enough did not appear to hold any strong anti-catholic views. 'We're all the same down there' he used to say while pointing between his legs. It was difficult to interest the rakers directly in discussions about what one would describe as important problems or interests that catholics and protestants had in common.

While acknowledging the many interests that both sides held in common, and these included things that were very important to the rakers (money, football, snooker, boxing, drugs, drink, not gettin' enough of it), they none the less recognized what they perceived as crucial differences. 'Breeding habits' exemplified this the most and they were forceful in stressing the significance of this fact ('ti get us all out ti fuck'). Sharkey maintained that some catholics thought Diet Coke was a contraceptive. When it was suggested to them that some protestant families had up to 20 children in them, Tommy replied, 'That's because they had no TV.'

Ned conceded that catholics and protestants were all the same: 'have the same blood and all, we're all human'. He had a realistic approach to life, however: 'It's gettin' everybody to realize that like.'

> NED: If you walk down the Falls like and you says 'don't hit me because I'm a human like you' they still knock the cunt out of you like. They'd laugh at ye an' knock yer fuck in. 'You're not like me yi bastard, you're an orange man,' they'd say.

One of the most significant developments at the time of the discussions was the increase in the Sinn Fein vote in West Belfast and the election of Gerry Adams. To Ossie this confirmed his explanation of why catholics were 'now gettin' the army out'.

> OSSIE: They're more powerful now than what the' were . . . You'd think they'd have enough men to get rid of them an' pick us off like.

For Ned, the rise in the fortunes of Sinn Fein was the result of a political stunt:

> NED: I guarantee . . . nine out a ten up there [in Ballymurphy] will say the' don't want a united Ireland an' I guarantee you go ti ten politicians up there an' they'll say they do want it.
> CAROL: But they're votin' them politicians in. The likes of Gerry Adams. The' voted him in.

All of those in the group were unable to solve the contradiction as to why people could support Sinn Fein and yet not believe in a united Ireland.

> SAM: If the' got it the' would regret it they know the' would. They'd say 'fuck this country was all right the way it was' . . . they're probably votin' for him because they're not too sure whether they're goin' ti get it or not. The' just want ti show us up and say, 'look at the votes we can get' . . . an' yi can picture a prod from the Shankill Road . . . you know the way he's our MP . . . you could picture goin' over an' sayin' somethin' ti him like 'we want this done til our house'. He'd chase yi ti fuck, 'stick your house up yer arse' like.

Catholics, according to most in the ACE project, turned against their politicians for helping protestants. They did admit that some catholic politicians (even, at times, Adams) had helped protestants on occasions:

> BARBARA: There's been people from Highfield that's went til him an' he's got them things.
> SAM: You know the best politician was ever out? A catholic one. Gerry Fitt. He done more for the protestants then he done for his own. That's why they put him out of his house an' all. Sure the' burnt him out an' all.

Catholics were perceived as the main, if not only, culprits when it came to sectarianism. Gerry Fitt's power waned after he refused to support the republican hunger strike in 1981, not because he helped protestants. In the Upper Shankill YTP the group thought that the catholics couldn't be trusted. They also thought that catholic instructors discriminated against protestants: 'they want to get rid of half of them taig supervisors' (Noel had been sent home for wearing a UVF badge, which he considered unfair). In fact it was not possible to convince the group that discrimination did act against catholics:

> NG: There are figures for the amount of people signing on at the dole offices each month and there are more signing on the Falls than the Shankill.
> NOEL: That's because they are spongers of the British Government . . . the taigs don't want jobs and then they moan. When they get a chance of one they won't take it . . . they take advantage of the British Government.

The 'taigs' tended to take the blame for a wide range of mishaps, even those which were unintentionally self-inflicted:

> NOEL: My uncle was blown up makin' a bomb an' I reckon if we weren't fighting the taigs that would't have happened.

Catholics were also seen as being vindictive.
Noel tended to be more suspicious than most about catholics:

> NOEL: That's the worst about here. Any of those taigs could go into reception and find out where you live.

The boys at the school were wary of attending the Upper Shankill YTP after they left because it was 'mixed' or, as one put it, 'they're all taigs'. Working with 'taigs' was not always perceived as a big problem. As Bill (school leaver) put it:

> BILL: Sure what's taigs? If you get a job you'll probably be working with taigs.
> ROY: I don't think there's any way you can get out of it.

Roy was regarded as a 'fenian lover' because he was keen to join the YTP in question. Unfortunately, for him, he had inadvertently become close friends with a catholic a few years previously.

Despite the apparent bitterness in many of the responses about catholics there were still a significant number of people (even including some who made the responses) who believed that catholics should be accommodated in the administration of the Province. The school group agreed that there should be a local devolved government in Northern Ireland in which catholics (but 'not ones like Gerry Adams') would have a say and be represented, 'but not high up'.

The group from the ACE project who frequented the city centre regularly and who were, on the whole, more outwardly mobile than most of the others held the most positive views about catholics. They did not feel that catholics, generally speaking, were dominated by the church although they agreed that perhaps 'one in five have been brainwashed'. They tended to agree that catholics in general did not sympathize with the IRA. They were, however, concerned with how catholics perceived them. Some thought that most catholics believed that most protestants were bigoted. They were quick to stress that although there were protestant bigots they were no worse, or no more plentiful, than catholic bigots. Almost all of them expressed the desire to send any children they may have to 'mixed schools' provided they were convenient.

While believing that catholic fears of protestant violence were justified they stressed that it was 'tit for tat'. They did, however, believe that there were major differences between catholics and protestants regarding attitudes to nationality and knowledge of history. Catholics, they felt, also tended to exaggerate the influence of the Orange Order in the protestant community and the extent of its involvement in anti-catholic discimination in areas such as employment policy.

Politics and 'the troubles'

This section examines the nature of the political and military crisis in Northern Ireland and how young people who are located in it experience its various forms and practices. The discussions took place at a time when there was an upsurge in tension as part of the reaction to the implementation of the Anglo-Irish Agreement.

Discrimination

Discrimination and the IRA, for the young people of the Shankill, are the two primary elements in the present phase of the 'troubles'. The 'discrimination', however, is perceived as discrimination not against catholics but against protestants. The discrimination, nearly all of them believed, would be exacerbated in a united Ireland, which would lead to a reversal of roles in the continuing conflict:

> DEE: If there should become a united Ireland we'd be like the IRA. The taigs are gettin' ev'rything as it is. Look at Andytown like. It's got a leisure centre and ev'ry fuckin' thing. The Shankill's got about six fuckin' shops. The fuckin' heap.

This is one example of what is clearly a distorted view of discrimination. The Shankill, too, has a leisure centre and considerably more than six shops.

There are, however, areas in which the perceived discrimination is much more plausible, such as in employment patterns:

NIGEL: Catholics go on about fair employment and all the rest of it but yet there's protestants that doesn't get employed in catholic firms . . . And this Fair Employment Agency . . . every case you hear is a catholic being discriminated against . . . you never hear of a protestant being discriminated against.

It was generally felt also by the group in the Upper Shankill YTP that catholics 'get better jobs than us so they do'. Matters, they pointed out, were even worse in the South.

NOEL: See Cherry Polish down South. They don't employ one prod.
DEE: So does Stork Margarine.

Security was another major issue here. It was thought that the security forces (the RUC in particular) were much more repressive in their treatment of protestants than of catholics. Relations between young people and the police were at a particularly low ebb at the time of the discussions. This was mainly due to the role of the police in implementing the Anglo-Irish Agreement (although relations had already deteriorated considerably since the supergrass trials). Popular Shankill graffiti at the time illustrated local feelings towards the RUC:

RUC paid in punts.

Garda short of recruits. Apply Tennant Street barracks.

To get into Tennant Street barracks you need O level Gaelic.

If pigs could fly Tennant Street barracks would be an airport.

The acronym ACAB (All Cops Are Bastards) seemed to be sprawled on almost every available space.

We shall consider attitudes to the police in more detail later. However, an ironic twist occurred in attitudes when the RUC started to use plastic bullets against protestant rioters and demonstrators. Catholics had been protesting against their use for years before this while protestants considered that this tactic was 'too soft' ('they should use live rounds'). Protestant reaction, however, to the use of plastic bullets against *them* was fierce and widespread. One of the groups in a YTP had held a one-hour strike in protest against plastic bullets.

MARTHA: It was good when we were all out on Thursday. We bate the fuck outta a Land-Rover.
DEE: All the taigs said 'that's not fuckin' right'. Fuck them.
MARTHA: Aye. They said we should get money takin' off us.

It appeared to the group that although catholics had protested so strongly against plastic bullets in the past they suddenly became much more acceptable once the police started to use them against protestants.

Politics

As with the population in general in Northern Ireland, the political outlooks of the youth in the Shankill were a reflection of the unionist/nationalist dichotomy, which dominates politics. While almost all of those we spoke to were unionist (with regard to the border) most of them did not support any specific political party. Political parties and politicans in general were not very highly regarded although most of those we spoke to supported the unionists of one kind or another because they wanted to remain British (or at least separate from the rest of Ireland).

The function of the border was perceived as 'keeping republicans out', although there was some suspicion that this was not being adhered to:

WILLIAM: If they did away wi'the border it would let the republicans in.
GREG: They're comin' in anyway. The border doesn't keep them out. I think the British Army is goin' hand in hand wi'the Provies an' turnin' a blind eye like.

Not everyone was absolutely clear on why some people wanted a united Ireland:

JANE: Because they want it to be called Ireland and not Northern Ireland.

Others were much closer to the point:

JOHN: Because they feel that they are being discriminated against.

While the thought of a united Ireland was generally feared, many did not believe it would be attained in the foreseeable future because of the opposition of unionists:

NED: There'll never be a united Ireland in our time.
SAM: There would be too many asking for political asylum at the same time.

Politicians on the whole were seen as being ineffective:

NED: The ones that get in don't do much. They just want in.
JOHN: I think they're just out for themselves. They have their job and to hell with yours.

Support for specific political parties, where it existed, tended to be for those of a militant variety, which were at least seen to be 'doing things' in areas that mattered most to the respondents. The National Front tended to have widespread support, as did Paisley's DUP and, to a lesser extent, the Progressive Unionist Party (which some people associated with the UVF). Noel underlined the stupidity of voting for more conventional politicians:

NOEL: After all, everybody asked for Maggie Thatcher and she was gonna do this and that and since she got in she's done an awful lot. She's wrecked the country.

Most of the local Official Unionist politicians in the area were not well regarded. Nobody thought it would make much difference if the MP for West Belfast (Adams's constituency) was a unionist, although this was not out of any regard for Mr Adams:

NOEL: They should have shot him that time with the UFF [they did shoot him but he survived]. I know the fella that shot him . . . He [the attempted assassin] should have been decorated.

It was widely believed that people only elected unionists because 'they're better than Sinn Fein'. It was generally considered a waste of time going to the polling stations by many of those in our study. Ned was asked if he thought politicians ever considered the views or interests of the young. 'I'm fuckin' sure they don't', was the reply. John said he threw his voting card 'in the bin' and that 'fuckin' Paisley talks too much'. Ned agreed, but added 'He's better than that fuckin' cunt Adams.'

Gerry Adams was generally regarded as 'head of the IRA'. There was some apparently grudging (and jealous) admiration for the success Adams achieved in 'stickin' up for them' (republicans/nationalists).

NOEL: Did you ever try to argue with Gerry Adams? . . . he's a hard man ti beat. He knows what he's talkin' about, doesn't he?

Probably the most popular politican on the Shankill at the time was George Seawright, although there was a significant opposition to him. Among the young it was a case of either admiration ('he's a man of action') or contempt ('he's a bin lid').

Ian Paisley, who is widely regarded as the natural leader of Ulster's protestants, was not popular at all among the young secular elements of the Shankill and was frequently the subject of ridicule.

ALEX: See Geordie Seawright, he should be a fuckin' MP . . . should be Prime Minister . . . Paisley he's a Christian bastard. I hate Christians. He's a fuckin' wanker.

Oddly enough, Seawright regarded himself as a 'born again Christian' but the fact seemed to be ignored by his secular adherents. One of the Christians from the Mission was able to explain why, in the past at least, he had supported Paisley:

CHRISTIAN: I remember a lot of years ago there was a day of action or something and I was listening to Paisley at the City Hall . . . I wouldn't say I was hard headed or bigoted but he was able to have my blood boiling by the use of language and terms and the way he put it across. If you're anyway intelligent it's easy to manipulate someone.

Another of the group suggested that 'maybe the guy didn't mean to provoke you but anyway at least he's there to be honest'. The first respondent replied, 'He always has the facts to back things up but at the same time it's very easy to get carried away.'

Orangeism

Orangeism is often presented as being the bulwark of Ulster protestantism and unionism. We have discussed the political significance of what is known as the Orange system in an earlier chapter. To the young people of the Shankill orangeism means different things. Certainly the stereotypical view of loyalists as being people wearing bowler hats and sashes at every opportunity just does not apply. Many of the young treat orangeism with contempt. Some mock it while others have no feelings at all. Some are active supporters or members while others are passive members.

The latter are commonly known as 'the Twelfth Orangemen'; that is, they participate in the Twelfth of July parade each year and that is basically the limit of their involvement. For others the Order is a whole way of life. For the latter it dictates their moral standards, political outlooks, who their friends are likely to be. It is also likely to dominate their social life and, on occasions, their work relations (and sometimes who they work for).

Bob, who worked in the ACE project, belonged to the latter group. Sam had been a member but claimed he had been thrown out and now preferred the 'crack' of belonging to a 'blood and thunder' band:

SAM: I was in it but got threw out . . . not payin' dues.
BOB: They didn't throw you out. You're suspended. When you're suspended you've only got to pay your back dues. Say you owe a fiver. You only have to pay the fiver.

While Sam was somewhat sceptical about the Order, Bob took it very seriously: 'I lap it up so I do.' He insisted that the tradition of marching past catholic areas should be retained as 'a show of strength against the rebels'. He attended meetings on a monthly basis and joined when he was six. There was a certain amount of antagonism between Sam and Bob, which was related to their views on the Order.

BOB: My father was in it.
SAM: All my family was in it.
BOB: Look where all your family is now. Long Kesh [prison].
SAM: Yi need a password an' all ti get in.
BOB: A different one ev'ry year . . . you have the parades . . . Easter Tuesday . . . then you have the Twelfth . . . and a couple of others. The first Saturday in August. The last Saturday in August is for the Black [Royal Black Preceptory – a 'higher' version of the Orange Order].
NG: Are you in the Black as well. What's the difference between the Black and the Orange?

SAM: The Black is stricter so it is. You've ti do tests an' all ti get inti that and then the' kick yer fuck in an' all . . . in the end yi get a wee badge ti prove yer in it an' all.

Bob was shaking his head at Sam and remaining tight lipped, obviously angry at Sam's disclosure of the form of the 'initiation tests'.

NG: Do you think it's not like that at all?
BOB: I'm saying nothin', I can't say. I done it two years . . . and I'm not sayin' what happened because that's between me an' inside the Lodge an' I can't say what was done outside the Lodge . . . See him there [points to Sam], see if he was in the Lodge, I guarantee I'd get him kicked out . . . I'd squeal because he said things out against the Lodge.
SAM: I'm not in the Lodge now so I can say whatever the fuck I like.
BOB: If I ever see you in the Lodge I'll report you because what you say is forbidden and you're wrong for a start.
SAM: Fuckin' bunch of hoods the' are. That's why I stick til the oul bands. Yi never get commotions and beatin's. . . . they're all good livin' an all [in the Lodge]. Some a them just walk on the Twelfth an' all an' don't really give a fuck about it. Just ti get walkin' . . . I like the oul Lodge like so I did, but I'm fuckin' payin' no more til it.
BOB: [getting excited and more angry at Sam]: You're comin' out and sayin' . . . yi got a kickin'. When was that? Yi can always get yer own back, if he's sayin' what's true. Yi wait til the next people come through an' then you give them a beatin' . . . but I'm sayin' yi don't.
SAM: The' fuckin' do! That's the God's honest truth . . . I've seen it get done.
BOB: You're talkin' outta yer arse. That's between the Orange Order. It's nothin' ti do wi'you.
SAM: It is ti do wi'me. I'm in the Orange Purple as well [another step in the hierarchy].
BOB: Fuckin' sure you're not.
SAM: I can prove it. I'll show my certificates. It says 'you've passed your Orange Purple' . . . they get yi in the dark an' kick yer fuck in . . . the' hit yi wi thorn branches an' all.
NG: You had to do that test. Get beaten with thorn branches in the dark?
SAM: Aye. Holly branches an' all.
BOB: You're sworn to secrecy.
SAM: I'll say whatever the fuck I like.

Derek (21) entered the room towards the end of the previous conversation. He raised a few eyebrows at Sam's remarks. Derek was quietly spoken but articulate. He took the Orange Order seriously. To him it was a 'way of life'.

> DEREK: It's religious. It says in the Orange Order that they follow God's word. So it does. I believe in God. I'm not a Christian but I believe in God. The Orange Order is dedicated to the Queen and Ulster and I suppose if it ever came to the crunch that the Orange Order had to take up arms in order to save the Queen, I'm sure they would. But no way it's paramilitary. It's more religious. . . . It's a religious type of protestantism. It says 'go to your church'. I go to church but I wouldn't call myself a regular.
>
> BOB: You don't have ti go ti church ti be a Christian. Yi can worship anywhere. Ev'ry one a us in here's not a loyalist . . . A loyalist is a Christian who pays respect ti his Orange Order.
>
> DEREK: Sure I do that.
>
> BOB: But you're not a Christian.
>
> DEREK: I believe in God, same thing.
>
> BOB: It's not really the same. I believe in God too. I don't class myself as a loyalist.
>
> SAM: You're a dickhead.
>
> DEREK: There's two forms of loyalists. Ones that believe in God and other ones believe in killin' catholics . . . The UDA class themselves as loyalists but I don't believe they're true loyalists because to me they're only interested in lining their pockets. The longer the troubles go on the more money they stand to make.
>
> BOB: I vote DUP like. Ian Paisley, he's in the Orange Order.
>
> DEREK: I support Martin Smyth [Official Unionist]. He's a true loyalist.
>
> NG: Do you agree then with ministers being involved in politics?
>
> SAM: A minister shouldn't be involved in politics . . . they're only in it for publicity.
>
> NG: Do you [to Derek and Bob] not think it's hypocrisy for Paisley and Martin Smyth to complain about Rome rule and all in the South when they're actually elected representatives here in the North?
>
> DEREK: It's a bit hypocritical of them like but they do what they think's right so they do. They're only doin' what they think's right . . . and everybody's entitled to their own opinion . . . Everbody's free to speak their mind.

Derek's argument may, of course, be used by anyone to justify any action. Possibly he did not believe that politicians in the South were not doing 'what they think's right'. He was however, definitely suggesting by his final statement here ('Everybody's free to speak their mind') that such was not the case in the South of Ireland. We shall consider attitudes to 'the South' later. At this stage we shall consider the more immediate concern expressed with the IRA.

The IRA

The continuing existence of the Provisional IRA campaign was not viewed as a reaction by militant nationalists to oppression, injustice or social conditions. The IRA was perceived unequivocally as a *sectarian* force. This view, although not entirely an accurate interpretation of the declared aims and methods of the republican movement, was nevertheless grounded in the social reality of the consequences of the IRA campaign. The Provisionals were considered an anti-British, and by extension anti-protestant, force. The IRA may state that protestant RUC and UDR personnel are not 'targets' because they are protestant but because they are the 'agents of the British presence in Ireland'. However, to the protestants in West Belfast (and Northern Ireland) this implies that they are all potential targets as it is they who are the 'British presence in Ireland'. It therefore follows that they have every right to support and join British security forces. The young people of the Shankill were in no doubt that when republicans called for 'Brits out' it was a demand to have all British subjects (almost the entire protestant population) forcibly removed.

The crucial variable in support of the continuation of the IRA campaign is seen as a combination of extortion and 'foreign' influences, rather than ideological and social conditions:

> GREY: It's people like in places like America support it and give them money and keep it goin' . . . The IRA gets more powerful weapons an' that from America like . . . Yi get a builder like in Ballymurphy or somewhere an' they have ti pay out. They're gettin' plenty of money outta it.

Although the Provisionals are universally detested and held in contempt it is conceded by some that they are an extremely successful organization, which accounts for much of the fear that protestants have of them:

> IAN: The IRA are the most best trained political force in the world.

Not everyone agreed with the above statement to the same extent. Nevertheless, it does indicate a measure of 'respect' for what is perceived as a powerful and dangerous enemy. Noel, who was always quick to tell jokes about the organization ('Who's the manager of Nuneaton Rovers? Bobby Sands') also treated them as formidable foes:

> NOEL: They are training with the PLO in Israel or Palestine. . . . They know everything that's goin' on.

It was not the case that the IRA were regarded as being selective about their victims. Theirs was perceived as a basically sectarian campaign being waged by ruthless (albeit well-trained) killers who had no regard for civilian casualties. It was suggested to the respondents that many of the victims were catholic members of the security forces (a catholic UDR soldier was killed two days before the following conversation was recorded):

DEE: It's bad any UDR man getting blown up . . . even when it's one of their own [a catholic] . . . They couldn't give a fuck anyway I think. Sure when the provos are sent out to shoot a peeler and he's in the car with his kids they aren't just gonna turn round and go away because of his kids. They'd blow the head off him and it's been proved before.

NG: Do you accept a lot of catholics support the security forces? Seeing as you are actually getting some of them prepared to join?

DEE: Not in areas like Ballymurphy.

Ballymurphy was generally regarded as a 'hive of IRA activity'. Catholics who lived in middle class, 'mixed' areas would tend to be less suspected of IRA membership or support.

Sectarian incidents involving the Provisionals (or one of their 'name of convenience' off-shoots) were quickly seized on and relayed to the researcher as 'proof' of the sectarian nature of their campaign:

NOEL: Did you see that programme on Monday night about the prods being shot coming home from work? [He was referring to the 'Whitecross' or 'Bessbrook' massacre in 1976 when the Provisionals killed ten protestants.]

There was a feeling of resentment that while protestant sectarian violence was condemned unequivocally throughout the world, catholic (IRA) sectarian violence was tolerated or even approved of in some places (particularly in Great Britain, the Republic and the United States).

The security forces and paramilitary organizations

It was generally accepted that the police sided with catholic paramilitaries against protestants:

NOEL: See whenever the prods shoot anyone? The peelers always get them. See when the taigs shoot someone? They get away with it.

The latter statement, if true, is probably more a reflection of the greater affinity between the police and the protestant community in general (despite events at the time) rather than the opposite. Certainly, relations with the police and paramilitary organizations tended to be flexible for most of those we spoke with. Some were openly hostile to paramilitaries. Jane blamed 'organizations' for keeping the troubles going, rather than people's attitudes:

JANE: I think it's more the organizations to blame going out and shooting people and admitting it. What do they want? A fuckin' medal?

Nicola agreed with these comments and added:

NICOLA: Sometimes the wrong people get shot. You could be walkin' down the street and just look like someone and end up getting shot.

Paramilitary leaders were widely believed to be cynical individuals intent on 'making money out of the troubles':

NED: I know people in it with fuckin' videos, wall to wall carpet and new cars. It's all themens who are always askin' for money. If they get no money they'd have to close and we'd get peace then.

Such sentiments were expressed, surprisingly, by some junior members of organizations, who nevertheless saw them, and their role in them, as necessary evils:

ALFIE (23, UDA MEMBER): We need somebody to defend the area if the crunch comes.

Alfie was fairly typical of a section of low-ranking UDA members whose involvement was limited to 'attendin' meetings' and 'payin' yer dues'. In return they received the security of being a member and the status attached to it without having to be effectively active. They frequently referred to other UDA members as being 'gangsters' and even made fun of some of the leaders.

There was an ongoing debate concerning the effectiveness and acceptability of the security forces (the police in particular) and paramilitary organizations (the UDA and UVF). Ned pointed out that although his 'ma hates the police, every time there's a burglary or something she runs to them'. Juke thought she would be better 'running to organizations, they get things done quicker', although he conceded that this was because 'they've a protection racket'.

Beverly (whose father was a prominent UDA man) thought that 'a majority of prods don't support the UDA and UVF because they're all stick men . . . they come up and . . . beat you with sticks.' Alex had thought the nickname 'stickman' was given because 'they're all oul lads walking on sticks'. Ian believed the UDA was 'a pack of animals'. Smithey thought that the difference between the main protestant organizations was that 'the UVF are cunts and the UDA are fuckin' shites'. To this Alex added that 'the UDA are a pack of bastards, I have to laugh at them uns. They get everybody to do their work, the UDA' (he meant that the commanders gave orders which they would not be prepared to obey themselves). Beverly said she would 'rather have the UDA because the UVF are just bastards'. She seemed to be under the impression that there was more than one UDA or that it was divided into various factions: 'It depends what UDA it is really,' she replied when asked if she would be prepared to join it in the event of a civil war (it is possible she was thinking of the Ulster Freedom Fighters or UFF, which is a 'flag of convenience' label for UDA assassination squads). 'See the bastards on the

Shankill Road? They get the kids to go out and do their fuckin' jobs. My brother an' my cousin's in jail for doin' jobs.'

Others in the same project (the Lower Shankill YTP) were generally supportive of 'organizations'.

> PAULINE: I'd love ti join them but if the' asked mi to do somethin' I'd shite miself.
> SHAWSY: My mate's brother got knee-capped for doing shops 'round our way.
> NG: Do you think they should knee-cap people?
> SHAWSY: Yes because it's a warnin'. . . Nobody gets knee-capped unless they're in the wrong.

Noel, who supported loyalist paramilitaries almost unconditionally, had one form of criticism of their actions:

> NOEL: They shouldn't go about knee-capping their own. Maybe in years ti come you'd need those men ti fight.

There was often some confusion about the various organizations. Ian (the fifth former) thought that 'the UVF are part of the UDA'. His friend William thought that the UFF was just another name for the UVF. Ian thought that 'the UVF is soft' (that is, lenient, which is absurd).

'Punishment' shootings and beatings were generally regarded with mixed feelings and aroused debate on several occasions:

> CLARKEY (17): If somebody done somethin' they'd find out who it is and then bang, they're dead.
> NED: What good does that do?
> CLARKEY: He doesn't do it again ti anyone else.
> JANE: Ned, what would you rather do, be knee-capped or be in prison for twenty years?
> NED: Knee-capped.
> NICOLA: With rape cases I think they should go to an organization. They're sick, anyone like that.
> CLARKEY: Fuckin' cut it off them.

Will, from the drop-in centre, thought that the 'local recruitment' aspect of paramilitaries was significant:

> WILL: Some peelers came on the Road just for the harassment of people. Local people wouldn't do that.

Alex, from Lower Shankill, who 'hated the UVF', said he would support the UDA (whom he also hated) in a riot against the RUC: 'I hate them more because they're bastards.' Pauline said that 'everybody in here hates the peelers except Ian' (whom she regarded as a 'snob'). Ian stressed that he disliked them sometimes.

Following the death of a rioter on the Falls, who was shot at close quarters by a police plastic bullet, it was suggested to the group from the

Upper Shankill that they should have condemned this as they condemned the death of a protestant plastic bullet victim:

> DEE: The peelers have got the right ti kill an' shoot a petrol bomber. If your life's in danger or your colleague's life is in danger you're allowed ti shoot ti kill. I know 'cause my da was in the UDR. Even if yi suspect they're goin' ti endanger yer life you're allowed ti shoot the bastards.
>
> NG: Do you think they should use plastic bullets on the Shankill during riots?
>
> DEE: It's right ti say the' should be usin' them all the time but the' shouldn't use them on our road . . . because the Shankill people don't shoot at the army an' the peelers, but the taigs do.

Support for the British Army was much more forthcoming than support for the RUC. It was generally assumed, however, that the hands of the army were tied.

> DEE: If the army got their way there wouldn't be much more trouble.

Noel thought that 'they should bring back the B Specials and the Black and Tans', although he conceded that the British Army 'seem to help us'. The police, on the other hand, were unpopular with most of those in the YTPs:

> PAULINE: The' beat us up an' the' won't go near the taigs. They're scared of them.
>
> WALLY: The' think the prods are just cowardly bastards but we're not. We'll knock the ballicks outta them.

There were of course exceptions. Some of the respondents had relatives or friends of relatives who were in the RUC and these were usually regarded as 'all right'.

The police were particularly resented for what was perceived as their anti-loyalist bias in controlling parades.

> NOEL: Sure the police don't stop the taigs when they have illegal marches. But if the prods were ti hold an illegal march like the one in Portadown the' wouldn't let them march through the Tunnel [catholic area]. The prods should wise up and start shooting them.

Those policemen who were not catholics (and few believed that the RUC contained only 10 per cent catholics) were referred to generally as 'fenian lovers', which is worse than being a 'fenian' as 'fenians don't know any better'.

Ned believed that 'peelers preferred to give rioters a kickin' than arrest them as it saved paperwork'. He was referring to the riots on the Shankill during the 'Day of Action' in February 1986. He also pointed out that when the television cameras 'were on the RUC they were prepared to lose an argument like wi' yer man who was given off because the' wouldn't force him through the crowd inti work . . . If the camera hadn't bin there he would have bin told ti fuck up or fuck off.'

The police became progressively unpopular in loyalist areas throughout 1985–7 as they appeared to be to the fore in coercing protestant reaction to the Anglo-Irish Agreement.

The Anglo-Irish Agreement

The Anglo-Irish Agreement, which was implemented in November 1985, was the result of a series of consultations between the British and Irish Governments. According to the British Government it merely increased co-operation between both countries in regard to Northern Ireland without undermining the constitutional position of the Province. To the Irish it was regarded as recognition by the British that they were entitled to a say in the affairs of the North. In the unionist/loyalist population it was widely regarded as 'a sell out' – at least giving a foreign hostile country a right to interfere in the internal affairs of the Province. To many more it was a first step in a process that would quickly lead to a united Ireland outside the United Kingdom. Most protestants felt that there should have been a referendum in Northern Ireland on the legislation before it was implemented.

Most of the young people from the Shankill thought that the South had most to gain from the agreement while the North had most to lose. They thought it could lead to a united Ireland, which they felt would be disastrous:

NOEL: Fitzgerald is laughing behind Thatcher's back because he thinks he's got our airport. The' can't even run their own state. The Gippos are comin' up here from the South ti get more money.

LILY: I was in Dublin one weekend. There was three year old kids sittin' in the street with blankets 'round them beggin' for money. Them bastards walked past them and gave them nothin'. In Blackrock it's supposed ti be comin' down with everything an' the' want more money from us. Fuck off.

The penultimate sentence is an interesting common-sense working class Northern Ireland protestant interpretation of the South's claim over the North. To Lily, the Southern ruling class, not satisfied with the complete exploitation of their own citizens, are now intent on the exploitation of the Northern citizens as well – a form of what may be called 'Southern Irish imperialism'.

Lily was adamant (and plenty of others agreed with her) that the prize the South sought through the Anglo-Irish Agreement and eventual reunification was the North's industry, and particularly Belfast's shipyard. The fact that Northern Ireland is an industrial wasteland had been lost. Dee contemplated this state of affairs and replied: 'they'd still want it'. Noel thought the South's intentions were more malicious: 'If they got a united Ireland they would take advantage of it and blow the fuck out of the whole lot.' Wilbur agreed with this analysis: 'They'd run amok. They'd burn us out 'cause there'd be no one ti help us.'

Sam was one of those who thought that there was going to be a united Ireland 'sooner or later' and that the 'prods will give in'. Such attitudes prompted the usual reactions to defeatism: 'never', 'no way', 'Ulster says NO'. Sam thought catholics would eventually outvote protestants in the Province. He was quick to add: 'I went away we them once an' the' were all talkin' about a united Ireland but the' don't want ti have it.' Ned added: 'Aye, there's a whole lotta them don't want it.' Sam noted, 'because you have ti pay for yer medical an' all'. Stewarty mentioned that 'beer goes up'. Carol was more concerned that 'ev'rything goes up'.

The above examples illustrate that the young protestant population of Belfast are aware of the economic grounds for partition and that such grounds are considered sufficient to induce a significant proportion of catholics to reject the reunification of Ireland. Indeed, they considered it an absurdity for anyone to change the constitutional status on Northern Ireland on economic grounds. Margaret Thatcher was considered the main culprit in implementing the Agreement:

> STEWARTY: I think Margaret Thatcher should be shot. That's all I have ti say. She sold us out.

Sam thought that a united Ireland would lead to 'a blood bath' in which Rob thought 'we'd be wiped out'. Macker thought that if a united Ireland did materialize, 'all the top men will get out. They'll not want ti know it.' Sam had already planned for a doomsday situation:

> SAM: It'd be like Beirut. Total chaos . . . But I'll tell yi what. Before I'd move outta the estate I'd say 'wait a minute'. I'd fuckin' put a petrol bomb right down in the house. I wouldn't let them take it. I wouldn't let no bastard take over my house.

Rob was quick at this point: 'You'd be hidin' under yer bed.' Billy (from the ACE project) was more optimistic: 'I imagine they'll come tigither an' be all right.' Derek, however, thought 'that's more wishful thinking'. Macker thought even republicans did not really want a united Ireland: 'Sure they're makin' a fuckin' fortune.'

Sam, Rob and Billy were all prepared to stay in the country in the event of a united Ireland although Sam said he would fight against it. Rob conceded that 'You'd be walkin' about the street wi guns', while Derek said he would 'prefer not using violence if I could possibly help it. . . . If it got to the stage that I had to if someone was going to shoot me it's a matter of self-defence.'

> SAM: If there was a united Ireland the provos would want ti run the country and want ti be the law and ti live by their law is ti fly the tricolour an' all. I wouldn't let no tricolour fly over me.

The tricolour, the flag of the Irish Republic, is associated by Northern Ireland working class protestants with triumphalist republicanism. Rob thought that an independent Ulster 'might end up bein' the case'. Derek had doubts:

> DEREK: Would Northern Ireland be strong enough to hold its own independence? You'll have no more government funds for Harland and Wolff or Shorts and they're two of the biggest employers in Northern Ireland . . . You would have no grants to attract industry and new jobs here.

Rob added 'No ACE schemes, no YTP.' Billy thought, 'It's still one of the options that's on the cards.' Macker was convinced: 'Sure it wouldn't work'. Rob considered it better than 'surrendin' to the South'. It was widely believed that there would be some form of violent reaction to a united Ireland being imposed on Northern protestants and that, therefore, uniting the country was not a feasible political option for ending the campaign of violence:

> SAM: The taigs have bin fightin' for an All Ireland for years . . . but yi see if the' get it then the prods would be fightin' for just as long . . . ti get [the Border] back.

Ned thought that 'nine out of ten' catholics would be against a united Ireland although nine out of ten catholic politicians advocated it. Sam thought that this was because catholics like protestants to think that they could get a united Ireland if they pleased 'just to prove that they're great'.

Some of the solutions suggested to the troubles tended to be simplistic, practical and even drastic although they seemed perfectly effective, straightforward and legitimate to their adherents: 'they should bring all the prods up from Dublin and throw down there all the taigs'. It was suggested, at one stage, that the Anglo-Irish Agreement may create more employment opportunities. Ned was sceptical about this: 'The only person that will get a job will be all the undertakers . . . Maybe I'll open me own fuckin' business . . . make a fortune.' The Agreement, in general, was not regarded as having any economic or social significance and was thought to be a political disaster. It was also blamed for the deteriorating security situation and an 'appeasement' policy towards republicans.

The British and Ulster loyalism

The Anglo-Irish Agreement has served to undermine further what was already an unstable relationship between Ulster protestants and the English. For all their professed loyalty to Britain, loyalists had already considered themselves deeply betrayed by the English (and Welsh) in particular. The Scots were not included in this 'wrong-doing' because of the long historical, kinship and cultural ties between the two countries. The introduction of British troops in August 1969 (initially to defend catholic areas from ultra-loyalist attacks) marked the beginning of the realignment of loyalism (which was considered to be caused by a mixture of English incompetence, failure to 'understand' the situation, political expediency and republican sympathizers in England).

Loyalists are also aggrieved that the English have failed to treat them any differently from the rest of the Irish despite their loyalty, religious and cultural similarities, common history and British ethnic identity:

> JANE: Sure over there they think the Irish is shit and dirt. My cousin went over and once they heard her accent she got a hiding and now she's paralysed down one side.

Lily believed that Margaret Thatcher would 'give us back ti the Irish timorra if she could'.

Although they were aware of the fact that Northern Ireland is constitutionally part of the United Kindom, it was widely believed that it was not treated as such on the mainland. Media coverage was considered one of the prime indicators of this discrepancy:

> DEE: Another thing like. Ev'ry time there's a bomb over there, like the Brighton bomb, yi never hear the end e it. But ev'ry time there's one here the' say fuck all about it.

It was also considered by the Upper Shankill YTP group that a separate British identity would not be possible in an independent all-Ireland state and that protestants who thought that they would be able to remain protestants (in the *ethnic* sense) were living in a fool's paradise:

> DEE: See if Thatcher handed us over ti the Free State? See all themens sayin' they'd be all right, they'd still be prods an' all. They wouldn't wanna be prods. Same wi all themens sayin' they'd still be British. Sure that's stupid. They wouldn't want ti be British.

The contempt that many young people felt for the Royal Family was one of the most striking illustrations of the growing disillusionment with Great Britain. The Royal Family had for generations been afforded unswerving respect and servitude from Ulster protestants. Mrs Thatcher, who at the time of the IRA/INLA hunger strike and Falklands War was probably the most popular British Prime Minister ever among Northern Ireland loyalists, came to be regarded as public enemy number one by them (as well as by republicans for different reasons). She was preferred to effigies of Lundy, the Pope, De Valera, Gerry Adams and Bobby Sands for decorating the top of the 'Eleventh Night' bonfires. The contempt in which the Queen is regarded is mainly due to her *alleged* inactivity. Political figures in general were regarded similarly:

> LILY: What's she ever done for us? Sits on her fuckin' arse all day.
> DEE: Ever hear the fuckin' Queen talk about Northern Ireland like?

LILY: It would take the Queen and Maggie Thatcher to come over to Northern Ireland ti know what was fuckin' goin' on.

DEE: If yi fuckin' brought them over here the' wouldn't know their arse from their elbows.

NOEL: It's a pity she wasn't on the fuckin' space shuttle.

DEE: They're all for a united Ireland now. Sure if ye ask me themens in government, sure all the' do when the' go in there is a lotta fuckin' slabberin'.

MARTHA: Sure all yi see in that House a Commins is a pack a lazy bastards lyin' sleepin'.

Resistance to the imposition of legislation such as the Anglo-Irish Agreement was not considered to be disloyal: 'It's the Government's disloyal ti us,' as Dee had put it. It was recalled, by Dee, that Churchill was in favour of 'handing us back to Dublin but brought us back because the war was comin''. Belfast's industry and Northern Ireland's ports were considered imperative for the war effort. Indeed, Churchill later admitted that the war would have been lost without them. There were many more like Dee who would not easily forget that fact, 'Now they're doin' the same again . . . if another war comes, fuck them.' Events have not only led to a disenchantment and a growing contempt for what were previously considered almost sacred loyalist institutions, they have also heralded a disillusionment with the British political system. It is not only the ultra-right of British politics, but also the left, that has come in for increasing criticism. Attitudes of many of those we spoke to resembled attitudes of young disillusioned youth who supported organizations such as the National Front in England. Indeed, all but one of the Lower Shankill YTP male group supported the National Front and not only because of its stance on Ulster. There were distinctive racist motives for their support:

ALEX: See the fuckin' niggers? Send them back ti their bastardin' country.

WALLY: If it wasn't for your man there would be no fuckin' niggers . . . no fuckin' chinkies or nothing. You know Ken Livingstone . . . he's one fenian dirty rat.

The ethnic problem in England was associated clearly with the problem in Northern Ireland and Ken Livingstone was viewed as a common denominator, as was the National Front.

There are times when almost any public figure who is not a loyalist is perceived as being a republican, 'fenian lover' or 'provo supporter'. This was particularly true if the figure was from the South or was a catholic. Rock stars came under suspicion, as did leaders of the Peace Movement. It was widely believed that most Americans 'give the provos money because the' originate from Ireland durin' the famine'. It was well known that 'President Kennedy's relations were from here'. The fact that Kennedy was one of the few US presidents of catholic Irish stock and that at least a dozen were of Ulster protestant descent was missed.

The 'Peace People' movement was seen as something that never enjoyed the level of cross-community support attributed to it by the media. Noel said that if they marched up the Shankill now he would 'brick the fuck outta them'. The media do have a habit of clinging on to any phenomenon that they see as 'uniting catholic and protestant in Ulster'. Events at which both sides attend are hailed as 'wonders of reconciliation'. Rock concerts are one example of this. The fact that people go to see a rock concert is not seen as the primary motive. One would be led to believe that they go to be reconciled. The most famous recent example of this attitude was the Barry McGuigan phenomenon. Ian, the fifth former, called it 'all a lotta oul shit. . . . People only go ti watch him beatin' the fuck outta the other fella.' The Northern Ireland football team is another example. The fact that some of the players are catholics is held as an indication of sport 'reconciling the two communities'. However, this does not dilute one bit the fiercely ultra-loyalist and anti-catholic fervour of the Windsor Park 'Spion Kop' supporters. The above are also examples of double standards being applied when it suits to accept catholics for mutual advantages or for ensuring the continuing success and reputation of the Province. Such double standards are most clearly illustrated in attitudes to civil disorder, which we will now consider.

The riots

There was intermittent rioting throughout the period of our research in the Shankill area. Mostly it involved attacks by young people on the police. The most serious rioting occurred in February 1986, which was during the actual period that we were involved with the 'unattached'. The riots were a reaction to the Anglo-Irish Agreement in general and alleged police harassment in particular (there had been continuous claims of police harassment since the supergrass riots 16 months previously).

Alan, who participated in the rioting, exemplified the double standards that are often applied in Northern Ireland. While he complained about the police using plastic bullets to disperse Shankill rioters he thought that 'it would be all fucking right to use lead ones on the other side'. Support for the rioting was fairly evenly divided. John was against it as he thought it was wrong to attack the police, which indicates the complexity of generalizing about those we talked to. John, from his previous statements, would probably have given the impression that it was legitimate behaviour to attack the police. There is also, of course, the flexible but special relationship that protestants have with the police. The RUC is a mainly protestant force and it is in the front line against the Provisionals.

The main riot followed 'a day of action', which was a Province-wide strike. Fervour had increased throughout the day as the RUC were unable effectively to stop intimidation. Intimidation was denied by the organizers although, as Martha put it, 'no bastard should have been at work anyway'. Noel thought that half the people who complained of having their cars hijacked only did this to get insurance money. Martha thought 'it was brilliant after the electric went out and we watched the cars burn'. Alice thought it was 'all right ti shoot at the peelers as they shot too'. It was suggested to her that the police only shot in self-defence to which she replied: 'Sure the fuckin' peelers are fenian lovers.'

Lily was against the riots on the grounds that 'they wrecked the Shankill'. She seriously suggested that if the rioters were prepared to move on to the Falls Road to attack the police then she would support them. The school group, however, told us two days before the riot: 'We're hopin' there's gonna be a riot wi'the peelers.'

As may be expected, the riots were roundly criticized by the Christians. As one of them explained:

> CHRISTIAN: I do not agree with the Anglo-Irish Agreement but at the same time I don't agree with the violence that's happened . . . you couldn't get down the Shankill. I was nervous. They're wrecking their own road and their own people's cars. I agree something has to be done but I don't think what happened on Monday night is the answer.

The same respondent did agree with the strike and thought that many of the rioters had been 'worked up' by politicians at a public meeting. Another respondent was critical of the intellectual and mental powers of the rioters:

> CHRISTIAN: I don't think people sit down and think about it. If you wreck a shop you're putting ten or fifteen people out of work. It's really crazy . . . they're probably so stupid they don't think about that.

Another respondent simply added that 'they've no respect for people's property'. The first respondent thought that 'it seems to me it gives them a kick'. He was also highly critical of the rioters:

> CHRISTIAN: If you look at the likes of Brixton and those places in England. If there's a riot there's an inquiry into why the riot occurred. I guarantee the group of people who are doing the enquiry would say it's because they're deprived. . . . I was brought up on the Shankill Road and times were hard, but at the same time you don't go around wrecking places.

Clearly, this respondent saw rioting as a personality trait inherent in some individuals while lacking in others. Sharkey thought a 'hell of a lot of people only went on strike for an excuse to get a day off work'. Nicola thought that most of those on strike would be afraid to go to work. Noel shouted this remark: 'You take it, there's 23 thousand members of the

UDA and there's a fuckin' lotta them work . . . and plus the UVF and other groups.' (The UDA did not formally support the day of action.)

The greatest dilemma in events such as these falls on those who work in a place almost exclusively of the opposite religion. If they attend work they are branded a blackleg by their neighbours. If they do not go they are facing the risk of being regarded as an extremist by their work friends:

> LILY: There's a girl I know works in the _____ [city centre pub] where there's all taigs in there and she's been told to go to work on Monday. My ma says 'let on yi got ti the bottom of the fuckin' street and someone threatened you' . . . and my ma says 'go down the road an' I'll fuckin' threaten yi'.

Ironically, the Anglo-Irish Agreement, which was supposed to help bring stability to the Province, has had the opposite effect. It was widely believed that people who were 'getting sick of the troubles' before the agreement have been incited to resume violent activity:

> FROGGIE: Before Thatcher made that agreement, I think it was getting on better than ever. There was no killings. It wasn't as bad as it is now.

This is an optimistic view of what conditions were like before the Agreement. Others, however, thought that there was a general trend towards rejection of violence in recent years:

> NED: People are just gettin' sick of it. It's goin' on too long. . . . I think most of it is breaking away . . . all this King Billy shit.

The contradictions in the unionist bloc were becoming apparent to some and this was serving to undermine traditional views of loyalism:

> BILLY: If you're a loyalist what are you loyal to now?

This is the paramount question that has dominated Ulster protestant political thinking since 1969. Before that the question would not have inspired much thought. Loyalty to Britain, to the Crown, was inherited, taken-for-granted and *apparently* unconditional. The continuing conflict since 1969 has served to remind the Protestants that there were conditions and it is these that are now being re-negotiated in the ideological and political spheres. Furthermore, rather than 'loyalty' meaning loyalty to Britain and/or the Crown, the emergence of Ulster nationalism has brought a new dimension to the debate. Increasingly loyalism has come to mean 'loyalty to Ulster', and this is a somewhat vague but much more pragmatic position for the loyalists. The final section in this chapter will consider the problem of identity, for young people of the Shankill, more closely.

Identity

One of the most dramatic changes in protestant political culture over the past 15 years has been that the old political certitudes provided by traditional unionism have disappeared, for the young at least. Our work with the formal youth work participants showed that class, club, age and gender were all significantly correlated with political affiliation and values. Identification with Ulster, as distinct from Britain or Northern Ireland, was more pronounced as one descended the class scale, attended less formal clubs, grew older (less parental influence) and with boys as distinct from girls. This trend, generally, was continued with the unattached.

One of the overriding patterns to emerge from our discussions with young protestants is that when they speak of Ulster they are not merely referring to a place. They are also implying a particular form of lifestyle, which they at times attempt to make explicit through formal and informal rituals and social practices. This would support and be supported by Bell's (n.d.) study in Derry. Consider the following reply by one of his interviewees when asked what the term 'Ulster' meant to them:

> Sometimes it doesn't mean anything if you see someone writing ULSTER say at Christmas or something . . . but when it comes up to the Twelfth (of July) it seems to mean more to everybody. Ye see more people writing, ye seem to notice it more. Like if ye went past a fence now and seen it you'd begin to notice it 'cause it's coming up to the Twelfth. . . . I don't think Ulster is meant to be a place . . . it's just meant to be the protestant people . . . it's the North of Ireland but it isn't any particular place – it's just protestant.

The 'youth culture' of the protestant young is a mixture of the trends, fashions and music of youth sub-culture throughout Britain and the unique ethnic identification with the symbols and rituals of being 'Ulster'. When asked their nationality, protestant youths (and many adults too) will frequently reply 'Ulster'. Ulster applies to much more than one's nationality, though. They are referring to a whole lifestyle, which encompasses a national/ethnic consciousness (which is neither British nor Irish though it contains elements of both), a religious identification (even with the secular 'prods'), political sympathies (the vague 'loyalist') and social behaviour (as distinct from what they perceive as catholic social behaviour).

Noel attended the 'Loyalist' (a UDA drinking and social club) but it was not to participate in paramilitary activity ('there was a good group there'). He listed his favourite music as Dire Straits, Big Country, Queen and UVF music (UVF music refers to rather up-dated versions of Orange traditional songs, some revamped contemporary popular tunes lauding the qualities of 'Ulster', and even some stolen 'rebel' tunes, with an appropriate re-wording process where necessary).

It was widely believed that, for all its problems, Ulster was the 'best wee place in the world'. One of the most noticeable characteristics of the

'Ulster' character is its parochialism. Many Ulster protestants believe that Belfast is the hub of the British Empire (which they believe still exists). They believe its shipyard, aircraft factory, linen industry and so on (despite their chronic recession) are the best anywhere. The Ulster countryside has the best scenery and Belfast the finest buildings. They believe they are the friendliest people in the world and that the food, social habits and climate here are 'hard ti whack'. They believe their sports teams are the best and that they are the most tolerant people you could meet. It follows from all this that there is an air of self-confidence about the Ulster character that at times borders upon arrogance. They are quite prepared to take on Britain even if it means going to war with Britain in order to remain British. This arrogance and self-importance (or delusion?) was exhibited by the unionist parliamentary candidates in the 1987 Westminster election, when they actually believed (or said they did) that the crucial issue in the campaign (on the mainland as well as in Northern Ireland) was going to be the Anglo-Irish Agreement, which the British people were going to reject (the great majority of British people had no interest whatsoever in the matter).

Lily was one of those who did not think the world ended at Belfast Lough. She frequently expressed a desire to go 'somewhere like Spain' although she was reluctant, as her father had wished, to emigrate to Australia: 'ye'd have ti start all over again'. Wilbur was adamant that she would 'get shot in Spain' as it was 'worse than here'. Lily thought there was 'nowhere worse than here'. Wilbur pointed out that 'the' don't like foreigners there, like the Irish or anything'.

Noel often said, 'I was born in this country an' I'll die in this country.' When asked what he thought was so good about it he replied: 'its scenery, its history'. Wilbur thought, 'there's nothin' good about it', but he was quite prepared to 'fight for it'. He did not know why he would be prepared to fight for something he thought had nothing good about it.

Lily said that she liked the friendship: 'There's cheeky bastards ev'rywhere else now. The Irish and the British are the best mannered people anywhere'. Lily referred to her sister, Martha, as a 'stupid cunt . . . had the opportunity ti go ti France an' all an' turned it fuckin' down'. Despite her ambition to travel Lily always maintained she would never live anywhere else.

Although the youth of the Shankill are vague about the reasons why they wish to remain there despite its limitations, we may assume that there is a definite identification with the area ('a great wee place') and that this is premised upon a certain lifestyle (kinship patterns, friends, community, social life, culture) that they inherit and develop. 'Being a prod' is part of this lifestyle. To different people this meant different things. Noel thought that 'ti be a prod you have to be loyal to your fellow citizens' (meaning 'fellow prods'). Lily thought that a 'true prod' would have to be 'in the Orange Order and go to church'.

In terms of national identity an affinity to Ulster was preferred to British. In some cases there was a definite aversion to being called British as this was seen as synonymous with the English. While some preferred 'Northern Irish' nobody seemed to identify themselves as 'Irish (although a few said that they were Irish as well as British). Alex hated the English to the extent that he at times disassociated himself from them: 'I'm an Ulsterman before I'm British . . . they're [the English] all bastards.' Wally shared this view: 'If someone were ti call me fuckin' British I'd kick the ballicks outta them . . . see the English I fuckin' hate them. They think they're fuckin' it . . . but I hate the taigs more.' Pauline indicated on a number of occasions that she 'didn't like fuckin' British people; while her friend, Beverly, was adamant to describe herself as an 'Ulsterwoman' although she was 'British before I'd be Irish'. One of the group did add that 'us Ulster are Irish', which was perhaps one way of solving the national dilemma, while others described themselves as 'Ulster British'.

The Irish in general were associated with Catholicism, which all of those in the Lower Shankill YTP group regarded as 'foreign'. Most distinctively Irish things were alien to them, such as the Gaelic language, 'It's a foreign language, it's like Jewish.' Nigel, though, thought that basically catholic interests were much the same as those of protestants 'They just want ti make a livin' that's all. That's all anybody wants ti do.'

Irish history, as taught in catholic schools, was considered by those in the ACE project as a distorted representation of fact. Tommy insisted that the catholics had 'stolen' heroes from Ulster history:

TOMMY: They had ti take our history like yer man Colhoun [Culhulin, who in legend defended the ancient kingdom of Ulster against the Gaels] . . . the' stole him. Sure he's outside the GPO down in Dublin . . . the' stole him from here.

Tommy also referred to Robert Emmet (leader of the 1802 Irish Rebellion) as a 'fuckin' good prod' and said that the 1798 Rebellion 'was nearly all prods too'. The role of protestants in Irish nationalist rebellions was a topic of some interest although, as John put it, 'things have fuckin' changed now'. Tommy also considered that 'yer fella James Connolly was a prod as well'. Sometimes specific incidents in Irish history involving protestants were recalled, although the names of the characters had been forgotten:

JUKE: Yer man was in jail as well an' the' fuckin' chopped his head off an' the' got a boat it was full of ammunition an' all. It was the British that fuckin' took over it.

Most of those in the ACE project were more inclined towards an Irish identity, which they thought was an important part of their heritage although it was being denied them because of the close affinity between Catholicism and things Irish:

TOMMY: We're all Irish.

JOHN: But they (the catholics) don't think we are.

JUKE: Originally we're all Irish.

Although they considered themselves Irish, however, they qualified this by stressing their British nationality:

NED: We are British because this is British territory we're in like. We have ti be British . . . catholics are British too because they were from here.

One of the males thought that Northern Ireland 'was an Irish state before protestants took it over – before King Billy took it over'. Ned considered that 'Gaelic used ti be a protestant language and then the catholics took that over'. 'Britishness' to Ned was just a fact of life, something he had been born into and he thought that 'everybody's the same . . . same blood an' all'. Nationality to him, like religion, was unimportant:

NED: They should stop the whole lot of it, catholic and protestant religion . . . All the countries are all the same too. Just all bits of muck and bits of land like. It's only border divides it. There's all there is till it.

Carol thought that catholics and protestants had much more in common than what divided them: 'sure some catholics fought in the world war'. Stewarty had doubts about King William of Orange: 'You never know. Sure King Billy was meant ti be a taig . . . for all yi know there could a bin catholics fightin' on his side' (there were). Ned thought it was 'a wonder the catholics don't celebrate the Twelfth' especially after he had been informed that William had the Pope's blessing. It was suggested that protestants should then celebrate the 1798 rebellion as protestants fought in that. Sam replied to this: 'No . . . that's anti–British isn't it?' Ossie did not understand why catholics commemorated Wolfe Tone: 'he was a prod wasn't he?' This was proof to Sam that 'the oul taigs don't know what they're at', while Stewarty thought that he was 'probably an oul provie in disguise lettin' on he was a prod'. When informed that the Presbyterians in the North had supported Tone and that some of the group's ancestors may have fought on his side, Sam quipped, 'Don't tell me that or I'll go out an' shoot miself . . . was there anybody called Mason there?' (Sam's surname).

National identity, for protestant youths, is much more complex now than in the past as a result of the ongoing political crisis. There were several quite common definitions of their nationality ranging from British, Northern Irish and Ulsterish to British Irish and, as Barbara put it, 'I wouldn't call myself nothing'.

Conclusion

What we have attempted to present in this chapter is an examination of the cultural content and practices of working class protestant youth in West

Belfast. Our intention here was to present a picture of their culture that would illustrate why the working class 'counter-culture' they inherit is contrary to the aims, objectives and practices of formal youth provision as it is presently structured. Basically, what we are saying is that a significant proportion of working class youth exclude themselves, or are excluded by others, from formal youth work because it is not relevant to their needs and aspirations.

The young people of the Shankill experience the institutions of society in everyday life, be they school, work, police or youth club. Their encounters with such institutions are often precarious and this is because they experience such bourgeois institutions from a working class position. An adequate understanding of their reaction would require an analysis of working class cultural contents and the position of the young in regard to these. This is what we have attempted here. The most striking feature of the behaviour (or cultural expression) of the unattached is its informality. It is through an informal approach to alien institutions that they are able to make sense of their position ('keeping things basic'), justify it ('we call a spade a spade') and perhaps improve it (through informal group or individual activities).

This has wide-ranging implications for those involved with youth work. Clearly youth provision (especially in the 16+ range) would need to be much less formal and should concentrate on preparing the young for adulthood. Activities are fine but the crucial problem for adolescents is growing to maturity. The informal group (or 'gang') provides the structure that is best suited to many working class needs at this age. It is in such groups that young people receive the recognition they need.

As Jane put it about 'anti-social' behaviour, 'I think it's got a lot ti do with attention.' Formal youth work has never really made any inroads in this direction. Perhaps it could, through providing more counselling and work in groups (discussions and practical or social activities).

Paramount, of course, to youth provision is the need to provide some sort of enjoyment. We would stress that this needs to be closely harnessed to the local environment and social aspirations of the would-be recipients. We recall our accounts of the overwhelming success (yet informality) of the early youth initiatives in the Shankill and Ballymurphy. Such initiatives 'worked' and had wide appeal because they grew out of and directly responded to particular environments and needs that the recipients were experiencing and could identify with. We must also get away from the idea that youth work must be preoccupied with 'getting the kids off the streets'. There are plenty of enjoyable, rewarding and sociable activities that young people can participate in 'on the streets'.

Our research has illustrated that the ethos of many clubs and organizations is alien to a large proportion of the young working class. Most of the clubs in the Shankill are church-controlled and it is difficult to imagine someone like, say, Dee finding those attractive. Most of the clubs have a list of rules that users must adhere to. One common rule is 'no swearing'.

That just about excludes all who are mentioned in this chapter (except the Christians). Furthermore, a formal youth and recreation provision falls far short of attracting a large number of girls (except, maybe, on disco night). It seems to be quite content with the idea of keeping working class girls 'in the home'. Clearly, the structural changes that have occurred in society (male unemployment, female employment and equality of opportunity, etc.) have not been mirrored by the social priorities. Surely it should be the role of organized youth work to correct this imbalance, where girls are still being encouraged to stay at home and 'mind the kids', 'help mother' and so on.

Youth clubs also tend to close early and that would be particularly unappealing to many in the 16+ age bracket who are just growing into adulthood and who prefer to stay out that bit later than, say, a 12 or 13 year old. They should also be given more responsibility. They are no longer 'kids'. They are young adults. This would be achieved through an integrated approach, which would harness youth to community work and local needs, thus fostering a closer identification with the youth club. As Jane said, 'you would look on it as your own house.' It is not that long ago since the streets were regarded in a similar manner.

Finally, as the discussions on social problems and conflict illustrated, there was a sense of confusion, misunderstanding and, at times, fear concerning the effects that these may have on the young. If we fail to understand and negate these it should come as no surprise when the reaction of those who are subjected to such impositions is confused, misunderstood and often violent.

7 WORKING CLASS YOUTH IN BALLYMURPHY

The field work for this chapter was carried out over a period of six months in the predominantly catholic Upper Springfield. A large percentage of the research was carried out with females, with a total of 50 being involved. They were drawn from the following categories: single parents, a school truant group attending a community house, unemployed females, females who attended a formal youth club, females who congregated in a leisure centre, females within their home and school attenders. They were aged 13–23 and five were married.

There were 30 males interviewed in the age range 12–33. They were drawn from the following groups: an unemployed group, a school group, leisure centre users, males congregating on street corners, those interested in a sport, school truants who attended a community house, formal youth club users and males who did not use any facility. Ten of the males were married.

Youth sub-culture and gender

Many theories of youth sub-culture ignore any examination of the role of women within this culture. These theories concentrate upon a patriarchal view of culture and in themselves are reticent about the role of women. Any mention of the female in relation to culture is and has always been linked to her position with regard to and relationship with males, as opposed to her individuality as a female. Her social class also labels her, in that working class women are seen as home keepers whose rights to independence are stifled.

As Janice Winship states, 'Woman is a feminine individual whose individuality and implied independence are recuperated by patriarchal relations . . . ideological constructions are still pervasively at work today' (Winship 1982: 11–12). In order to examine the reason why woman's individuality is recuperated by patriarchal relations it is necessary to examine the culture of those working class males who represent patriarchality.

The sub-culture of males

This section will offer an insight into the culture of young males from catholic West Belfast. It will deal with such issues as their attitudes to work and unemployment, school, relationships, social activities and delinquency. It will not be as detailed an analysis as that of the culture of females. However, it will offer a general overview of the culture of young males from West Belfast. Most of the males were interviewed on street corners, although a few were interviewed in structured group sessions. The majority of the males were generally enthusiastic about being inter-viewed and enjoyed talking about subjects not normally discussed at the street level. Most of them were good conversationalists and they were always keen to challenge views. It is through such an examination of the male culture that we are able to examine the culture of females and their relationship with the patriarchal structure of society. Neither cultures can be examined in isolation from the other as they are intertwined.

Male attitudes to work and unemployment

> Well, it's hard to talk about work. I've never had a job. I can only talk about the kind of job I'd like. I've been unemployed for two years now, dead boring. I'd love to work on a building site, it would be great crack, great loyalty from your mates, then going out on Fridays for a pint with your mates, plus feeling that you're doing something important.

Most of the males interviewed, although unemployed, did want to find a job. Many of them talked about wanting to be 'breadwinners' and feeling bad about not having a job. They wanted a job that offered them comradeship, self worth, 'good crack' and money. They seemed to lack confidence when dealing with females and could only relate to them with a very domineering, sarcastic and patronizing manner. This cultural tradition was forced upon most males by their working class fathers. In turn the females related to them by shouting and competing for the limelight. This aggressive attitude has become a new trait of the working class woman, who uses it to get attention. Consequently, most of the unemployed males lacked social skills such as communicating their thoughts, needs and wants.

The majority of these males suggested that they only attended the 'unemployed club' because there was nowhere else to go. They often expressed the feeling of boredom and frequently talked about doing potentially exciting things. They spent their dole money on buying bottles of cider or drinking at the street corners at weekends. The trait of drinking at the street corners has a particular significance, which gives an image within their own communities. They often went to a local disco but once they went there they had no money left for the remainder of the week – they would often spend £30 in a night because spending vast amounts of money proves your worth within such cultural groupings.

Many had relationships with females and were already engaged. Yet they felt it was important to 'get out with the mates' as well. This 'going out with the mates' was an integral part of their culture. They presented the image of not caring for their female counterparts, but when this attitude was challenged many of them did admit to caring for their girl-friends. The traditional pattern of men not showing their feelings was reinforced by females who did not want a man 'to act like a wimp'.

In general most of these males were resentful of the police force (RUC) and the British Army. They felt that the police force and the army were unduly antagonistic towards them, stopping them in the streets, searching their clothes and asking questions. Many had been involved in riots with the police and army and this was seen as an expression of the young catholic male's political feelings about 'the Brits' in Ireland.

They felt that aggression was an important part of their male image. It was important to 'fight for a cause', 'defend a mate in a fight', fight for a girl and defend members of their family. This was an integral part of their male culture and there was a tremendous degree of loyalty among them. The group, its culture and the parent culture were the main influences on shaping their identity.

Consequently the unemployed males felt threatened by females who had achieved more in educational terms than themselves. Hence they treated such females with contempt and were usually patronizing and abusive towards them. Similarly, females who had jobs were treated with con-tempt, joked about, abused and laughed at. The patriarchal base of the males' socialization process was threatened by this role reversal. Their sense of male pride and masculinity always seemed threatened by females who had achieved more than they had. Many dealt with the situation by physically and verbally abusing their women, which in turn would keep their women 'in their proper place'.

The effects of being unemployed were devastating for most males. Not only did it threaten the whole base of their socialization but it also placed them in a position of vulnerability, where their role as breadwinner, provider and ruler seemed threatened. The consequences for their personal lives and social standing in the community were severe.

Male attitudes to school

'School is crap, it doesn't prepare you for life. Anyway I always hiked off school. I've been expelled a few times as well. Who wants to learn about history and all that crap. The teachers are useless in my school – they can't teach.' Most of their attitudes to school were negative. They talked about 'messing around' and 'getting a good rake' – 'that's the best thing about school'. As Paul Willis (1979) noticed: 'it is during the 3rd or 4th year that many males rebel against the rules . . . it is during this stage when the individual develops an analysis of his social position vis-a-vis the school and the people in it.' Many of the males interviewed were 14 and 15 year olds who would fall into this category. Willis defines such males as 'the lads never listening, always doing'. Most of these males opted out of class work. In a sense they may be viewed as protecting their alternative culture against the pressure of the school. Their alternative culture consisted of smoking, kidding and 'taking the piss out of' schoolmates or teachers, and joyriding. By no means were the least able the only ones involved in this counter-school group. In fact many of the males interviewed were street-wise and had a well developed interest in contemporary politics. But their main interest in attending school was to mess around and have a laugh. The act of studying for exams was frowned upon by the anti-school group members. Most of the males interviewed belonged to this anti-school group, and were often anti-family, anti-female and anti-law.

The culture of this anti-school group offered much excitement and adventure and they met outside of school hours and maintained many of the same cultural practices. Male or female teachers had little or no control over the escalation of their cultural practices within the classroom. Their actions would appear to be a reaction to either the negative teaching methods or their negative view of the value of what was being taught, alongside a confusion about how education affected their lives as young catholic males in a working class community with no future.

Male attitudes to relationships

An integral part of the masculine culture is seen to be carrying out the roles of boyfriend, husband, provider, dominator, breadwinner, political activist and community leader. When these roles are altered by the impact of unemployment, relationships are inevitably affected. When the female is slotted into the position of provider and breadwinner, the relationship between male and female is greatly affected. Although this is prevalent in working class areas, 'doing the double' (working illegally while claiming social security) becomes the alternative that offers the male his role as a working class man with money in his pocket.

Many of the female partners of the males we interviewed were in the position of earning money and this had severe consequences for the male. Consequently, many expressed the feeling of being useless and less independent. In return this greatly affected the culture of the specific males whose patriarchal hegemony had been threatened. Many felt they were 'losing control over their relationships', 'losing control over their female partners', 'females were wanting too much freedom', 'females going out with their mates' and so on.

The male's threatened social status as head of household and bread-winner had profound effects on how he approached and dealt with relationships. Many of the males felt that the best way to regain this control was verbally or physically to abuse their female partners. This was a phenomenon accepted by quite a number of males and females. Many felt that once they became engaged to their girlfriends their degree of control should be increased. Likewise, the act of marriage was seen as possession in many eyes. 'Well, now that you are my wife it's different, you do exactly as I say.' All these attitudes are an integral part of the working class culture, particularly for unemployed males whose social standing is threatened.

In the area of romance many males laughed at other males who talked about buying their girls flowers or cards, or taking them out for a romantic meal. As one male said: 'I take my girl to the Chinese for a curry chip and that's as far as she gets.' Yet many younger males were romantic although they were afraid to express it and did not have steady relationships.

Most believed that sex was a very important part of their relationships and that the Catholic religion would not prevent them from experimenting with sex and having pre-marital sex. It was apparent that sexual exploits were another integral part of the male culture and quite acceptable within their social class.

Most believed that women should stay at home and look after the children. They thought that their freedom should be uninterrupted by an act of marriage. Some of the males felt that faithfulness was a very important part of their relationships while others did not. Being faithful is becoming a very controversial issue, with many changing to this belief because of AIDS. Some of the males were verbally abusive about females who had more than one relationship at a time, calling them names like 'slut', 'whore' and 'slag'. Yet they felt it was a commendable asset for a male. In their words, 'Males are allowed to sleep around, it's OK, it's expected from him, it's different for women.' The act of enjoying sexual exploits was considered to be a totally male phenomenon.

Many of the younger males, aged 15 and 16, felt that 'wee girls' were a waste of time: 'Who wants a girl?' This attitude was common among the anti-school group, who preferred to spend their free time raking and having fun. The older males felt, on occasions, that they had been forced into relationships.

> Because your mates all split up and go their separate ways especially when you're about 17 . . . then you think to yourself . . . well, I suppose I had better get a girl . . . because my mates will think I'm a fruit [homosexual] if I don't . . . but wee girls can be too demanding.

Therefore, it would seem that the issue of homosexuality is one of the reasons why a few of the males form relationships with females. It is interesting to note that many of the males found females to be demanding and those females interviewed found the males to be demanding.

Many felt it was their duty as a male to get married and reproduce. The act of reproduction and becoming a father gave many young males the status they lacked as an unemployed male. Hence, many of the males interviewed were already young unmarried fathers. Being able to impregnate a woman is of the utmost relevance to their gender and culture.

Most older males interviewed had negative views about relationships, whereas many of the younger males were more optimistic. The majority of males felt that they were forced into relationships as the strong peer group disbanded. Yet even within relationships most males felt that it was crucially important to maintain contact with their 'mates'. The majority of them viewed women as slotting into the role of traditional girlfriend, wife and mother, where she was to remain submissive regardless of her individuality, job or ambitions.

> They keep you down, always nagging and telling you not to go out, always asking where you've been, wanting to know every bloody thing that goes on. I've hit my girl a few times, it does her good to be hit, beat some sense into her, give her a few kicks and then you can go out with your mates whenever you like.

Male attitudes to social activities and leisure

'Well we spend most of our leisure time in the social clubs, at the leisure centre, hanging about the streets, drinking and doing other things we can't mention to you.' This comment reflects the attitudes of the males we interviewed to leisure and social activities. These attitudes to leisure ignore an important facet: the role of females within it. They are culturally socialized to distance themselves from including women in their leisure time pursuits. It is significant that males define their leisure time without any mention of women. Yet most of the females interviewed defined their leisure time as centring on the male. However, these attitudes to leisure serve to reiterate the male culture: drinking, hanging about the streets and becoming involved in activities that can't be named. Such activities may range from illegal membership of paramilitary organizations to an indulgence in 'anti-social' activities which are further used to convince working class males of their position as working class males in that area.

Leisure is very important for males. 'I wouldn't go to any local youth club or anything. In our free time we like to hang about the streets, drink cider, get a chase from the police. Can't do that in a youth club, too strict. Prefer to hang about streets, more fun.' This youthful drinking is an aspect of the more general search for excitement, male group solidarity and occasional confrontations with authority. These activities are an integral part of the male cultural group. Without such 'leisure' activities many of these groups would cease to exist. The very existence of leisure facilitates the reinforcement of male cultural exploits.

Many of the younger males who belonged to the anti-school group were involved in anti-social and illegal activities. It might be that they become involved in these delinquent leisure time activities as a result of their disappointment with their failures in school, or the class/ethnic pressure that achievers are not real males. On certain occasions it would appear that such males may turn this disappointment into a blaming of the system, hence delegitimizing previously subscribed social mores. They then become involved in joyriding (stealing cars) and robbing local shops.

Many of the older males were secretive about their anti-social activities and did not wish to disclose any information about them. Yet most of them spent most of their leisure time hanging about on local street corners. Their degree of geographic mobility was very limited and they were very territorial. Much of their leisure time was spent patrolling their local streets in order to investigate the whereabouts of potential strangers. Many admitted to 'protecting their area from those ones up the road or down the road'. This territory provided them with a strong bond and these strong bonds often developed into gang rivalry, which preoccupied the leisure time of many of the young males. Most of those interviewed said they would not go into a protestant area (females were more willing to move in and out of different religious areas).

Some of the males interviewed belonged to specific sub-cultural groups, such as skinheads or trendies. These sub-cultural groups spent most of their leisure time reinforcing their specific cultural practices. As Hall *et al.* (1978) says: 'Skinheads may be a reaction against contamination of the parent culture by middle class values and a reassertion of the integral values of working class culture through its most recessive traits, puritanism and chauvinism.' In fact many of the skinhead males were puritanical and chauvinistic in their attitudes, but not all were. The group of trendy males may be viewed as representing the popular trend in fashion. Their social activities encompassed things like weight training, disco dancing and night clubbing. This group were more socially mobile, whether employed, unemployed or attending school. They appeared to be more idealistic in outlook, searching for females from different social backgrounds. Many of this group were older, with a few of them having been involved in criminal activities in the past. They were very socially skilled in their dealing with people, particularly skilful in communicating with females. Yet their attitudes to females reflected those of their counterparts, although many were married.

Generally speaking most of the males interviewed spent a great deal of their leisure time in the company of other males from their particular cultural sub-groupings. These sub-groupings offered them a constructive outlet in leisure time. They had much to offer: common attitudes, solidarity, similar music tastes, similar dress sense, similar outlook on life, similar age range and comradeship. These facets can be found in both the trendy and skinhead groups. This feeling of making use of leisure time was vitally important for most males interviewed, regardless of their age. It is interesting to reiterate the apparent absence of females in their recollections of leisure time. It is obvious that the male culture is of vital importance to all the males interviewed. Their cultural variations into youth cultural activities were tolerated to the extent that phases of growing up were controllable and finally they would return to their real roots and develop the image expected of them from their fathers. This culture gives males greater freedom in that their male cultural syndrome is a microcosm of the larger community and society within which patriarchal social relations are deeply embedded.

The sub-culture of females

The culture of femininity has been structured in relation to the dominant culture and many assertions of femininity are based upon male attributes. As Janice Winship states,

> Women are ardent consumers of products by virtue of being women; their class position is only secondary. . . . Women's structural subordination in the site of the family where motherhood throws you back into the natural and economic dependence on men is displaced from view.
>
> (Winship 1982: 13–14)

As the interviews with the young females below indicate, the female's free choice is associated with femininity. Her individuality is subjected to femininity and patriarchal relations. The female is an individual whose individuality and implied independence are mediated by patriarchal relations, particularly in working class communities. These assumptions will be explored under the following subject areas: females and leisure; females and work; females and education; fashion and style for females; females – marriage and romance; females and roles (roles within the family and roles within the local community with reference to relationships).

Females and leisure

There was until recently an apparent absence of literature on females in research on youth. In terms of leisure, females can be seen killing time in streets, shopping centres and in town. Consequently women are perceived as objects of leisure by men: 'men's pleasure is women's leisure'. Men's leisure often depends upon female participation. Women's leisure patterns are subordinate to and supportive of those of men: 'Well I'll have to wait to see what he's doing before I can decide what I'm doing'. The central factor in the nature of leisure for women is gender and for most girls choosing the right mate is a vital part of unwaged work and leisure.

The construction of femininity itself can take a considerable amount of leisure time, both inside and outside waged or unwaged work. Females service men's leisure and they are an integral part of it, as they see it: 'I love to get my make up on especially when we're going out to get a boy.' Most of the females interviewed felt that it was important to 'look good for men'. This vicious trap causes tension for women who want a different leisure world to participate in but are not allowed to deviate by mothers, friends or sisters because it is not 'culturally' acceptable.

It seems then that females are not totally free to enjoy leisure activities, such as the television, the radio or going out, because of the constraints attached. As one girl said, 'I sometimes never get a chance to listen to the radio or TV because I'm always being hassled by someone in the house to do something else.' The tensions of being a female in a working class community are enormous.

Another constraint facing the young female's leisure time is her lack of money. Material inadequacy can prevent the young working class female from enjoying her leisure time. Very often a female's leisure time is restricted by housework. It is this experience of femininity, its construction in relation to men, that determines her leisure patterns and what kind of activities leisure involves. If she doesn't do housework she is classified as dirty or 'a trollop'.

Most of the females interviewed did attempt to find some time for leisure and when they did they were more than willing to move out of their immediate environment in search of it. They were more likely to do this than boys. Many of them were particularly mobile in that they would use their leisure time to venture into town, where 'both religions' meet. The phenomenon of a girls' night out was something more common to the older girls. This phenomenon of collective taxis home, dancing together, staying overnight with friends and singalongs seems to indicate that an autonomous and supportive female culture exists among working class females. In fact this is commonplace for many groups of working class females. Although the girls' night out seemed a quest for autonomy, this movement was tolerated as an integral part of the cultural world of the males, who viewed this as a means of having a good night with the lads instead. The older females interviewed did seem to enjoy leaving their male partners for one evening. However, this evening out caused many disagreements and tensions between partners, particularly when males had nothing organized.

Within these communities many females had strong friendship networks in which sisterhood and solidarity were important. Yet the central thrust of the females' leisure time was spent searching for the right mate. Most of the girls interviewed had found boyfriends within their local area, which often meant that leisure time activities were spent indoors with male partners. Yet it is this sisterhood that reminds the woman of her roots, her culture, her role and her gender, and does not allow her to deviate from them.

Females and work

Janice Winship (1982: 14) has stated 'that the feminine appearance is linked to work'. Yet many of the females in the study would not provide evidence to substantiate such a claim. Many of the females interviewed were unemployed, single parents, working on Youth Training Schemes or had very menial jobs and never had the opportunity to experience work. Despite this they were immaculate in appearance and well 'made-up'. They did not view housework as 'work': 'It's just a normal thing that you have to do when you're a girl. Our brothers don't have to do anything.' It is the very privatized nature of housework that reinforces the isolation of the individual woman in the home. This is one of the most recognizable sites of her oppression. The laborious nature of this kind of housework often isolates many females from contact with the world outside their front doors. Many females feel that the tension of their gender creates a situation in which 'it's better to do housework than to be called lazy'.

The females who did work were often employed as cleaners, shop assistants, storepersons in local supermarkets, cafe workers, or in other poorly paid jobs. Such jobs are commonplace to the majority of working class women. As Winship (1982: 14) states: 'Working class women tend to get the invisible work, they are workers who do the menial and monotonous jobs . . . middle class white girls tend to get jobs which are visible symbols of male prestige.' However, although many of the working class girls interviewed did have low-paid menial jobs, they expressed pride and appreciation at having 'any kind of job'. In this sense they were conditioned to accept their lot.

In a sense the origin of the girls' pride at having jobs stemmed from the fact that many of their male partners were unemployed. This created a situation whereby many of those females who worked were less financially dependent upon their male partners. Resulting from this a strong degree of conflict and tension arose within their relationship. Yet many females believed that holding the purse strings was a form of power.

Most of the females were supportive of their male counterparts, often buying clothes for their partners and offering them money to go out with 'the lads' drinking on a Friday night. This financial independence gave many of them a sense of security, which was not visible among the females who did not work. Yet it did not give them a sense of emotional security and independence. It did provide many with an opportunity to buy clothes, magazines, make up, etc., and to become active participants in a mass consumer market, where the female has become a major target. Many of them said things like 'OK, we have jobs but they're not well paid and it doesn't mean you don't have to do the housework, you must be kidding. When I come home from work I always have to do the housework.'

Housework is an integral part of a woman's working week and it is always unpaid work regardless of a female's commitments, whether they be caring for sick members of her family, a full-time paid job or being a single parent. The patriarchal system that dominates the structure of working class communities demands that women remain in the sub-ordinate position of doing unpaid housework. This is an integral part of the working class girls' socialization process. This theme is reflected in many of their comments about work:

> Women shouldn't have to work, but they need the money. . . . They should be able to stay at home with the kids. . . . Anyway, it's terrible for my sister who works at night, does the housework and looks after four kids. . . . Sitting in the house is boring . . . but it's the way you're brought up like . . . dolls, washing dishes and housework.

Females and education

Many of the girls in the study had resisted the school structure either by opting out or by refusing to take exams. This cultural tradition was further complicated by the assertion that 'women aren't supposed to be educated.' The subject of education seemed of little interest to them.

Resulting from this, many of them concentrated on their appearance, which was often immaculately tailored and trendy. As Chris Griffin (1982c: 25) states: 'Some young women adopt forms of femininity which involve defying school rules and authority and centre on appearance.' The majority of these girls were in constant competition with each other about hairstyles, shoes, make-up and general appearance. Many took a certain degree of pride in deviating from the school uniform by wearing the wrong coloured socks, shoes, blouses or skirts. Those females found a certain amount of excitement and fun in this. As Griffin (1982c: 25) says: 'Non academic girls at school try to relieve boredom by having a laugh and generating excitement.'

Such deviations from the school uniform were seen by the non-academic girls as resistance to the school's rules and discipline. Many of these girls were aware of their position and the consequences of their actions. Griffin (1982: 28) continues: 'The young woman's resistances in school are not seen in terms of disruptive aggression but in relation to their presumed deviant sexuality . . . perhaps male teachers see disruptive girls as common.' The non-academic girl often rejects the image of the middle class girl by resisting parental and educational pressures to 'be nice'. It is no longer a rebellious thing 'not to be nice', it is a cultural artefact shared by working class women. This involves a complex range of individual and collective cultural practices, such as 'mitching' from school, leaving school early, taking longer breaks, swearing, showing an interest in the males within the school and 'messing around' in the classroom. This 'messing around' may be viewed as the female's attempt to construct leisure within the classroom, resulting in these females being labelled as 'trouble makers'. Similarly they are like the 'lads'.

Most of the females interviewed felt that school was either irrelevant or a waste of time.

> School doesn't teach you anything you don't already know, it doesn't even prepare you for life, and those careers teachers, they really are a waste of time. Careers teachers for what, a life on the dole. There should be more education about sex, drugs, having children etc., subjects are useless. The teachers are out of touch completely.

Many of them resisted school in a variety of ways. They felt that school was irrelevant, inadequate and removed from reality because it challenged their role, ethnicity and class. As one female said, 'Well, I've no choice but to attend so I may as well pass my time as easily as possible . . . get a bit of a laugh and that. . . . I hate school.'

Fashion and style for females

Dressing up is an important part of feminine cultural practice. Many of the girls adored dressing up and wearing make up. This resulted in socialization patterns that had been largely influenced by their mothers, who in turn were largely pressurized by their male partners to 'look good at all costs'. Consequently even 'battered' females had to 'look good'. The females interviewed were fashion conscious and concerned with wearing the latest styles. They were under considerable pressure to conform to the latest trends as 'part of the mating game. No boy wants to take you out if you're wearing old fashioned, out of date clothes.' The creation of their style involved a selection of certain objects, clothes, hairstyles and music that were relevant to the focal concerns of this group, and chosen for males. Other groups of females had a separate system of style codification that was special to their group: leather jackets, tight jeans, hair tipped blonde and cut short, stiletto-heeled shoes and a keen interest in disco music. These visible and symbolic elements of style were not separate from the group who created them, but were shaped by the group and were constantly carried and re-affirmed in the group situation. Even females who deviated from the world of make up, colourful fashions and attractive hairstyles often belonged to other sub-groups that re-affirmed their individual style. Although 'looking good' was expected of females, drawing a male's attention when one looked good was often considered 'common' and an unacceptable moral practice for a girl.

There are many contradictions related to style. Some styles are rejected in the classroom, the youth club and other institutions in society, but are at the same time displayed in shops, such as outrageous hairstyles and unattractive and sexually suggestive clothes. It may be argued that the diffusion of these sub-cultural styles can be viewed as one of the main reasons for their loss of subversive power.

Many females feel threatened by styles that promote individualism. They often find a degree of security and comfort in their efforts to look like their friends, dress like their friends and adopt their friends' mannerisms, because such mannerisms are acceptable forms of behaviour for a working class girl. This socially constructed sub-cultural definition of style and fashion is central to the lives of many females. They will even resort to the mail order syndrome and parental financial support to satisfy their insatiable desire for style, resulting in serious debt problems for many young females. Style is seen as a crucial resource in the construction of the gender identity, providing opportunities for the completion of the process of taking on one or other of the roles constituting the family. It is an integral part of the female's culture.

Females, marriage and romance

> Well I'd love to get married one day, so would I, but not too young. But I'd love a white wedding. Anyway if I don't marry him I might not find anyone else . . . it's not stupid it's true. Many girls around here get pregnant because a lot of the fellas will marry them . . . others are left with the child. Not my idea of romance.

Romance is central to the ideologies of working class adolescent femininity. Most of the females did seem to be isolated and divided against each other in competition for a 'fella'. Consequently this served to undermine the young women's friendships and their cultural autonomy from the dominant male groups in school, clubs and on the street corner. The characteristic of cultural autonomy is, however, central to the young males' sub-culture, in which males are seen to use their leisure time socializing with each other, often ignoring the existence of females. It is often the reverse for females.

Many of the girls competed for males and when they did meet a 'fella' they often talked romantically about their relationship together. Girls who had been involved in relationships for longer than six months were less romantic and more interested in other things. One problem that most of the females encountered was this pressure to formulate heterosexual relationships. Although many of them planned to stay faithful to their friends the force of ideological and cultural pressures towards having relationships with males was considerable; at the same time the labelling process of being a 'slut, whore or slag' was implanted if they went too far!

The majority of the females interviewed believed in marriage as opposed to cohabitation. All of the females viewed a white wedding as romantic: 'something to look back upon when you are old'. Most felt that romance was central to their relationships but their boyfriends did not see it as important. 'It would be nice to receive flowers, soppy cards, be taken out for meals and treated like a lady, but the wee lads up here wouldn't dream of doing any of those things.' Therefore, they believed that romance was an integral part of engagement or marriage, but it just didn't happen. The idea of marriage was viewed as romantic by most females, because of security and its acceptability within the working class area. Those who realized the disadvantages of marriage believed they should marry 'because every girl gets married someday'. As Christine Griffin (1982c: 30–1) points out: 'The sexual market overlaps with what has been called the marriage market for women in which women are judged as potential wives, mothers, working for emotionally and sexually serving men and their families'.

Females and relationships

The majority of females interviewed had relationships with males, although there were a few who did not seem to have a specific interest in males. The latter females had other cultural and social interests and were generally older. This small percentage of females spent more time with other females and indulged in such social activities as drinking, dancing, baby sitting, going to discos or sitting at home. However, many of them felt pressurized by their peers into forming relationships with males (women who drank too much were considered alcoholics by the community, whereas similar men were not considered alcoholics).

Females who did have relationships with males were in the majority. They frequently discussed their relationships and many of the problems they encountered with their male partners, and felt that their male partners were too domineering (most of the male partners were older than the females) and too demanding. Yet if men were not aggressive or demanding they considered them 'wimps', as 'men are supposed to be able to fight in this area'. The male partners expected the females to have sex (even though many of the females were virgins and afraid of sexual intercourse), to dress according to their wishes, to wear lots of make up, to see them on most evenings (even though many worked, were doing schoolwork or other things), not to speak their mind, to know their place in company, not to have career ambitions and to spend as little time as possible with their friends. Many of the girls felt that such demands created a strain upon their relationship although many succumbed to it. They could not cope with such demands, yet they felt compelled to maintain the relationship. Some of the girls did reveal that their boyfriends had physically attacked and abused them on occasions. Yet they felt powerless when they were confronted with terminating the relationship. Other females were more assertive but were not involved in long-term relationships.

Many of the females interviewed felt guilty about enjoying their leisure time (when they had any) and also felt unable to claim space away from their male partners. Consequently they enjoyed what time they did have away from their male partners. They enjoyed spending time with other females as a possible way of managing the tensions and contradictions in their lives. As Griffin (1982b: 21) states, 'Women would appear to have some power together'. Yet their time together would be spent discussing men and what their partners would be doing.

The women enjoyed their relationships with each other because of their common bond, friendship ties and mutual understanding of each other's lives. These relationships, although limited by the male partners' demands, were seen to be a significant part in young women's lives. This patriarchal dominance is reflected within the community structures, where the separation of women from other women may be seen as a way of maintaining control over young females. Hence many females had limited time to spend with their female friends. Such limitations were placed upon females by the demands of their male partners, who believed that women had a place because they were women; working class women did not deviate from this.

Females in working class communities are given status according to the relationships they have. A young married female is accepted within the community because her status is ascribed to her through her husband. A female who cohabits with a male partner is either respected or slandered according to her male partner's occupation, reputation or verbal accounts of his life with her. An unmarried mother is less frowned upon when she is having a steady relationship. A lesbian or an unattached female is seen to pose specific threats to patriarchal social relations. They are unacceptable because they have an individual status linked to their femininity that excludes the status of males. A female without a relationship is the subject of local gossip.

Many females are forced into heterosexual relationships regardless of their personal desires for careers. Many girls felt that they were trapped and unable to get out of the rut. Relationships were expected from them and they in turn had to form them. Yet there were females who expressed a genuine desire to form relationships. 'Well I think it's only natural to have a relationship with a man . . . anyway I feel I need one. I'd rather be going with a boy than hanging around with my mates.'

Whatever the reason, the majority of females felt they should be involved in relationships with males. They all felt that their female friends were important, but not as important as a boyfriend. Many agreed that their communities and families expected too much from them in the way of getting engaged and married, and having children. Yet others felt that it was a status symbol to be married or to have children. Most of them were politically unaware of their social position in relation to the patriarchal society because this was so well disguised as 'just the way things are'.

Females and roles

It appeared that the females who were interviewed saw their roles in a variety of different ways: their role within the family, their role in school, their role within the social network of the local community and their role within relationships.

Roles within the family

Many of the females felt that their role within the family was fairly traditional in that they were expected to behave in a traditionally feminine way. Some of the girls mentioned that when they were being brought up they were given the traditional things, like dolls, prams or toy washing machines, and rarely ever allowed to play with toys that their brothers played with. Many of the females recalled being forced into the position of 'doing housework' at an early age, before puberty. As one female said, 'I've been doing housework since I was eleven years of age, helping with the washing and all that. You see there are six males in our house and it's expected of me. It always has been and it causes constant rows.' They felt that it was not fair that they were burdened with the housework and such things as it restricted their freedom. Many came from families where there were more males than females, and it was assumed that they should look after the males regardless of their minority positions. Although many had tried to rebel against being slotted into this traditional role they felt that it was almost impossible to break free. Many did not want to break free because the role was culturally reassuring.

Fathers tried to exert control over their daughters – to advise them on 'how to dress, you shouldn't wear clothes like that, you should wear those nice clothes, your hair is too short, your hair is too long, you shouldn't wear make up, you shouldn't wear tight jeans'. Many of the girls felt that their fathers were too judgemental. As one girl says: 'He always wants me to wear skirts and look pretty, he wants to dress me like a kid. I'm not a kid anymore.' It would appear that the fathers' attitudes and attempts to exert control over their daughters caused many problems for the females. Some of these females enjoyed having a feminine appearance, but they resented being told how to go about attaining this.

The female's role within the family unit was one of traditional femininity as dictated by the community. The relationship between father and daughter was of considerable significance, in that it caused tremendous problems for the females concerned. Most of the females felt trapped by their fathers' discipline and attitudes. This attempt by parents to control their daughters by traditional practices associated with femininity serves to reinforce the patriarchal systems that operate within such working class communities. The specific function is to remind females that they are objects of male consumption: 'to serve, honour and obey thee'.

Roles within the local community with reference to relationships

The majority of females felt they were slotted into a very traditional feminine role within their local community. Their status was ascribed to them through the actions of a male world. They were deemed significant only in the eyes of their fathers, boyfriends or husbands. Much of the female's status within the local community was attained according to the type of relationships she had. If a female was involved in local community activities, local organizations, local youth clubs, local schools, local churches or local centres and had achieved considerable status as a result of her membership of these, local people would refer to her as: 'the daughter of such and such is a great girl, the wife of Mr ____ is a marvellous woman, she's done so well for herself, Mr ____'s wife does a lot of good work for the community, yes, she's a really good worker, didn't she used to be married to John?' Comments like this are often heard in the community. They remove the individuality from the woman and transfer her success, status and achievements to her male partner.

A female is awarded her status not by her personal achievements but by her achievements for her male partner, and within the local community the female is awarded a secondary role with reference to the status of her relationships with males. The patriarchal ethos, profoundly embedded within the community, is unable to view the woman as a separate entity, a woman within her own right.

Conclusion

The emergence of new cultural styles has become a symbolic one for many young people. Such styles manifest themselves in new fashions, new attitudes, new morals and new beliefs. Although young males' and females' attitudes to issues such as work, unemployment, leisure, the church, the family, the youth club and the law would seem to challenge the existing attitudes held within their local community, it is apparent that much youth culture is intertwined with the parent culture. Young males find it difficult to free themselves from the patriarchal stereotyped image of the male as breadwinner, provider, wife beater, macho man. Others are unaware of the pressures of the parent culture. Likewise, young females find it difficult to free themselves from the patriarchal view of the women as housewife, child bearer, mother, servant, burden carrier.

It is obvious that the lives of the young are muddled with complexities, contradications and problems. Many young males are forced to depend upon their female counterparts for provisions and financial support; thus role reversal is one example of the many contradictions inherent in patriarchal working class culture.

8 Conclusions

Taken by itself the 'culture' described in these chapters would appear to be contradictory, senseless and incoherent. There are, of course, contradictions, illogicalities and incoherence. However, as a whole, when placed within the frameworks of political economy and ideology outlined in the earlier chapters, the culture of working class youth in West Belfast becomes comprehensible. To them the contradictions lie in a society that preaches the virtues of Christianity, individualism, democracy and equality of opportunity while presenting them with a very different reality. There is no equality of opportunity or democracy for the youth of West Belfast and little scope for meaningful individual expression. There is plenty of religion but a serious lack of apparent Christian policy and practice. It is therefore of little wonder that attitudes to the institutions of society (school, government, church etc.) are frequently negative.

The alienation of youth from society is not to be examined in a vacuum. The alienation process, like Camus's plague, has afflicted all. How often have we heard older members of the community refer to 'everyone going mad'. Alienation must be explained in terms of what is happening within working class neighbourhoods at the cultural as well as the physical levels. This can be explained by reference to the transformation in the British and Irish economies since the Second World War. Within this context, youth work strategies can best be described as part of the 'acculturation' process, and as long as this is the case they will always meet a hostile, or at least apathetic, reaction from a large section of working class youth.

'Giving young people something to do' is not a solution to the problems of West Belfast but naive youth work practitioners and policy formulators would have us believe that it is. Neither will providing 'acceptable alternative forms of activity' discourage a significant element from engaging in forms of what is regarded as 'anti-social' behaviour. Rioters, hoods, glue sniffers and boozers are such because the acceptable alternative forms of activity hold no appeal for them. This is not the result of some inherent personality defect, as many professional commentators (clerics, community workers, teachers, social workers, youth workers, politicians, police and army personnel) would have us believe.

The section of the youth population that gives rise to most concern is that which does not participate in formal youth provision, and we are talking about 60–70 per cent of the population. When we consider this, and the clear class bias that exists in formal youth work, then the nature and extent of the problems facing the Youth Service become glaring.

The recent sophisticated attempts at curbing the informal activities of youth are a reflection of the changing social and economic structures. Urban redevelopment and the destruction of local economies have left their mark. On the one hand there is the reality of the corrosion of the traditional working class neighbourhood and all that went with it (sense of belonging, capacity for common action, a high degree of face-to-face interaction, shared goals and interdependence). On the other hand there has been a failure to deliver the promised 'consumer society' that increased geographical and educational mobility – not to mention changes in production – were to bring.

Formal youth provision, in its present form, will never be able to recreate the values and integrity of traditional working class communities upon which the stablility of the class depended. Neither can it hope to compensate adequately for the glaring lack of the basic necessities of life, such as jobs, money, meaningful education and a pleasant environment. Fifty years ago the American community organizer Saul Alinsky noted

> You don't, you dare not, come to a people who are in the gutter of despair and offer them . . . not security, but supervised recreation, handicraft classes and character building. Yet that is what is done . . . we come to them with handouts of bats and balls.
>
> (Alinsky 1969: 58)

It would appear that to a large extent that is also what is being done in West Belfast. It is little wonder that social policy-makers and practitioners are continually wringing their hands and crying 'what more can we do?' The most basic characteristics when one enters a youth club in West Belfast are the video games, the television and the pool tables. The most consistent activities on the programmes are games of one kind or another. A large proportion of youth workers may be aware of the pressing needs in the area – such as finding job security – but few will claim that their club is in any way meeting these needs.

Youth provision in West Belfast appears to be one of the major forms of provision of mass entertainment, which permeates working class social life generally. The emphasis on providing mass entertainments in deprived areas is more of an attempt at moral evasion rather than an attempt at alleviating the causes of despair.

Mass entertainments tend towards a view of the world in which progress is conceived as a 'seeking of material possessions, equality as a moral levelling, and freedom as the ground for endless irresponsible pleasure' (Hoggart 1976: 340). The aim of such activities is to ensure the continuation of a spectators' world. They are not designed to tax the mind, and serve to stifle development of the intellect among those who have most to gain from that. They also assist the undermining of positive and co-operative kinds of enjoyment in which one gains much by giving much.

Seabrook (1982: 15–16) has noted that the market place is the instrument whereby the dependency on such activities is created. The material advantages that young people are given ensure that they achieve satisfaction of needs without effort or struggle. This leads to a systematic under-use of their cognitive powers and possibilities, the suppression of their energies and abilities, and passivity and subordination. This helps them to accept the under-employment of their skills and intelligence. By this process it is ensured that there will be an absence of purpose in their lives, an eroded sense of identity, the lack of function and definitions, and recurring bouts of boredom.

As we stated earlier, the Shankill, post-redevelopment, is a sort of 'mad Disneyland' of leisure centres, bingo halls, sports complexes, slot machines and car parks against a back-drop of social despair on an unprecedented scale. The anticipation is, of course, that social consciousness – the perception of the conditions of existence – will be distorted in the hall of mirrors, and it works. Some youth club participants in Ballymurphy and Shankill actually stated that provision of more slot machines was one of the most pressing needs in their area. It is a case of 'the people wanting what the people get'. Traditional youth work provides part of this process no matter how well intentioned the workers are and how much emphasis they place on social or personal development. If we look at the emphasis on personal development, as it is preached and practised by the Youth Service, a little more closely, it becomes apparent that what we are seeing is really Baden-Powell's 'character building'. Spiritual development (which was particularly prevalent in the Shankill clubs) is another form of this and serves to prepare the disillusioned youth for the life he or she will supposedly inherit hereafter, although he or she would probably rather have settled for it now.

It is apparent that the Youth Service falls far short of meeting the needs of the one-third of young people who participate in formal youth provision, never mind the other two-thirds. Neither does it know where to begin. The departure point for the implementation of any social policy that is designed to alleviate a particular problem must be to ascertain the nature and extent of the problem. But the Youth Service does not appear to know what this is. 'Keeping kids off the street' does not alleviate a problem or meet a need. It just keeps kids off the street. There is nothing problematical about them being there providing they so choose.

The central issue with which this study is concerned is the interest of young people. The Youth Service would claim the same and this leads us ultimately to the consideration of how the Youth Service can best meet the needs of young people of West Belfast (or elsewhere for that matter). The latest 'in' concepts in youth work regarding the needs of the young appear to be those of political and social education. Attention has been drawn to the position that when one seeks clarification of what terms like 'social', 'political' or even 'participation' mean in regard to the young as posed by the Youth Service 'they seem elusive and contradictory' (Sawbridge 1983/ 84: 37). The same source has drawn attention to the tendency to avoid a focus on class as a central factor in youth work despite the fact that most of the problems associated with young people are distinctly related to their social class.

The 1986 Youth Service Report for Northern Ireland concluded that 'it is important to stress that one of the main themes of the report is the extent to which the Youth Service should be meeting the specific needs of young people against a background of rapid social change' (Youth Committee for Northern Ireland 1986: 31). Clearly, the most pressing need arising out of this rapid social change is the need to find a job. In our survey area fewer than one in five young people were finding a job within a year of leaving school. The greatest draw-back is their social class and the Youth Service is absolutely powerless to meet this need because it is a class issue. Most of the young people we talked to both informally and in structured interviews did not know what class they belonged to or what the concept meant. It is little wonder that we are inheriting a 'confused' generation when they are not even aware of the cause of their greatest plight. Surely it must be essential to the personal development of young people for them to have at least some conception of the nature of their predicament. Should this not come under the heading political education? Clearly in terms of the Youth Service it does not, which leaves us with the irresistible assumption that the 'non-political' Youth Service is political and that it exists to serve not the needs of young people but the needs of a state that depends upon the accumulation of capital for survival at the expense of the increasing degradation (due to their position in the 'reserve' pool of labour) of those at the lower end of the social class scale. The role of the Youth Service then becomes one of fostering the reproduction of class relations by facilitating young people in their acceptance of the effects of unemployment while ignoring its causes. This is achieved through 'personal development, social education and recreational provision'. The 1986 Youth Committee Report is permeated with references to the changes experienced in youth work to meet the problems associated with unemployment. A hundred years ago religion was the 'opium of the masses'. Then it became 'character building'. Nowadays it is videos, slot machines and social education.

We are not saying that an organized youth service does not have a part to play in areas such as West Belfast. On the contrary, youth work, if it is used to tackle the *real* problems of inner city decline, communal disintegration, adolescent insecurity, miseducation and so on, could have a positive and meaningful function. This would involve harnessing itself more closely to the needs and aspirations of the communities it serves through a much increased level of organizational participation by local people and the fostering of more imaginative and relevant programmes of *popular* education. We would refer the reader again to our conclusions and recommendations presented in Chapters 4 and 5. We would again emphasize the points made in Chapter 6, specifically those relating to the complexities of working class culture. It is imperative for the success of youth clubs based in working class communities that workers have an understanding of, and are sensitive to, *all* the cultural characteristics of an area. To view non-participants in a negative manner will merely exacerbate the problems associated with the unattached. Youth work should reach out to them before the often tragic consequences of a failure to do so are devastatingly brought home to us all. Courses on formal youth work need to include a substantial content of working class culture rather than the mere churning out of theories of youth sub-cultures (which often imply delinquent sub-cultures). Bernstein (1971: 225) made a point about teachers that would equally apply to youth workers: 'If the consciousness of the teacher is to be part of the culture of the child then the culture of the child should be part of the consciousness of the teacher.' The young people of Ballymurphy and Shankill have some unique characteristics that are not common to their parents, but they have so much more in common. Lifestyle, status, environment, needs, aspirations, cultural values, mobility and so on are constants whether one is aged 16 or 60.

All these points need to be considered if formal youth provision in West Belfast is to make a significant impact on raising the living standards of the people who live there. The alternative is to continue the ineffective exercise of limiting the role of the Youth Service to a 'tarting-up' operation that conceals the real problems and thus hinders realistic approaches to solving them. The Youth Service is in effect colluding with the state in general to 'prepare' young people for a future of unemployment, no opportunities and powerlessness. This is carried by an implementation of an ideology of leisure stressing individual 'freedoms' to replace the older, now archaic, belief that an essential indicator of one's personal success was to 'work for one's keep' for the 'communal good'.

This has been replaced by the slot machine culture of the 1990s – a culture that offers the freedom to participate in a vast array of leisure activities at the expense of the sense of purpose that has traditionally been associated with the demands of the labour movement. The problems of West Belfast can only be understood by reference to political economy. To say that they are the result of personality defects peculiar to the majority of people in such localities is an obscene absurdity. Any analysis of the role of the Youth Service in Northern Ireland, or elsewhere for that matter, must firmly locate it within an analysis of the historical transformation and present implications of the nature of the state.

For as long as the problems of inner-city areas, including 'youth problems', are divorced from the overall problems of political economy, governments will be desperately trying to fill up the 'gaping holes' with bits of 'plastic padding' in the form of the odd grant here and a few bats and balls there.

Furthermore, we are left in an age of consumerism in which access to material goods has been blocked for a large portion of the population; for those with access to them the predicament is not much better. We were led to believe that the power of money could be made to cure the sufferings of the lower classes and that by ending primary poverty an emancipation (and embourgeoisement) of the working class would occur. The price to be paid for this was that

> the determining process of the market place has been substituted, a dependency on it so complete, that the social identity of a whole generation has been formed by it. In this way, one of the most significant aspects of human development – the social part – has been subordinated to, and determined by, the selling of things.
>
> (Seabrook 1983: 193)

The market relations of production as promoted by the state are not neutral in the terms of a class society. The role, however, of the state ideological aparatuses (particularly education and youth work) is to obscure the real position of the state by presenting it as a neutral mediator rather than the producer or facilitator of the capitalist system. Money is the means by which the market relations are presented as a system of equal exchange (a fair day's pay for a fair day's work) and the worship of money has become the cult of the 1990s. An *independent* youth service, committed to fostering the needs of working class communities, would need to distance itself from such processes.

Political education within the framework of a 'service' (who or what does it really serve?) that is concerned with the reproduction of exploitative social relations is bound to be treated with scepticism, at least by those who are exploited. What youth work with working class people is seriously lacking is a political perspective that allows young people to consider the possibility of changing their life conditions and expectations. We may continue to campaign for a purpose-built club here and there but we must also ask what the function of that club is to be in terms of the 'real' needs of the youth involved. It should not be surprising, given the lack of a coherent explanation of the needs of young people today, that the pages of our tabloids are forever filled with 'horror stories' of adolescent delinquency, mugging, murder and at times worse, as an entire generation seemingly runs amok. It is the price to be paid for the imposition of the superstition of money. That the consequences of this imposition are often disturbing and the reactions of its victims unhappy, often violent and, at times, destructive is not because of the world having gone mad. It can be explained within the parameters of political economy and an understanding of ideology and its relation to action. An explicit recognition of these points is crucial for anyone who claims to care about the youth of today. Only then can we proceed to prepare the programmes that will ensure that the generations of the future will inhabit a world which has meaning to them and to which they will feel they belong.

Recommendations

Following from our own conclusions we are broadly in agreement with the findings of a previous study in another marginalized region of the UK (Coffield *et al.* 1986). This study, based on research carried out in the north-east of England, suggested a proposed social contract for young people. This would include:

1 A strong regional dimension in all aspects of government policy.
2 Training linked to jobs and jobs to training, whenever possible.
3 A comprehensive system of 16+ education, training and employment.
4 The close involvement of employers in the training of young people.
5 Alteration of the model of learning at the heart of MSC and DES initiatives (in Northern Ireland we would refer to ACE and YTP specifically).
6 Community education to combat racism (in Northern Ireland, we would add sectarianism and, generally, sexism).
7 Programmes of positive discrimination in favour of young women.
8 Young adults being involved in the formation of social policy about young adults and given the freedom to develop alternatives.

We feel that the necessity for such a contract has been supported by our own study. We feel, however, that certain specific points need to be made in regard to youth work in general and Northern Irish youth work in particular.

While the Youth Service acknowledges the fact that present provision does not meet the needs of all young people in areas like West Belfast, we feel that this is not necessarily something that should be considered as inevitable.

1 As we have shown, the young confront a barrage of social and economic problems, most of which are outside their control. Many of them are faced with the prospect of long-term unemployment in a society where money is the major means of access to status and a comfortable standard of living. Simultaneously, they confront in society major problems associated with changing moral attitudes and values, not to mention the omnipresent sectarian social relations and conflict of Northern Ireland. All of this is experienced by them at a time when they are

attempting to come to terms with the physical and psychological trans- formation from childhood to adulthood. Non-participants are not unattached, unclubables, undesirables or uncontrollables. They are basically ordinary young people experiencing, confronting and reacting to a somewhat (to them anyway) confused social structure. We have attempted to present the culture of working class youth (not merely 'youth culture') in order to illustrate how it is often contrary to the aims, objectives and practices of formal provision as it is presently structured. We suggest that a significant proportion of working class youth exclude themselves, or are excluded by others, from formal youth work because it is not relevant to their needs and aspirations. We feel that to date the youth service has not adjusted itself to what these needs and aspirations are, let alone how they may be realistically met.

As we have illustrated, the most striking feature of behaviour (or cultural expression) of the non-participants is its informality and the very nature of this informal (it is not apathy, laziness, irresponsibility, absent- mindedness or negative thinking) characteristic of working class youth has been grossly misunderstood by those involved in a vast array of youth provision. As we argued, such behaviour is an inevitable outcome of a trajectory of influences common to working class youth culture of the 1980s and 1990s.

Providing games is fine but the crucial problems concerning young people are those associated with growing towards maturity in an environ- ment in which many of those expectations (having money, freedom, power etc.) and responsibilities (a steady job, home etc.) of being mature will be denied.

2 It was found that formal youth provision in West Belfast did not appear to cater sufficiently for people aged over 16, particularly females. We would suggest that this is because of the past preoccupation of the youth service with providing 'alternative acceptable forms of activities' for young working class males. Hence many working class females find they do not fit into these alternative acceptable forms of activities, which are dominated by a patriarchal ethos. Many females who participate in the youth service feel that it does not meet their immediate needs. Most of the females we interviewed only participated in formal youth club provision because it kept them off the streets. Young females feel that formal youth provision caters for males or for very young females. Females who participate in the youth service over the age of 15 want the youth service to relate to their needs, providing programmes on health education, sex education, relationships, childbirth, careers, etc. Females who did not participate in the formal youth service share common attitudes and activities with participants and many of these are not unusual, including socializing, the importance of peer groups, concern for the handicapped and elderly, their love of fashion, music, going out, a sense of adventure, fun and excitement, their desire for male attention and their idealistic

career ambitions. A modern progressive youth service would need to consider problems that they encounter in achieving its aims in an *informal* setting. In the 1990s it is no longer fashionable (let alone structurally practical) for girls over 16 to be expected to stay at home. They should be encouraged to participate in a regenerated youth service that will provide an environment that does not leave them feeling threatened or excluded by the traditional male dominance.

3   The issue of what is provided should be re-examined with regard to males. A majority of young males still do not have any desire to participate in organized programmes. Attempts should be made to provide programmes that they find attractive. First of all, it is necessary to discover what they want or need (and we do not simply mean what they have been led to believe they want or need). This would involve a harnessing of youth provision to the educational (in the broadest sense of the term), social, cultural and economic aspirations of local communities – and we mean the entire community, not simply those who are easily accessible. This would, of course, require an adventurous approach to social planning, which would be preceded by a radical programme of participatory research. The benefits of such a programme could be enormous.

It is interesting that youth workers in the Shankill thought that young people did not use youth clubs and organizations because of their formality and social influences. When they say 'social influences' they are referring to a cultural phenomenon (aspirations, attitudes, values, behaviour). We appear to have a further illustration of the need for clubs to be made less formal and for workers and officials to be more sensitive to the cultural composition of the entire community.

4   There is still an apparent reliance in protestant areas on uniformed organizations and church clubs as a means of providing for the needs of youth. They do, of course, offer a degree of excitement for sections of the population who enjoy drilling, wearing uniform, religion and so on. However, we must remember that their origins lie in a long past era of nationalistic jingoism, imperialistic social relations, militarism and, more recently, widespread religious practice. They do not seem to be so relevant to a de-militarized, post-imperialist, internationalized and secularized society. We are not suggesting they should be discouraged. On the contrary they do provide an important social function. However, a progressive and modern youth service would need to re-evaluate its position in relation to them. We suggest that the function of statutory youth provision in areas where uniformed organizations dominate should be to offer an alternative. We do not think it is feasible to say that a community does not need a statutory youth club because there are already plenty of uniformed organizations and church clubs in the area. It is apparent from our findings that an emphasis on drill, rules, uniform, religion and so on is

not the sort of provision that most young people are likely to be attracted to.

5   It is apparent that youth clubs and organizations tend to provide activities that will maximize the number of 'acceptable' users. Individual youth leaders are under some pressure to maximize attendance and membership numbers (and to exclude 'undesirables'). This inevitably presents the temptation to provide easily organized and managed 'mass' activities that will promote the optimal level of participation by the 'respectable' sections of working class youth. Quantity rather than quality of provision becomes the main objective and we are heading back to the traditional, and often criticized, negative motive of youth provision: 'keeping the kids off the streets'. Provision also fails ultimately in this objective, in that the section of working class youth who spend most of their time on the streets – the so-called unattached – are excluded by bureaucracy or exclude themselves because of the unattractive programmes.

Those involved in youth work need to be more aware of the needs of young people and of the community in which they work. Our findings indicated clearly that youth workers generally had a serious lack of aware- ness of the needs of the people they worked with, or of how they could be met. Professionally qualified youth workers were more likely to have an awareness of what real needs were, but were much more reluctant to claim that their project made a significant impact in meeting those needs. Officials in the youth service also suffered from a similar discrepancy. One official had removed the section on sex education from a respectable BBC publication designed to help young people grow to maturity. This occurred in an area with at least 15 per cent of one-parent households.

6   Youth workers should be allowed to spend more time counselling young people and have some of the burden of managing the centre removed from them. The workers themselves expressed a definite pre- ference for this type of activity (they are youth workers after all, not managers) and the young people tended to agree that this should be so.

7   There seem to be differences between the most unsatisfying aspects of youth work, depending on the type of youth work practised and/or the area. The Springfield workers (who were mainly qualified professionals) were most dissatisfied with 'constraints', while the Shankill workers (who were mainly unqualified volunteers) were dissatisfied with what they called 'negative' behaviour. We would suggest that the reason for this discrepancy is that there are less constraints placed on voluntary workers than on those in paid employment. It would also follow that voluntary workers would be less inclined to tolerate 'negative' behaviour (they are not being paid to do so and probably expect more co-operation for their efforts). The difference probably has a lot to do with ethos. The uniformed

organizations in the Shankill, for instance, all have mottos and 'laws' that emphasize 'positive' thinking, such as 'to do my best' (Scouts' promise). It also has a lot to do with the 'spiritual development' role that is prevalent in most Shankill clubs.

8   Youth workers in the Springfield thought that non-participation was mainly caused by the existence of 'undesirable alternatives' (such as drinking). There does appear to be evidence that as the young approach the legal drinking age they lose interest in formal youth provision. We must, however, consider why activities such as drinking appeal more to them (and bear in mind that it is a perfectly acceptable adult activity – many youth workers themselves are no mean drinkers) than formal youth club activities. We should raise the issue here that, like it or not, drinking is an important element in working class culture. It should therefore not be surprising when the young are so keen to emulate the adult culture. Perhaps provision should be made whereby the young people who do insist upon drinking should be allowed to do so under close supervision and counselled on alcohol abuse. We would suggest that such a strategy of controlling under-age drinkers is much preferable to excluding them. Drink is available in youth clubs on the continent where there is no serious drinking problem (with either youth or adults), relatively speaking. It would also help to discourage activities such as drug and solvent abuse.

9   We found that 'public relations' came very low down the scale of youth workers' activities and that they generally felt that they would like to be granted more time for this. This seems a reasonable request given the somewhat poor image that formal provision has with a substantial proportion of the population. It is significant that voluntary clubs spend more time at this than statutory clubs, and this may account for their greater popularity.

10   We feel that youth work would have much wider appeal if it were made more democratic. Young people should be encouraged to participate more in organizing the activities and also in deciding the nature of the programmes. This would be made more effective by initiating pro- grammes designed to boost the self-confidence of those who would not normally participate in such activities through apathy or lack of self- esteem.

11   The majority of youth workers in our survey were against the youth service being a part of the education system and we feel that this was because of a fear of it becoming too formal or institutionalized as a result. However, this fear would be removed if youth work adopted an informal community education role.

12   There appeared to be a lack of flexibility from the BELB towards support for small informal youth initiatives, such as those attached to

community associations. Such units make valuable contributions to youth provision and usually come closest to catering for the 'unattached' because of their informality and close identification with the local community.

13   We feel that more imaginative programmes of social education and personal development are required and should reflect the needs and problems of local areas and also the individual characteristics of the participants. Attempts at implementing social education programmes have so far tended to be peripheral and unattractive to the participants (never mind the non-participants) in youth clubs. The whole educational role of the youth service needs to be examined. Indeed, the stated aims of the youth service tend rarely to be implemented through the individual youth club programmes. This is partly due to the ambivalence that appears to exist between youth workers and youth service officials and partly due to the restraints and limitations that youth workers confront in their working roles. There is also the question of relevance, and we would warn against the youth service becoming an extension of the formal education system. As we have seen, the structure of the school system is rejected and resisted by a large proportion of working class 'kids' and it is the same kids who reject the youth clubs and organizations. This is not a coincidence and it is not a case of 'personality pecularities' (such as maladjusted, disruptive, ill-mannered, negative thinking, trouble-making) in the non-participants. There is clearly a dichotomy between the cultural values of the working class and the structure, and to some extent the curricula or programmes, of the schools and youth organizations and clubs. There is nothing to indicate that working class people reject education for itself. On the contrary, an extension of educational services has always been one of the main demands of that class and there was recently a bitter campaign aimed at resisting school closures in our study area. We feel that the youth club could be the vehicle for promoting educational activities in an atmosphere avoiding those aspects of the school structure that the young people resisted.

14   We feel that the youth service does not tackle the questions of inter-communal relations in a divided society. We are not necessarily advocating more integrated holidays or visits for protestants and catholics. The youth club should be a centre for neutralizing sectarian attitudes and prejudices. This could be attempted through a programme of community education that confronts frankly the contradictions in sectarian ideologies and practices and that promotes the issues and interests that working class protestants and catholics have in common. Such a programme would differ from traditional approaches in that it would confront prejudices within the community and tackle their origins at source.

15   The youth service does appear to be somewhat haphazard and unco-ordinated in its structure. One official told us that 'there is no youth

service'. We feel that the structure should be more clearly defined, which would offset the lack of co-ordination in providing specific services for youth (and informing them of what is available).

16   Youth workers were not content with the amount of time spent in in-service training and we would suggest that this is an area requiring further extensive consideration. They were, after all, admitting that they were not adequately prepared for the job they were required to do. We would suggest that such training should concentrate on issues that are important to it. Youth workers should also be trained to do the job in question. Managerial skills are not something that professionally qualified youth workers should be assumed to possess. They are, however, an important aspect of the work in organizing a modern youth club. Perhaps youth work courses should include an element of managerial studies. We would suggest that in a youth and community centre there should be a division of responsibility between those responsible for management and administration and those responsible for community education and development.

17   We would propose that youth clubs should be 'powerhouses' for local community activities – we prefer the term youth and community centre – and should be concerned with issues that affect young and old alike. Young people are becoming more isolated because they do not meet adults as much as in the past. This inevitably leads to structural problems, which are often accredited to the psychological (and simplistic) 'generation gap' concept. It is not natural for young people to be structurally separated from adults and this will inevitably lead to them seeking out adult company. In working class communities this often means frequenting the places where adults meet – pubs and drinking clubs.

General comments

The results of this study have clearly shown that there is a compelling argument for the development of a much more relevant youth and community service with an emphasis on community education, community development and counselling. A greater priority should also be placed on community relations, starting with the promotion of self-examination (in the social sense) for young people. This would involve them in realistic activities where they would confront community problems and cultural contradictions. The next step would be for them to examine the nature of differences between their own and other cultures and communities, and what they have in common. The same also applies with regard to gender. Indeed, we would stress that much more attention needs to be directed towards females and problems concerned with sexist attitudes towards them. We also feel that there should be much more emphasis placed upon promoting links between youth and adults in their community. This could be achieved by using youth clubs as centres for community development as well as for recreational purposes.

Research and development is continuing along these lines at the Community Education and Development Centre, University of Ulster, and the Ulster People's College (where this project was based), particularly in curriculum development work concerned with the use of materials on working class culture, a focus on community education as a progressive force and an emphasis on democratic models of participation.

GLOSSARY AND ABBREVIATIONS

Glossary

bin lid   idiot, stupid person
down south (the south)   the Republic of Ireland
eejit   idiot
fenian   derogatory term for catholic
free state   the Republic of Ireland
gurnin'   crying or complaining
oul doll (oul lad)   elderly female (male)
peeler   police officer
plastered   intoxicated
prod   derogatory term for protestant
raker   someone who persistently 'messes about'
raking   'messing about'
rebel   catholic
taig   derogatory term for catholic
tricolour   flag of the Republic of Ireland
the Twelfth   12 July, the anniversary of the Battle of the Boyne in 1690
windies   windows

Abbreviations

ACE   Action for Community Employment
BELB   Belfast Education and Library Board
BTA   Ballymurphy Tenants Association
CDC   Citizens Defence Committee (Ballymurphy)
NIHE   Northern Ireland Housing Executive
IRA   Irish Republican Army
RUC   Royal Ulster Constabulary

SDLP   Social Democratic and Labour Party
UDA   Ulster Defence Association
UFF   Ulster Freedom Fighters
UVF   Ulster Volunteer Force
YTP   Youth Training Programme

BIBLIOGRAPHY

Albemarle, Lord (1960) *The Albemarle Report*. London: HMSO.

Alinsky, S. (1969) *Reveille for Radicals*. New York: Vintage.

Althusser, L. (1969) *For Marx*. London: New Left Books.

Althusser, L. (1971) *Lenin, Philosophy and Other Essays*. London: Monthly Review Press.

BAN (1976) *Belfast Areas of Social Need Report*. Belfast: HMSO.

BAN Sub-group (1980) *Ballymurphy: a Survey and Action Report Prepared by the Belfast Areas of Need Sub-group*. Belfast: HMSO.

Bell, D. (not dated) *Acts of Union: Youth Culture and the Reproduction of Sectarianism in Northern Ireland*. Dublin: National Institute of Higher Education.

Bernstein, B. (1971) *Class Codes and Social Control*. London: Paladin.

Birley, D. (1987) *The Birley Report: Opportunities at Sixteen*. Belfast: HMSO.

Blach, B. (1980) 'Imperialism, nationalism and organised youth', in C. Clarke, C. Critcher and R. Johnston (eds) *Working Class Culture: Studies in History and Theory*. London and Birmingham: Hutchinson and Centre for Contemporary Studies.

Burton, F. (1978) *The Politics of Legitimacy: Struggles in a Belfast Community*. London: Routledge and Kegan Paul.

Clarke, J., Hall, S., Jefferson, T. and Roberts, B. (1976) 'Subcultures, cultures and class: A theoretical overview', in S. Hall and T. Jefferson (eds) *Resistance through Rituals: Youth Sub-cultures in Post War Britain*. London and Birmingham: Hutchinson and Centre for Contemporary Cultural Studies.

Clarke, C., Critcher, C. and Johnston, R. (eds) (1980) *Working Class Culture: Studies in History and Theory*. London and Birmingham: Hutchinson and Centre for Contemporary Cultural Studies.

Clarke, J. (1982) 'Defending ski-jumpers: a critique of theories of youth sub-cultures', stencilled paper no. 71. Centre for Contemporary Cultural Studies, Birmingham.

Coffield, F., Borrill, C. and Marshall, S. (1986) *Growing Up at the Margins*. Milton Keynes: Open University Press.

Cohen, P. (1972) 'Sub-cultural conflict and working-class communtiy', working papers in cultural studies no. 2. Centre for Contemporary Cultural Studies, Birmingham.

Cohen, S. (1972) *Folk Devils and Moral Panics*. London: Paladin.

Corrigan, P. and Frith, F. (1976) 'The politics of youth culture', in S. Hall and T. Jefferson (eds) *Resistance through Rituals: Youth Sub-cultures in Post War Britain*. London and Birmingham: Hutchinson and Centre for Contemporary Cultural Studies.

Department of Economic Development (1986) Press release. Belfast: HMSO.

Department of Education Northern Ireland (1987) *Policy for the Youth Service in Northern Ireland*. Belfast: HMSO.

Field, D. (1959) *Study of Unsatisfactory Tenants*. Belfast: Belfast Council of Social Welfare.

Finnegan, G., Jardine, M. and Palmer, D. (1982) *What Next? From School to Work*. Belfast: Standing Conference of Youth Organisations in Northern Ireland.

Fraser, M. (1973) *Children in Conflict*. Harmondsworth: Penguin.

Frazer, H. (ed.) (1980) *Community Work in a Divided Society*. Belfast: Farset.

Gillespie, N. (1983) *The Vital Statistics: Shankill Employment Report*. Belfast: Shankill Community Council.

Goldthorpe, J. H., Bechhofer, F. and Platt, J. (1969) *The Affluent Worker in the Class Structure*. Cambridge: Cambridge University Press.

Government of Northern Ireland (1949) *A Publication of Youth Organisations in Northern Ireland*. Belfast: HMSO.

Government of Northern Ireland (1962) *The Book of Government Statutes*. Belfast: HMSO.

Griffin, C. (1982a) 'Cultures of femininity: romance revisited', stencilled paper no. 69. Centre for Contemporary Cultural Studies, Birmingham.

Griffin, C. (1982b) 'The good, the bad and the ugly: images of young women in the labour market', stencilled paper no. 70. Centre for Contemporary Cultural Studies, Birmingham.

Griffin, C. (1982c) 'Young women and work: the transition from school to the labour market for young working class women', stencilled paper no. 76. Centre for Contemporary Cultural Studies, Birmingham.

Hall, S., Critcher, C., Jefferson, T., Clarke, J. and Roberts, B. (eds) (1978) *Policing the Crisis: Mugging, the State, and Law and Order*. London: Macmillan.

Hall, S. and Jefferson, T. (eds) (1976) *Resistance through Rituals: Youth Sub-cultures in Post War Britain*. London and Birmingham: Hutchinson and Centre for Contemporary Cultural Studies.

Hoggart, R. (1976) *The Uses of Literacy*. Harmondsworth: Pelican.

Jeffs, A. J. (1985) *Young People and the Youth Service*. London: Routledge and Kegan Paul.

Jenkins, R. (1983) *Lads, Citizens and Ordinary Kids: Working Class Youth Life-styles in Belfast*. London: Routledge and Kegan Paul.

Leslie, W. B. (1985) 'Time: the subtle thief of youth', *Youth and Policy*, (11), 26–8.

Milson, F. W. and Fairburn, A. N. (1975) *Youth and Community Work in the Seventies*. London: HMSO.

Northern Ireland Assembly (1983) 'Minutes: Education Committee, April'. Belfast: HMSO.

Northern Ireland Housing Executive (1978) *Northern Ireland Household Survey*. Belfast: NIHE.

Northern Ireland Youth Committee (1973) *The Northern Ireland Youth Services Act*. Belfast: HMSO.

Northern Ireland Youth Service (1965) *The Youth Service: the Way Forward*. Belfast: HMSO.

Northern Ireland Youth Workers Association (1987) *Social Education in Practice*. Belfast: Standing Conference of Youth Organisations in Northern Ireland.

St Johns and Corpus Christi Parish Council Steering Committee (1975) *Open the Window, Let in the Light*. Belfast, July.

Sawbridge, M. (1983/4) 'Political education, inequality and training', *Youth and Policy*, 2(3), 36–8.

Seabrook, J. (1982) *Working Class Childhood*. London: Gollancz.

Seabrook, J. (1983) *Unemployment*. London: Granada.

Shankill Community Council (1977) *Annual Report 1976–7*. Belfast: SCC.

Spencer, A. (1972) *Ballymurphy Survey: the Spencer Report*. Belfast: Ballymurphy Tenants Association and Northern Ireland Community Relations Commission.

Springhall, J. (1985) 'Rotten to the very core: leisure and youth, 1830–1914', *Youth and Policy*, (14), 30–2.

Townsend, P. (1979) *Poverty in the United Kingdom*. Harmondsworth: Penguin.

Tressel, R. (1985) *The Ragged Trousered Philanthropists*. London: Panther.

Wiener, R. (1980) *The Rape and Plunder of the Shankill*. Belfast: Farset.

Willis, P. (1979) *The Culture of the Shop Floor*. Birmingham: Centre for Contemporary Cultural Studies.

Willis, P. (1983) *Learning to Labour: How Working Class Kids Get Working Class Jobs*. Aldershot: Gower.

Winship, J. (1982) 'Woman becomes an individual – Femininity and consumption in women's magazines'. Birmingham: Centre for Contemporary Cultural Studies.

Young, M. and Wilmott, P. (1971) *Family and Kinship in East London*. Harmondsworth: Penguin.

Youth Committee for Northern Ireland (1977) *Report for the Period Ending 1977*. Belfast: HMSO.

Youth Committee for Northern Ireland (1981) *Report for the Period 1977–1981*. Belfast: HMSO.

Youth Committee for Northern Ireland (1986) *Report for the Period 1982–1986*. Belfast: HMSO.

Interviews

Interviews were conducted in 1985–6 with the following people:

Cahill, F.; Ballymurphy Tenants Association.
De Bariod, C.; Ballymurphy Tenants Association.
Donnelly, D.; Belfast Education and Library Board.
Galbraith, J.; 'Save the Shankill' Campaign.
Green, R.; Northern Ireland Youth Forum.
Hearst, N.; Belfast Education and Library Board.
Hewitt, J.; Farset Youth and Community Project.

Johnston, G.; Northern Ireland Association of Youth Clubs.
McDermott, P.; Department of Education Northern Ireland.
Morgan, P.; Community Services Department, Belfast City Council.
Redpath, J.; *Shankill Bulletin*.
Steven, R.; Belfast Education and Library Board.
Stewart, J.; Crumlin Road Opportunities.
Teacher (anonymous); St Louise's, Belfast.
Warm, D.; Department of Youth and Community Studies, University of
 Ulster at Jordanstown.
Wilson, Father D.; Springhill Community House.

INDEX